AF689782

A Practical Guide to Extradition Law Post-Brexit

Second Edition

A Practical Guide to Extradition Law Post-Brexit

Second Edition

Editor:

Daniel Sternberg

Contributors:

Nicholas Dobbs, Kathryn Howarth,
Anisa Kassamali, Nancy Kelehar,
Émilie Pottle, Benjamin Seifert,
Saoirse Townshend

Law Brief Publishing

Published 2025 by Law Brief Publishing, an imprint of Law Brief Publishing Ltd
30 The Parks
Minehead
Somerset
TA24 8BT

www.lawbriefpublishing.com

Paperback: 978-1-916698-56-7

FOREWORD

The British public have by now perhaps become inured to the UK's departure from the European Union, while recognising it has been a seismic political development. The political consequences will be long-lasting and profound. But Brexit is also a major legal event, indeed a change of the first order. As this book spells out, extradition is an area of law where the impact will immediately be seen, and I wonder if there will not be a good deal of continuing change.

Departure from the EU has meant departure from the widespread reciprocal arrangements between the continuing member states and the UK. Although the best-known slogan of those who campaigned for departure was that Britain must "take back control", that phrase may evoke a feeling of irony, when we contemplate aspects of the successor arrangements. As the authors explain, a considerable number of member states have given notice that they will no longer be extraditing their own nationals to Britain, whereas HMG has indicated that the UK will not invoke a nationality bar. As this book also delineates, the European legal order continues to permeate our extradition law, channelled through the European Convention of Human Rights, the Strasbourg court and the provisions of the Extradition Act 2003. Since the European Convention and the EU Charter are in essence co-terminous, it may be that the arrangements now reached through the Trade and Cooperation Agreement ("the TCA") for extradition from the UK will produce rather similar results to the pre-Brexit law, albeit by formally different routes. Over time, it will be interesting to see if that situation changes, and how. One reason for change may be the approach to interpreting domestic legislation, when considering conformity to the TCA (or any European directives cited as parallel provisions).

This book is timely, and practitioners will find it of great use. Reading through the script, it is clear that it is well-researched, well-expressed, easy to follow and practical in its focus. Sometimes the description 'practical' carries the implication of the great tradition of the Nutshell guide, but not here. This book is erudite as well as accessible. I commend it to all lawyers in the field.

The Right Honourable Sir Stephen John Irwin,
former Lord Justice of Appeal
August 2021

PREFACE TO THE SECOND EDITION

Since the first edition of this book was published in 2021, rumours of the demise of extradition following the UK's departure from the European Union have turned out to be greatly exaggerated. Any drop off in the volume of requests from EU states appears to have been compensated for by a rise in Part 2 requests and Westminster Magistrates' Court, the Administrative Court and the Supreme Court all remain busy with extradition litigation. It is a case of *plus ça change, plus c'est le même chose.*

In particular, since the first edition was published, the Supreme Court has continued to reshape UK extradition law in seismic ways. In the past two years alone, in *Popoviciu* the correct standard for a breach of articles 5 and 6 in conviction cases was confirmed. *Bertino* and *Merticariu* introduced a much more rigorous approach both to deliberate absence and retrial rights in assessing conviction in absence. In *El Khouri* the harm doctrine, settled law for over 20 years, in deciding where conduct occurred for the purposes of determining extradition offences, was set aside. At the time of publication, *Andrysiewicz* on the relevance of the prospects of early release in the requesting territory awaits judgment.

I echo the thanks contained in the preface to the first edition to the authors. Each of them has sacrificed their own time around busy practices to make their contributions. Great thanks to each of them and their families for those efforts.

Finally, much gratitude is due to Myles Grandison, the editor and originator of the first edition of this work. The work of preparing the second edition has been made much easier thanks to his tireless labours in 2020-2021.

The law is stated as up to date from May 2025. The responsibility for errors or omissions lies with the authors and the editor.

Daniel Sternberg
1st May 2025

PREFACE TO THE FIRST EDITION

This book has been written over the months from June 2020 to May 2021, during a period of significant change in our relationship with the European Union ('EU'). In the early months, the contents were premised upon the expectation that extradition with our European partners would be governed by the European Convention on Extradition 1957 ('the Convention'). Parliament was clearly preparing for this eventuality, as evidenced by the hastily passed Extradition (Provisional Arrest Act) 2020 and the Law Enforcement and Security (Amendment) (EU Exit) Regulations 2019. Experts from academia to law enforcement were sceptical of the Convention's suitability for the task in the current era, leading the Home Affairs Select Committee to state that it would be "catastrophic" if we had to revert to the Convention.

However, with one week to go before the end of the transition period, the EU and UK brokered the Trade and Cooperation Agreement ('TCA'), which contained an agreement governing extradition between the UK and the Member States. Superficially, the agreement is remarkably similar to the Council Framework Decision 2002/584/JHA. However, upon closer inspection, there are some fundamental differences which are likely to impact extradition arrangements for years to come.

The purpose of this book is to address the law that has developed under the Extradition Act 2003 ('the Act'), whilst also introducing readers to the significant developments that have been brought about by the TCA. Where possible, we have tried to assess how the Act and the TCA can be read in conformity with one another. However, to date, there has only been one reported decision which analyses the impact that the TCA has had on the Act. Consequently, readers should be mindful that this is a rapidly developing area of law. We have tried to ensure that the law is up to date and accurate as of 1st May 2021.

I would like to take this opportunity to thank the authors who contributed to this book, without whom it would not have come about. I would like to show my gratitude to Paul Erdunast for offering his experience and expertise in proof-reading this textbook. His help and support has been invaluable. I would also like to thank the clerks at Temple Garden Chambers for their support and understanding in allowing me to devote sufficient time to editing this book. Finally, I would like to thank my wife, Kim, for her patience and forbearance whilst I spent many an hour putting this book together.

Myles Grandison
23rd July 2021

CONTENTS

TABLE OF CASES

Nemeth v Hungarian Judicial Authorities [2022] EWHC 273 (Admin) … 170

Nika v The Douai County Court, France [2020] EWHC 3335 (Admin) … 69

Nikonovs v Governor of Brixton Prison [2005] EWHC 2405 (Admin), [2006] 1 WLR 1518 … 227

Niziol v Poland [2023] EWHC 3252 (Admin) … 97

Nobre v Portugal [2024] EWHC 417 (Admin) … 78

Norris v Government of the United States of America [2009] EWHC (Admin) 995, [2009] Lloyd's Rep FC 475 … 191

Norris v The Government of the United States of America [2008] UKHL 16, [2008] 1 AC 920 … 39

Norris v Government of the USA (No 2) [2010] UKSC 9, [2010] 2 AC 487… 81, 121, 171, 172, 175, 178

Nur v Public Prosecutor [2005] EWHC 1874 (Admin) … 19

O'Connor v Greece [2017] NIQB 77… 205

O'Connor v Greece [2022] UKSC 4, [2022] 1 WLR 903 … 205

O'Keeffe v Ireland (App. 35810/09) [2014] ECHR 28 … 144

Ode v High Court, Criminal Courts of Justice, Dublin, Ireland [2013] EWHC 3718 (Admin) … 178

Olah v Regional Court in Plzen, Czech Republic [2008] EWHC 2701 (Admin), [2008] Extradition LR 278 … 227

Oncel v the Governor of HM Prison Brixton and Turkey [2001] EWHC Admin 1142, [2002] ACD 17 … 65

Opalfvens v Belgium [2015] EWHC 2808 (Admin) … 207

Oprea v The Constanta Tribunal, Romania [2021] EWHC 223 (Admin) … 100, 101

Osso v Germany [2023] EWHC 1728 (Admin) … 108

INTRODUCTION

On 24th December 2020, the United Kingdom and the European Union ('EU') agreed a Trade and Cooperation Agreement ('TCA') that will govern the UK's relationship with the EU and its Member States across myriad sectors: from fishing rights to public procurement and from air transport to law enforcement. At around the same time, the authors were putting the finishing touches to a book that had hoped to guide practitioners through the European Convention on Extradition 1957 in the expectation that, with one week to go before the end of the transition period, the prospects of a deal to govern extradition between the UK and the EU appeared remote and the parties would therefore be reverting to the 1957 Convention.

However, contrary to our expectations, the EU and UK did reach an extradition agreement, which is contained in Part 3 of the TCA, at Title VII. The agreement governs extradition between the UK and EU Member States and applies to all those who are arrested after 2300 on 31st December 2020.

The aim of this book is to provide practitioners with a guide to the operation of the Extradition Act 2003 ('the 2003 Act') post-Brexit. To this end, it provides a précis of the jurisprudence that has been generated under the 2003 Act, gives an update on the amendments to the 2003 Act, and attempts to set out the relationship between the 2003 Act and the TCA. However, at the time of writing, there has only been one reported decision which analysed extradition under the TCA (*Polakowski and others v Westminster Magistrates Court and others* [2021] 1 WLR 2521). Consequently, whilst this edition will assist in setting out the current legal position, there will undoubtedly be a number of significant cases in the near future which will examine the impact of the TCA on our extradition arrangements with our closest neighbours.

The agreement contained within the TCA provides a model for extradition, similar in terms to the Council Framework Decision 2002/584/JHA ('2002 Framework Decision'). In large parts, it is materially identical to its predecessor, whilst in others it is radically different. With regards to the differences, the following are of note:

Proportionality

The principle of proportionality (Article 597) could be described as one of the "cornerstones" of the TCA, appearing as it does at the beginning of Title VII, just below the agreement's Objective. This is in stark contrast to the 2002 Framework Decision which made no mention of the principle. Instead, it was left to the amended handbook on how to issue a European Arrest Warrant, which was published by the Council of the European Union in 2010 in an attempt to dissuade judicial authorities from issuing EAWs for minor offences where there existed less coercive measures. The Council of the European Union, however, was of the opinion that it could not compel Judicial Authorities to undertake a "proportionality check" prior to the issuance of an EAW. The UK therefore took matters into its own hands by enacting its own proportionality bar in July 2014, albeit solely in relation to accusation warrants under Part 1. Article 597 is in strikingly similar terms to our domestic bar, providing:

> *'Cooperation through the arrest warrant shall be necessary and proportionate, taking into account the rights of the requested person and the interests of the victims, and having regard to the seriousness of the act, the likely penalty that would be imposed and the possibility of a State taking measures less coercive than the surrender of the requested person particularly with a view to avoiding unnecessarily long periods of pre-trial detention.'*

The importance of requests being "proportionate" is reinforced by the Joint Political Declaration on Title VII [Surrender] of Part Three [Law enforcement and Judicial cooperation in criminal matters], which provides:

> *"Article LAW.SURR.77[1] [Principle of proportionality] of Title VII [Surrender][of Part Three [Law enforcement and judicial cooperation in criminal matters] provides that cooperation on surrender must be necessary and proportionate, taking into account the rights of the requested person and the interests of the victims, and having regard to*

1 The numbering to the TCA was amended in April 2021.

the seriousness of the act, the likely penalty that would be imposed and the possibility of a State taking measures less coercive than the surrender of the requested person, particularly with a view to avoiding unnecessarily long periods of pre-trial detention.

The principle of proportionality is relevant throughout the process leading to the surrender decision set out in Title VII [Surrender]. Where the executing judicial authority has concerns about the principle of proportionality, it shall request the necessary supplementary information to enable the issuing judicial authority to set out its views on the application of the principle of proportionality.

Both Parties note that Articles LAW.SURR 77 [Principle of proportionality] and 93 [Surrender decision] enable the competent judicial authorities of the States to consider proportionality and the possible duration of pre-trial detention when implementing Title VII [Surrender], and note that this is consistent with their respective domestic laws."

It is arguable that Article 597 is drafted in broader terms than section 21A of the 2003 Act, and is not confined to "accusation" cases[2]. How, if at all, this wider protection will be given effect domestically remains to be seen. Section 21A has not to be amended.

Dual criminality

Whilst the threshold as to whether conduct constitutes an extradition offence by reason of the length of sentence imposed/imposable remains the same as it was under the 2002 Framework Decision (4 months/at least 12 months). Under the 2002 Framework Decision there was a possibility of dispensing with the need to satisfy the dual criminality criteria where the framework list had been ticked. However, it is apparent that the UK has decided not to waive the dual criminality requirements under the TCA. It has both repealed sections 64(5) and 65(5) and has

2 The term "arrest warrant" is defined, at Article 598 as incorporating both "accusation" and "conviction" cases. Had it been intended to limit the scope of the proportionality bar, one would have expected the draftsman to state this explicitly.

not notified the Specialised Committee on Law Enforcement and Judicial Cooperation pursuant to Article 599(4) that it intends to waive this requirement.[3]

Nationality bar

One of the more striking differences between the 2002 Framework Decision and the TCA is that the latter provides for a "Nationality exception" contained at Article 603. Whilst the starting point is that, like the EAW, the execution of an arrest warrant cannot not be refused on the grounds of nationality, Article 603(2) permits States to notify the Specialised Committee on Law Enforcement and Judicial Cooperation that that '*State's own nationals will not be surrendered or that the surrender of their own nationals will be authorised only under certain specified conditions.*' Such notification must be based on reasons related to the '*fundamental principles or practice of the domestic legal order*'. Where a State has refused to extradite its own national it '*shall consider instituting proceedings against its own national which are commensurate with the subject matter of the arrest warrant, having taken into account the views of the issuing State.*'

Thus far: Germany, Greece, France, Croatia, Latvia, Poland, Slovenia, Slovakia, Finland, Sweden have notified the Specialised Committee that they won't be extraditing their own nationals to the UK. A number of other Member States have indicated that they won't extradite their own nationals in certain circumstances. Only Belgium, Ireland, Spain and Italy have stated that they will not be submitting a notification under Article 603(2).[4] As has been widely reported, the UK will not invoke a nationality exception.

Whilst this exception is unlikely to impact the work of practitioners at Westminster Magistrates' Court, it is bound to affect the ability of the

3 https://eur-lex.europa.eu/legal-content/EN/TXT/HTML/?uri=OJ:C:2021:117I:FULL&from=EN

4 https://eur-lex.europa.eu/legal-content/EN/TXT/HTML/?uri=OJ:C:2021:117I:FULL&from=EN

UK to obtain the surrender of numerous Requested Persons from across the European Union.

Assurances

Article 604 provides for guarantees that may be given by the Issuing State in particular cases. The first two (a guarantee that a life sentence will be reviewed after 20 years in custody have been served, and an undertaking that the Requested Person, upon conviction, will be permitted to serve their sentence in the executing State) reflect Article 5(2) and (3) of the 2002 Framework Decision. However, the third, Article 604(c) is a new addition which formalises the provision of assurances as to e.g. prison conditions in which a Requested Person will be held in the Requesting State. Article 604(c) provides:

> *'if there are substantial grounds for believing that there is a real risk to the protection of the fundamental rights of the requested person, the executing judicial authority may require, as appropriate, additional guarantees as to the treatment of the requested person after the person's surrender before it decides whether to execute the arrest warrant.'*

Whilst the providing of such assurances had become commonplace across the European Union, the 2002 Framework Decision did not contain an express provision drafted in terms similar to those used in Article 604(c). It therefore fell to the CJEU to clarify the position in a number of cases, starting with *Criminal proceedings against Aranyosi* [2016] Q.B. 921.

Rights of a Requested Person

Article 609 provides for certain rights that should be afforded to Requested Persons upon their arrest. Article 609(1)-(3) (right to be informed of the contents of the warrant and the ability to consent to extradition, access to an interpreter and the right to a lawyer in the executing State) grant the same rights that were provided for by Article 11 of the 2002 Framework Decision. However, Article 609(4) provides the right to instruct a lawyer in the issuing State for the *'purpose of assisting the lawyer in the executing State in the arrest warrant proceedings'* and Article 609(5) affords the right to communicate with consular authorities. Whilst these two rights were previously contained in EU

Directive 2013/48, the UK did not opt in to this Directive on 1st December 2014.

On the face of it, the right conferred by 609(4) will be particularly useful to extradition practitioners. However, at this stage, it is unclear how this right can be invoked domestically, as the TCA includes a provision (Article 5) which states that the agreement does not confer any additional enforceable rights upon individuals in the UK. This led the House of Lords' European Union Committee to assert, at paragraph 141 of its 25th Report of Session 2019–21:

> *"The Government has welcomed the inclusion of a principle of proportionality and the provision addressing a range of individual rights. We note, however, that these rights are all made subject to national law and that the Trade and Cooperation Agreement explicitly states that it does not confer any rights on individuals to be directly invoked in domestic courts, but the EU is exempt in this regard by virtue of Article COMPROV.16. We call on the Government, therefore, to explain the extent to which UK citizens subject to extradition requests under the terms of the TCA will be able to rely upon the rights set out in the Agreement in UK courts. We also ask the Government to provide the rationale for the apparent imbalance embodied in Article COMPROV.16 between the rights enjoyed and enforceable by citizens in the EU before their national courts in comparison to those who are resident in the UK."*

Status under domestic law

Arguably the greatest impact that the TCA could have on extradition, is the manner in which our courts construe domestic legislation in light of it.

Practitioners will recall that the relationship between the 2003 Act and the 2002 Framework Decision changed over the years.

It had originally been thought that our courts were obliged to adopt a "conforming interpretation"[5] when construing the terms of the 2003 Act

[5] See *Criminal proceedings against Pupino* C-105/03 [2006] QB 83, at [43].

in accordance with the Framework Decision (see *Dabas v. High Court of Justice in Madrid, Spain* [2007] 2 A.C. 31 at [76]. However, this misunderstanding was rectified by Lord Mance in *Assange v. Swedish Prosecution Authority* [2012] 2 A.C. 471, where he pointed out that the "conforming interpretation" obligation only arose if the Framework Decision came within the definition of "the Treaties" contained in section 1 of the European Communities Act 1972. Having considered the history of the European Treaties and the extent to which they had been incorporated into domestic law, Lord Mance was able to demonstrate that the Framework Decision did not fall within that definition.

However, the position changed on 1st December 2014, when the UK opted back in to the Framework Decision, along with 34 other measures. The effect of this opt-in was that it brought the Framework Decision within the European Communities Act 1972. Consequently, from that date, the UK was obliged to interpret its domestic legislation as far as possible in light of the wording and purpose of the Framework Decision in order to achieve the result which the latter pursues (*Cretu v Local Court of Suceava, Romania* [2016] 1 WLR 3344).

The TCA has been implemented into domestic law through the European Union (Future Relationship) Act 2020 ('EUFRA'), which amends the 2003 Act. Ostensibly, the only amendments have been to: the designation of Member States as Part 1 territories, dual criminality and the effect on "old cases". Consequently, it might be thought that extradition will continue almost unchanged.

However, on the assumption that the *Pupino* principle of conforming interpretation no longer applies, how are we to construe our domestic legislation so that it is consistent with the TCA? One view is that we revert to "*the weaker canon of statutory construction that Parliament does not intend to legislate contrary to the United Kingdom's international obligations*" (see *Cretu v Local Court of Suceava, Romania* [2016] 1 WLR 3344, at [16]). An alternative is that, by reason of section 29 of EUFRA, the TCA now has supremacy over existing domestic law (subject to limited exceptions). It is apparent that the courts will need to grapple with this issue, along with many others, during the coming months.

CHAPTER ONE

THE INITIAL HEARING

Arrest under certified request/warrant

Powers of arrest

The 2003 Act provides for a range of powers of arrest in order to give effect to extradition requests.

In Part 1 cases, the position is relatively straightforward since no domestic arrest warrant is required in order to arrest a Requested Person. Instead, it is the Part 1 warrant itself that is executed, provided that it has been certified under section 2 of the 2003 Act by the "designated authority" (currently the National Crime Agency ('NCA')). Additionally, there is a power to arrest without a warrant (known as 'provisional arrest'), which applies where the arresting officer has reasonable grounds for believing that a Part 1 warrant has been or will be issued, and the warrant and accompanying section 2 certificate are provided to the Court in very short order (48 hours, extendable to a maximum of 96 hours).

Part 2 cases are more complex, since not only is a domestic arrest warrant required in order to give effect to an extradition request by a category 2 territory, but there are also two separate schemes for provisional arrest in Part 2 cases.

Arrest in Part 1 and 2 cases

Where a Part 1 warrant has been certified by the NCA under section 2 of the 2003 Act, it may be executed by a constable or customs officer under section 3. Service police officers may only execute a warrant if the Requested Person is subject to service law or is a civilian subject to service discipline (s.3(3)). A warrant may be executed even if the arresting officer does not have a copy of it in their possession at the time of arrest (s.3(5)).

A Part 2 request which has been certified by the Secretary of State under section 70 of the 2003 Act may be executed once the appropriate Judge has issued a domestic arrest warrant, having received the request and certificate pursuant to section 70(9).[6] The appropriate Judge may issue a domestic arrest warrant where they have reasonable grounds for believing that the offence is an extradition offence (s.71(2)(a)), and there is written evidence[7] which would justify the issue of a warrant for the arrest of a person accused of the offence in England and Wales (in an accusation case),[8] or which would justify the issue of a warrant for that person's arrest if unlawfully at large after conviction (in a conviction case).[9] Section 71(5)-(7) sets out who may execute the domestic arrest warrant, and where. Again, the warrant may be executed even if the arresting officer does not have a copy of it in their possession (s.71(5)(b)).

A copy of the Part 1 warrant or domestic arrest warrant under Part 2, respectively, must be given to Requested Persons as soon as practicable after their arrest.[10] Failure to serve a copy of the Part 1 warrant or Part 2 domestic arrest warrant entitles the Requested Person to apply for their discharge at the initial hearing. The appropriate Judge has a discretion to grant discharge.[11] However, if no prejudice has been suffered by the Requested Person, it will be a reasonable exercise of the Court's discretion to refuse the application.[12]

The Requested Person must also be produced before the appropriate Judge as soon as practicable following their arrest[13] (unless in a Part 2 case the arresting officer grants the person bail).[14] The hearing at which

---

6 Section 71(1).

7 If the Requesting State has been designated by the Secretary of State In section 3 of SI 3334 of 2003 as amended, then "information" will be read as replacing the requirement for "evidence" (s.71(4)).

8 Section 71(3)(a).

9 Section 71(3)(b).

10 Section 4(2) and 72(2).

11 Sections 4(4) and Section 72(5).

12 BH and KAS or H v The Lord Advocate [2011] HCJAC 77.

13 Sections 4(3) and 72(3).

14 Section 72(4)(a); or if the Secretary of State decides under section 126 that the extradition request is not to continue: section 72(4)(b).

they are produced is known as the 'initial hearing' or 'initial appearance', discussed further below. If the Requested Person is not produced as soon as practicable, the appropriate Judge <u>must</u> order their discharge.[15] Whether or not the person has been produced as soon as practicable is a question of fact.[16] In deciding this issue, it is not necessary to show that the arresting officer could have produced the Requested Person themselves, account must be taken of the arrangements in place to transport arrested persons from police stations to Court.

<u>**Provisional arrest**</u>

Provisional arrest in Part 1 cases

A constable or customs officer may provisionally arrest a person under section 5 of the 2003 Act without a warrant if they have reasonable grounds for believing that a Part 1 warrant has been or will be issued by a judicial authority of a category 1 territory.

A person provisionally arrested under section 5 must be brought before the appropriate Judge within 48 hours of arrest (s.6(2)). A Part 1 warrant and section 2 certificate must be produced to the judge, also within 48 hours of arrest (s.6(2A) and (4)). If, when the arrested person first appears before the judge, the Part 1 warrant and section 2 certificate have not yet been produced, the representatives of the category 1 territory may apply to extend the time to produce the documents by a further 48 hours (s.6(3A)). The judge may grant such extension if satisfied on the balance of probabilities that the requirement to produce the documents could not reasonably be complied with within the initial 48-hour period (ss.6(3B) and (3C)). In such circumstances, the judge must remand the person in custody or on bail (s.6(5B)). If and when the documents are subsequently produced, the arrested person must be brought before the judge (again) (ss.6(2B) and (3)).

If the person is not brought before the judge within 48 hours, or if the warrant and certificate are not produced within 48 hours and no

15 Sections 4(5) and Section 72(6).

16 R. (on the application of Nikonovs) v Governor of Brixton Prison [2005] EWHC 2405 (Admin); [2006] 1 WLR 1518.

extension is sought, or if the person is not brought before the judge when the warrant and certificate are produced, he may apply to be discharged and the judge must order discharge (s.6(6)). For the purposes of section 6 of the 2003 Act, Saturdays, Sundays, Christmas Day and bank holidays do not count towards any 48-hour time limit (ss.6(8A) and (8B)).

As with arrest under sections 3 and 71, a copy of the Part 1 warrant must be given to the person as soon as practicable after their arrest (s.6(5)). Failure to do so means the Requested Person can apply to be discharged, although this power is discretionary (s.6(7)). A person discharged under section 6(6) or (7) must not be arrested again under section 5 on the basis of a belief relating to the same Part 1 warrant (s.6(9) and (10)).

Provisional arrest in Part 2 cases: section 73 of the 2003 Act:

Section 73 enables provisional arrest in Part 2 cases. This power is particularly useful where a person suspected or convicted of an offence in a category 2 country is believed to be in the UK, but there has not been time to complete the sometimes lengthy process of preparing a full extradition request, certification by the Home Office, and issuance of a domestic arrest warrant by an appropriate judge. Thus, section 73 provides that a provisional arrest warrant may be issued under section 73 of the 2003 Act if a judge[17] is satisfied (on information in writing and on oath) that a person is accused or convicted of an offence in a category 2 territory,[18] and is believed to be in the UK or on their way to the country.[19] As with domestic arrest warrants issued under section 71, there must be reasonable grounds to believe that the offence is an extradition

17 The judge may be any justice of the peace, not just a District Judge (Magistrates' Courts) who has been designated as an "appropriate judge" by the Lord Chief Justice under sections 67 and 139. In practice most warrants under s.73 are Issued by Judges designated under sections 67 and 139.

18 Section 73(2).

19 Section 73(1).

offence, and there must be written evidence[20] which would justify the issue of a warrant for the arrest of a person accused of the offence in England and Wales (in an accusation case),[21] or which would justify the issue of a warrant for that person's arrest if unlawfully at large after conviction (in a conviction case).[22] The powers of arrest on a provisional warrant are the same as if it were a full request.[23]

Section 74 requires that the person must be given a copy of the arrest warrant and be brought as soon as practicable before the appropriate Judge (s.74(2) and (3)), unless granted police bail.[24] Failure to produce the Requested Person before as soon as practicable or to serve a copy of the arrest warrant on them can found an application for discharge under section 74(6) and (5) respectively. As before, the power to discharge for non-service of the warrant is discretionary, whereas discharge for non-production of the Requested Person is mandatory.

Sections 74(10) and (11) make provision for the judge to be provided with the full extradition request, together with the Secretary of State's certificate, within the required period. That period is 45 days starting with the day on which the person was arrested, or longer[25] for territories designated by an Order made by the Secretary of State.[26] Pending this, the judge must remand the Requested Person in custody or on bail (s.74(7)(c)). Assuming the documents are received within the required

---

20 If the Requesting State has been designated by the Secretary of State, then "information" will be read as replacing the requirement for "evidence" (section 73(5)).

21 Section 73(4)(a).

22 Section 73(4)(b).

23 Section 73(6)-(8).

24 Section 74(4)(a); or unless the Secretary of State decides that a competing extradition request should take precedence: s.74(4)(b).

25 Section 74(11)(b).

26 See article 4 of The Extradition Act (Designation of Part 2 Territories) Order 2003 SI 3334 of 2003 for a list of Part 2 territories where the required period is longer than 45 days, and relevant period for each territory.

period, the Court may proceed to fix a date for the final hearing and issue case management directions (see further below); but if the documents are not received within the required period, section 74(10) provides that the judge must order the person's discharge.

Provisional arrest in Part 2 cases: section 74A of the 2003 Act

The Extradition (Provisional Arrest) Act 2020 (which came into force on 22 October 2020) created a new scheme of provisional arrest in Part 2 cases, by inserting sections 74A-E into the 2003 Act. In essence, section 74A permits arrest on the basis solely of a certificate issued by the NCA, where the request emanates from one of a number of particularly close and trusted extradition partners (the "specified part 2 territories" listed in Schedule A1 to the 2003 Act, currently Australia, Canada, Iceland, Liechtenstein, New Zealand, Norway, Switzerland and the USA), and the offence in respect of which the request is issued is a "serious extradition offence".

When the 2020 Act was drafted, the intention was that it would apply also (indeed, principally) to requests emanating from EU Member States, in the event that no deal was reached and such States were re-designated as category 2 territories following the end of the transition period. This could have led to a sudden influx of applications to District Judges to issue Part 2 arrest warrants for individuals sought by EU Member States, and the Extradition (Provisional Arrest) Act 2020 was enacted in part to avoid this. Even though the new provisions do not apply to EU Member States, as they are still designated as category 1 territories, this legislative history is worth bearing in mind as it helps to explain some aspects of the new scheme, which are modelled on Part 1 provisions.

Section 74A of the 2003 Act provides constables, customs officers and service police officers the power to make arrests without a warrant, based solely on a certificate issued under section 74B by a "designated authority". The "designated authority" is defined in section 74B(4) as the NCA.[27]

27 Although section 74B(5) provides that the Secretary of State can change the "designated authority" by regulations.

The NCA may issue a certificate if:

- it receives a "valid request", made by an authority of a specified category 2 territory, for the person's arrest (s.74B(1)(a)). A request is "valid" if the requesting authority is one which the NCA believes has the function of making such requests in that territory (s.74C(6)), and if the request contains the statement and information referred to in section 74C(2)-(3) (in an accusation case) or (4)-(5) (in a conviction case). These provisions are similar to sections 2(3)-(4) and (5)-(6) of the 2003 Act, respectively, discussed in detail elsewhere in this book.

- it is satisfied that a warrant has been issued in the category 2 territory for the person's arrest, or they are alleged to be unlawfully at large after conviction by a court in the category 2 territory (s.74B(1)(b)).

- it has reasonable grounds for believing that the offence specified in the request is a "serious extradition offence" (s.74B(1)(c)). In an accusation case, an offence is a "serious extradition offence" if the requirements of section 137 are satisfied, save that where subsections (3) or (4) are relied on, the conduct must be punishable by at least three years' imprisonment if it was committed in the UK (s.74B(10(d)).[28] In a conviction case, the definition of "serious extradition offence" is satisfied where the requirements of section 138 are made out, except that where subsections (3) is relied on, the conduct must be punishable by at least three years' imprisonment under the relevant UK law

28 Although the offence need only attract a sentence of at least 12 months in the Requesting State (s.74B(10)(e)). These requirements do not apply where section 135(5) is relied on, i.e. the offence is listed in section 137(6) (e.g. crimes within the jurisdiction of the International Criminal Court).

(s.74B(10(d)).[29] Sections 137 and 138 are discussed further below, in the section on dual criminality.

- it is satisfied that the seriousness of the conduct makes it appropriate to issue the certificate (s.74B(1)(d)).

The certificate issued by the NCA must (s.74B(2)):

i) state the category 2 territory, the form of the request, and the date on which the request was made;

ii) certify that the category 2 territory has been specified;

iii) certify that it is a valid request;

iv) certify that the offence is *"serious"* and that it is appropriate to issue the certificate; and

v) set out the statement and information referred to in section 74C(2)-(3) (in an accusation case) or (4)-(5) (in a conviction case).

The certificate must be given to the Requested Person as soon as practicable after arrest (s.74A(2)), and the Requested Person must also be brought before an appropriate Judge as soon as practicable pursuant to section 74A(3).

At the initial appearance, the Requested Person may apply for discharge if:

- there were no reasonable grounds on which the designated authority could have issued the certificate under section 74B(1) (for example, if it was clear that the offence could not constitute a "serious extradition

29 Although the actual sentence imposed need only be 4 months or more: s.138(3)(c). Where sections 138(4) (extra-territorial offences) or 138(5) (offences listed in section 136(6)) are relied on, there is no requirement that the conduct must be punishable by at least three years' imprisonment if it was committed in the UK.

offence"). If there were not, the Judge must discharge the Requested Person (s.74D(10)(b)(i)).

- the certificate does not comply with the formal requirements of section 74B(2), in which case the Judge may order discharge (s.74D)(10)(a)(ii)).
- the certificate was not given to the person as soon as practicable after the arrest. As we have seen elsewhere, the Judge may discharge in such circumstances; he is not obliged to do so (s.74D(10)(a)(i)).
- the Requested Person was not brought before the appropriate Judge as soon as practicable after arrest. As we have already seen, this is mandatory; the Judge must order the person's discharge if they are satisfied that section 74D(10)(b)(ii) is made out.

If the Requested Person does not fall to be discharged under the above provisions,[30] the appropriate Judge must decide whether, on the basis of the evidence or information before him,[31] a warrant for the person's provisional arrest would be issued under section 73 of the 2003 Act, discussed above (s.74D(1)). As we have seen, the question here is whether there are reasonable grounds for believing that the offence which the person is accused of or has been convicted of is an extradition offence, and whether there is written evidence or information that would justify the issuance of a warrant in this jurisdiction. If the judge decides that a

30 It should be noted that section 74B(3) provides that a certificate may be withdrawn and reissued on the basis of the same request, so long as the Requested Person has not yet been arrested. Thus, if a certificate is imperfect or incomplete, the NCA can simply withdraw it and issue a new one at any time before the Requested Person has been arrested in reliance on it. But if the Requested Person has been arrested, and the appropriate Judge discharges them, then the NCA would only be able to issue another certificate in relation to a freshly issued request.

31 Under section 74D(4), (7) and (8), if certain criteria are met the judge may adjourn the proceedings for up to 72 hours (excluding weekends and bank holidays) to allow for more evidence/information to be produced to show that a warrant would have been issued under section 73.

provisional arrest warrant would not be issued, section 74D(2) requires them to order the person's discharge.

If the judge decides that a provisional arrest warrant would be issued, they must proceed with the initial hearing under section 74E.[32] Inter alia, this provides for the full extradition request and Secretary of State's certificate to be provided to the appropriate Judge within the period specified in section 74(11) (45 days in most cases), failing which the Requested Person must be discharged (s.74E(4)).

Requirements at the initial hearing

The initial appearance is the hearing at which the Requested Person is brought before the Court for the first time. It serves a number of functions, including to open proceedings, determine a number of preliminary issues and identify the likely issues in the case, determine custody and bail issues, and manage the case going forwards. Exactly what steps are required to be taken at the initial hearing, and what issues are to be considered, varies depending on whether the case is under Part 1 or Part 2, and on what provision the Requested Person has been arrested under.

Production and service of the warrant

As has already been noted, the Requested Person must be produced for their initial hearing, and the relevant documents must be served on them, in short order after their arrest. If this is not done, then one of the first issues the appropriate Judge will have to consider at the initial hearing is whether they fall to be discharged. Practitioners should note that applications for discharge on these grounds must be made at the initial appearance, as they cannot be revisited at a later stage.

32 Section 74D(3)

Identity

In a Part 1 case the judge must decide on a balance of probabilities whether the person arrested is the subject of the warrant.[33] If the judge decides that they are not, they must be discharged. This issue must be addressed at the initial hearing, and cannot be reopened at the extradition hearing.[34]

In Part 2 cases, the judge is not required to consider identity at the initial hearing. It is an issue for the extradition hearing,[35] considered in chapter 2 later in this book.

Procedural requirements

In addition to any preliminary issues that are required to be dealt with, there are a number of procedural steps which must be taken at the initial hearing.

For example, the appropriate Judge must inform the Requested Person of the contents of the request for their extradition.[36] Further, they must give them the required information about consent.[37] This is considered further below.

If the Requested Person does not (at that stage) wish to consent, the Court will likely proceed to identification of the issues and case management (discussed further below), with a view to complying with the statutory requirement to fix a date on which the extradition hearing is to begin.[38] The date fixed cannot be later than the end of the permitted

---

33 Section 7(2) and 7(3).

34 *Nur v Public Prosecutor* [2005] EWHC 1874 (Admin), at [19].

35 Section 78(4)(a).

36 Sections 8(1)(b), 72(7)(a), 74(7)(a), and 74E(1)(a).

37 Sections 8(1)(c), 72(7)(b), 74(7)(b), and 74E(1)(b).

38 Section 8(1)(a)) and 75(1). In a Part 1 case, section 8(4) provides that the date fixed cannot be later than the end of the permitted period, which is 21 days starting with the date of arrest. In a Part 2 case, the permitted

period, which is 21 days starting with the date of arrest in a Part 1 case,[39] and two months starting with the date of the first appearance in a Part 2 case.[40]

The only exception to the requirement to fix a date is where the Requested Person has been provisionally arrested under Part 2. In such circumstances, the date for the extradition hearing is not fixed until after the full extradition request and accompanying certificate has been received.[41] The permitted period within which the hearing must begin is two months, starting with the date of receipt of the documents.[42]

Finally, the appropriate Judge is required by the statute to remand the Requested Person in custody or on bail at the conclusion of the initial hearing (as indeed they are at the conclusion of each hearing at which the Requested Person appears before them). Bail is considered in more detail below.

---

period is two months starting with the date on which the person first appears or is brought before the judge (s.75(2)). If, before the date fixed for the extradition hearing, a party to the proceedings applies to the judge for a later date to be fixed and the judge believes it to be in the interests of justice to do so, they may fix a later date (s.8(4) and 75(3)). However, if the extradition hearing does not begin on or before the date fixed under this section and the person applies to the judge to be discharged, the judge must order their discharge (s.8(7) and 75(4)). In a Part 1 case, this power need not be exercised if "reasonable cause is shown for the delay" (s.8(7)). An application for discharge on this basis must be made at the first hearing after the deadline for opening the extradition hearing: *R. (on the application of Asliturk) v City of Westminster Magistrates' Court* [2010] EWHC 2148 (Admin); [2011] 1 W.L.R. 1139. In reality, such applications can be easily avoided by formally opening the extradition hearing and adjourning without any rulings.

39 Section 8(4).

40 Section 75(2).

41 Section 76(1) and (2).

42 Section 76(3).

Consent to extradition

The information which the Requested Person is required to be given about consent is that they can consent to their extradition, but that by doing so they will lose the right to appeal against the appropriate Judge's decision. Consent must be giving in writing and is irrevocable.[43]

In *An application by Marc Ballan for Judicial Review* [2008] NIQB 140, Kerr LCJ ruled that consent to surrender must be voluntary and made in full awareness of the consequences. He said that voluntariness in this context has the following characteristics:

- The person must deliberately agree/acquiesce to their surrender.
- The person must be free from duress/coercion.
- The person must be of sufficient age/mental capacity to give their mind freely to the course chosen with sufficient comprehension of the nature of the decision to be taken.
- They must not be under any misapprehension as to the factual/legal basis on which the decision to consent is taken.

Therefore if the Requested Person subsequently challenges the voluntariness of consent, an enquiry should be undertaken. Such enquiry need not be elaborate but should include ascertaining:

- Whether the person had been given to understand that they had no option but to consent.
- Whether the person had appreciated that consent meant there would be no investigation as to the possible bars to extradition or whether extradition would be ECHR-compatible.

If consent is found to be involuntary then the question of irrevocability does not arise because the consent is ineffective.

In *Celczynski v Polish Judical Authority (No. 1)* [2019] EWHC 3450 (Admin) Dove J held that the Requested Person's consent to his extradition was not lawful on the basis that he was not legally represented

---

43 Section 8(3) and 72(8).

at the time that he purported to give his consent. Dove J therefore quashed the order for his extradition. The principles applying to such a challenge were further analysed by Fordham J in *R (on the application of Marc Salomon) v Westminster Magistrates' Court* [2022] EWHC 83 (Admin).

Case management

After the court has considered consent it is necessary to identify the challenges to extradition, which are dealt with in greater detail elsewhere in this book.

As a matter of practice, the advocate representing the Requested Person must complete a form containing details of the requested person at the initial hearing where extradition is contested. This is to put the Court and CPS on notice of the essential facts and the challenges likely to be raised, and to assist the court in exercising its case management powers under Criminal Procedure Rules 50.3 and 50.4. Paper forms (historically printed on blue paper and sometimes referred to as a 'blue form') are available at Westminster Magistrates' Court. It is important to complete the form as fully and as accurately as possible.

Having appraised the likely issues, the court will make various directions, including setting a date by which any application for legal aid must be made; a date for the service of a statement of issues and evidence upon which the Requested Person wishes to rely; as well as the date by which the Requesting State must serve its evidence and/or assurances.

When fixing the date for the hearing, the advocate ought to provide a realistic estimate of how long it will take to prepare the case and the amount of court time the full hearing is expected to take. The court may list a case management hearing before the substantive hearing, especially in cases where a significant number of complex challenges are raised. In practice, if a Requested Person is remanded in custody, the court is likely to review the progress of the case every 28 days when the person appears to be further remanded in custody.

Bail

After dealing with all other issues at the initial hearing the court will consider the question of bail. In accusation cases there is a presumption in favour of bail[44]. If an advocate believes that they need more information in order to make a full and proper bail application, they should not pursue an application at the initial hearing but rather apply to adjourn the case (and have the Requested Person remanded in custody under Paragraph 5 of Schedule 1 of the Bail Act 1976) for the shortest possible period, usually the next working day.

Paragraph 2 of Schedule 1 of the Bail Act 1976 provides that a Requested Person need not be granted bail if there are substantial grounds for believing that whether or not they were released on conditions, they would fail to surrender to custody, commit an offence while on bail, interfere with witnesses or otherwise obstruct the course of justice, whether in relation to themselves or any other person.

Section 198(13) of the 2003 Act amends the Bail Act 1976 to include a further ground for refusing bail. Paragraph 2B of Schedule 1 provides that the defendant need not be granted bail in extradition proceedings if the conduct would, if carried out in England and Wales, constitute an indictable offence or an offence triable either way, and it appears to the court that the defendant was on bail at the date of the offence.

Examples of conditions commonly imposed in extradition cases are:

- Pre-release security, surety or both;
- Pre-release surrender or retention of travel documents.[45]

---

44 Section 198 of the 2003 Act, amending the Bail Act 1976 to insert section 4(2B) to the Bail Act 1976. This removes the presumption in favour of bail in relation to a person who is unlawfully at large after conviction of an offence in the requesting territory.

45 In some cases, the court has imposed a condition of bail that the Requested Person's partner and, potentially, children, also surrender their identity documents. However, the power to require the surrender of such

- Residence and an electronically monitored curfew,
- Not to apply for international travel documents,
- Reporting at a police station,
- Not to go to any airport, seaport or international rail station.

The Requested Person will need to persuade the court that they have strong ties to this jurisdiction and little incentive to abscond. In the vast majority of extradition cases they are unlikely to achieve bail without a pre-release cash security. The amount of the security will vary according to the Requested Person's means and the seriousness of the offence for which their extradition is sought.

Securities need to be paid into Westminster Magistrates' Court. Once bail is granted a reference number can be given to the person paying the security who can then make the payment electronically. If the security is to be paid in cash the person must comply with anti-money laundering regulations. The Requested Person is not usually released from custody until after the court has received the cleared funds into its account. However, some District Judges are amenable to granting post-release securities in limited circumstances.

Where a Requested Person has been refused bail by the Magistrates' Court, they can make a fresh bail application at the next hearing which, unless they consent to be remanded in their absence, will be within eight clear days.[46] This will be a *de novo* hearing usually before a different judge, at which all arguments previously made can thus be repeated.[47] If the second bail application is unsuccessful, at subsequent hearings the

---

documents, especially If not offered voluntarily, is unclear and some Judges will not impose such a condition of bail. Whilst the Court cannot refuse to return these documents on request, the fact that they are surrendered can go some way towards allaying fears that the Requested Person might abscond.

46 Section 128(6), Magistrates' Courts Act 1980.

47 Schedule 1, Part IIA, Paragraph 2, Bail Act 1976.

court does not need to hear arguments which it has previously heard.[48] This is so even though the court must consider the question of bail at each hearing.[49] Thus, if there has been no material change in circumstances since the last application, the defendant is not entitled to make a further application for bail. Thereafter, the Requested Person is remanded in custody to be produced no later than every 28 days (unless they are serving a sentence of imprisonment in this jurisdiction, as set out below).

Bail 'appeals' by the Requested Person

Section 22(1A) of the Criminal Justice Act 1967 provides that where the Magistrates' Court withholds bail in extradition proceedings or imposes conditions in granting bail, the High Court may grant bail or vary the conditions imposed. As a matter of practice, an application under this provision is made to the High Court by submitting form EX244 to the Administrative Court Office along with the requisite fee. The notice should also be served on the CPS. Legal aid in the High Court is not means tested and a paper CRM14 form should be submitted to the Administrative Court Office to apply for legal aid.

Even though applications to the High Court for bail under section 22(1A) are commonly referred to as appeals, the application is considered *de novo*[50] rather than as an appeal against a District Judge's refusal to grant bail.

Prosecution appeals against the grant of bail

If the Requested Person is granted bail by a District Judge, section 1 of the Bail (Amendment) Act 1993 provides that there is a right of appeal against such a decision to the High Court. Oral notice of appeal must be given as soon as the decision is made to grant bail and before the person

---

48 Schedule 1, Part IIA, Paragraph 3, Bail Act 1976.

49 Schedule 1, Part IIA, Paragraph 1 Bail Act 1976.

50 Janet Tighe v High Court Dublin, Republic of Ireland [2013] EWHC 3313 (Admin).

is released.[51] Thereafter a written notice of appeal must be served on the Court and the person concerned, within two hours of the conclusion of the hearing before the Magistrates' Court.[52] The Magistrates' Court will then remand the person in custody until the appeal is resolved.[53] If the prosecution fails to serve the notices within two hours then the appeal is deemed to have been dismissed.[54] The appeal hearing shall be held within 48 hours of the date of oral notice being given, excluding weekends and public holidays.[55] The appeal against the grant of bail is a rehearing and the Court has the power to remand the person in custody or on bail subject to any conditions it sees fit.[56]

Outstanding domestic proceedings/sentence

Sections 8A and 8B of the 2003 Act (in Part 1 cases) and sections 76A and 76B (in Part 2 cases) deal with the situation where the Requested Person has been charged with an offence in the UK, or is already serving a sentence here, before the extradition hearing begins.[57]

If the person is charged[58] with a domestic criminal offence then the extradition hearing must be adjourned pursuant to section 8A or 76A

---

51 Section 1(4) of the Bail (Amendment) Act 1993.

52 Section 1(5) of the Bail (Amendment) Act 1993.

53 Section 1(6) of the Bail (Amendment) Act 1993.

54 Section 1(7) of the Bail (Amendment) Act 1993.

55 Section 1(8) of the Bail (Amendment) Act 1993.

56 Section 1(9) of the Bail (Amendment) Act 1993.

57 See also sections 22-23 (Part 1) and Sections 88-89 (Part 2), which apply where the appropriate judge is informed that the Requested Person has been charged with an offence or is required to serve a sentence in the UK, after the extradition hearing has opened but before it has ended; and sections 36B (Part 1) and 118C (Part 2), which make similar provision where the appropriate judge is informed of a domestic charge or sentence after an extradition order has been made, but before it has been carried out.

58 Cf. R (on the application of Nekrosius v Government of Switzerland [2009] EWHC 3080 (Admin).

until either: the charge is disposed of (as defined in section 214); the charge is withdrawn; proceedings in respect of the charge are discontinued; or an order is made for the charge to lie on the file. The Requested Person will not be asked if they consent to their extradition and the court will proceed straight to the issue of bail.

If the person is serving a sentence of imprisonment for a domestic offence then the case may be adjourned until the sentence has been served or until the person is eligible for release. This discretion is engaged only where the Requested Person is in custody; it does not apply where they have been released on licence from a domestic sentence.[59] If the Court exercises its discretion to adjourn, the Requested Person will be produced and the case reviewed every 6 months (unless, of course, the release date is sooner than that). The relevant principles applying to a decision to adjourn under section 8B were considered by the High Court In *Brockwell v Westminster Magistrates' Court* [2022] EWHC 1662 (Admin).

In some cases, the Requested Person may be subject to a lengthy sentence in the UK. In such circumstances, the CPS may obtain instructions from the Requesting State as to whether it wishes to seek the person's temporary surrender. If so, the Requesting State would be required to provide an undertaking that the person will be kept in custody pending their trial and then returned to the UK after the proceedings have concluded in the Requesting State. They would then, if the court agrees, be returned to the UK to serve the rest of their sentence.[60]

It is clearly desirable to avoid a long interval between an extradition order being made and the order being carried out; the Requested Person's circumstances might have changed in the intervening time in such a way as to render extradition inappropriate or disproportionate. For this reason, in *Robert Slator v Bow Street Magistrates' Court and the High Court of Dublin* [2006] EWHC 2628 (Admin), it was held that the District Judge's refusal to adjourn the extradition hearing in circumstances where

59 Maksimas Proskinas v Ministry of Justice of the Republic of Lithuania [2012] EWHC 4126 (Admin).

60 Sections 52 and 119 of the 2003 Act.

the domestic sentence would not have been completed for at least 3 years was irrational.

Competing requests

Under section 44 of the 2003 Act, the appropriate Judge is empowered to regulate competing Part 1 warrants, by ordering that the proceedings under one of the Part 1 warrants be deferred until the conclusion of the other (or, where an extradition order has already been made in respect of one of the Part 1 warrants, by ordering that extradition be deferred until the other Part 1 warrant has been disposed of). Where one or both of the competing requests is governed by Part 2, the Secretary of State has the power to decide which set of proceedings should be deferred.[61]

In reaching this decision, the judge must take into account the criteria set out in section 44(7), namely:

a) The relative seriousness of the offences concerned;

b) The place where each offence was committed (or was alleged to have been committed);

c) The date when each request was issued;

d) Whether, in relation to each offence, the Requested Person is accused of its commission (not convicted) or is alleged to be unlawfully at large after conviction.

Where extradition proceedings or extradition (if this was already ordered) were deferred in order to make way for a competing extradition claim, but the competing claim was resolved in the Requested Person's favour, there is scope to once again enliven the deferred proceedings or order. Resumption of deferred proceedings is governed by section 180, and the carrying out of a deferred order is dealt with in section 181. In either case, there is a strict window of 21 days (starting with the day on which the other extradition claim is disposed of), within which the judge may order that the deferred proceedings be resumed, or that the deferred order

61 The provisions under Part 2 are covered in the chapter dealing with the Secretary of State's role.

be carried out.[62] If no order is made within this period, the Requested Person must be discharged.[63]

Legal aid

Lastly, a word should be said about applications for legal aid. Legal aid in extradition proceedings is means tested at the Magistrates' Court, and applications can be submitted online using the LAA Online Portal[64] or in writing with form CRM14 (or, if required, CRM15). It is essential that the relevant forms are filled out carefully and accurately with the Requested Person at the initial appearance, since mistakes and omissions can lead to severe delays in applications being made, processed and/or accepted.

Certificates for counsel

Where a Requested Person is granted legal aid, the starting point is that the representation order will only cover work done by a solicitor, not by counsel. However, section 27 of the Legal Aid, Sentencing and Punishment of Offenders Act 2012 and the Criminal Legal Aid (Determinations by a Court and Choice of Representative) Regulations 2013 enable the Court to extend the representation order to include representation by an advocate as well as a litigator. Such an application can only be granted if there are circumstances which make the proceedings "unusually grave or difficult" and representation by an advocate would be "desirable" (regulation 16). Regulation 17 provides that Queen's Counsel can be instructed where the court determines that the Requested Person would not be adequately represented except by a Queen's Counsel or more than one advocate.

Such applications must be made in writing via the International Jurisdiction Office at Westminster Magistrates' Court to one of the

---

62 Sections 180(6) and 181(6).

63 Sections 180(5) and 181(5). The judge also has a discretion to order discharge on the deferred matter, even where the period for ordering resumption has not yet elapsed, and even where extradition on the deferred matter was previously ordered: sections 180(4) and 181(4).

64 https://portal.legalservices.gov.uk

appropriate Judges who are empowered by the Senior District Judge to consider them. It should be noted that where an application to extend the representation order is granted, this will take effect from the date of the judge's decision, or, if a different date is specified in the decision, that date. An application which is refused on paper can be renewed to an oral hearing before a different Judge.

CHAPTER TWO

THE EXTRADITION HEARING

The District Judge's powers

Under section 9 (in Part 1) and section 77 (in Part 2) of the 2003 Act the District Judge at the extradition hearing has the same powers, as nearly as may be, as if they were hearing the summary trial of an information against the person whose extradition is requested. That power necessarily includes the power to adjourn the proceedings and, if the judge does adjourn the hearing, to remand the Requested Person in custody or on bail (ss.9(4) and 77(4)). In the same way that a judge at a summary trial could hear evidence and submissions and give directions to ensure proper case management, the judge at the extradition hearing can exercise the same powers.

The District Judge's powers at the hearing also include the power to proceed in the absence of the Requested Person. In *Griffin v Westminster Magistrates' Court* [2011] EWHC 943 (Admin), [2012] 1 WLR 270, Collins J considered a challenge to an extradition hearing which took place in the absence of the Requested Person on the basis that there was no power in law to hold such a hearing. Collins J held at [33]:

> *"While there is nothing in the 2003 Act which expressly permits the court to proceed in the defendant's absence, there is nothing which expressly requires his presence and the importation of the powers of magistrates when trying an information summarily clearly recognises that s.122 of the 1980 Act*[65] *will apply. Since this deems presence where the defendant is represented, it clearly overrides s.11(2A)."*

The Divisional Court confirmed that an extradition hearing could proceed in the Requested Person's absence, provided that it was procedurally proper and fair.[66] In practice, this is likely to require the

---

65 The Magistrates' Courts Act 1980

66 Lagocki & Tarabanovs v Regional Court [2015] EWHC 3641 (Admin)

Requested Person to have been warned that the hearing could proceed in their absence if they do not attend and, in the case of a Requested Person who is remanded in custody, sufficient evidence being placed before the court from the prison to satisfy the judge that the reason for their non-attendance at the hearing is their deliberate choice rather than, for example, ill health or genuine confusion about the date of the hearing. Requested persons are routinely warned at the Initial Hearing that the Extradition Hearing can proceed in their absence and extradition can be ordered In their absence If they do not attend and there is no good reason for their non-attendance.

Uncontested hearings and consent

A Requested Person can consent to their extradition to the territory which has requested them at any time. Persons subject to provisional extradition requests may consent if they wish. Under sections 45(4) and 127(3) of the 2003 Act consent must be given in writing and is irrevocable. Consent to surrender on a Part 1 warrant must be given before the appropriate Judge (s.45(4)(a)). If the Requested Person consents to their surrender on a Part 1 warrant, section 46 requires the appropriate Judge to remand them in custody or on bail and to order their extradition within 10 days starting on the day that consent is given (s.46(6)). If a date for the extradition hearing has not been fixed the judge is not required to set a date and if the extradition hearing has begun the judge is not required to proceed or continue further with the hearing (s.46(4)-(5)). Similar provisions apply to consent to a Part 2 extradition request in section 128(2)-(3).

If a Requested Person consents to their extradition to a Part 2 territory before their case is sent to the Secretary of State, consent must be given at a hearing before the appropriate Judge. If their case has already been sent to the Secretary of State they must give their consent to the Home Secretary. If a person consents before the appropriate Judge, the judge must send the case to the Secretary of State for their decision on whether the person is to be extradited (s.128(4)).

Sections 45(5)-(6) and 127(6)-(9) of the 2003 Act require that, for consent to be valid, a Requested Person be represented by counsel or a solicitor, have had the right to apply for legal aid and have failed or refused to apply, had their application for legal aid rejected or have been granted legal aid which was subsequently withdrawn.

By virtue of sections 26(2) and 103(2) a person who consents loses the right to appeal the decision of the appropriate Judge to order their extradition (under Part 1) or to send their case to the Secretary of State (under Part 2). Similarly, by virtue of section 108(2) of the 2003 Act a person who consents also loses the right to appeal the decision of the Secretary of State to order their extradition on a Part 2 extradition request.

Whilst there is no right of appeal where a person consents to their extradition, the High Court has shown a degree of latitude to Requested Persons who subsequently claim not to have understood the requirements of consent or to have had ineffective legal assistance (notwithstanding the requirements of the statute that a person give consent in writing and be represented or to have had the opportunity to obtain representation)[67].

As an alternative to consenting, it is open to a Requested Person to indicate that they raise no bars or other issues in opposition to extradition. In such circumstances the case will proceed to a short, uncontested hearing at which the advocate appearing for the Requesting State will summarise the request and the issues the Judge must resolve under sections 10-21A under Part 1 or sections 78-87 under Part 2 of the 2003 Act and will result in extradition being ordered under section 21(3) or 21A(5) on a Part 1 warrant or the case being sent to the Secretary of State under section 87 on a Part 2 request. The advantage of such a course to the Requested Person is that it preserves the right to appeal the District Judge's decision. Under Part 2 it also preserves their right to make representations to the Secretary of State and to appeal the decision of the Secretary of State if they so wish. However, any application for permission to appeal following an uncontested extradition hearing would

67 An Application for Judicial Review by Marc Ballan [2008] NIQB 140, Celczynski v Polish Judicial Authority [2019] EWHC 3450 (Admin) and Salomon v Westminster Magistrates' Court [2022] EWHC 83 (Admin) discussed in greater detail in Chapter 1.

necessarily have to explain why no issues were raised before the District Judge.

Initial Stages of the Extradition Hearing

At the initial stage of the extradition hearing, the Judge must consider whether the requirements of section 10 in Part 1, or 78(2), in Part 2, of the 2003 Act have been met. If extradition proceedings originate from a British Overseas Territory, the 2003 Act must be read alongside the Extradition Act 2003 (Overseas Territories) Order 2016

Section 10 requires the Judge to consider whether the offence contained in the Part 1 warrant is an extradition offence and whether there are any bars to extradition under sections 11-19B of the 2003 Act. These issues are considered in further detail below and elsewhere in this book.

In Part 2, the requirements of section 78(2) are whether the judge has received the request and certificate from the Secretary of State, whether there are sufficient particulars of the Requested Person and the offence alleged, and whether there is an arrest warrant or certificate of conviction.

Of these issues, barring any obvious missing documents in the request such as an arrest warrant or certificate of conviction, the most frequently raised challenge is that there are insufficient particulars of conduct under section 78(2)(c).

Sufficiency of particulars

Section 78 of the 2003 Act should be read alongside and consistently with the more onerous requirements of section 2(4)(c) under Part 1 of the 2003 Act.[68] A '*broad omnibus*' description of the conduct alleged will be insufficient to satisfy the statutory requirement.[69] In *Ektor v The Netherlands* [2007] EWHC 3106 (Admin), [2008] Extradition LR 28, a Part 1 case, King J held, at [7]:

---

68 *Dudko v Russia* [2010] EWHC 1125 (Admin at [16]

69 *Von der Pahlen v Government of Austria* [2006] EWHC 1672 (Admin), [2006] Extradition LR 197, at [21].

> *"In particular, the description must include when and where the offence is said to have happened and what involvement the person named in the warrant had. As with any European instrument, these requirements must be read in the light of its objectives. A balance must be struck between, in this case, the need on the one hand for an adequate description to inform the person, and on the other the object of simplifying extradition procedures. The person sought by the warrant needs to know what offence he is said to have committed and to have an idea of the nature and extent of the allegations against him in relation to that offence. The amount of detail may turn on the nature of the offence. Where dual criminality is involved, the detail must also be sufficient to enable the transposition exercise to take place."*

In *King v France* [2015] EWHC 3670 (Admin), [2016] ACD 34, Collins J summarised the general position at [16] and [22]:

> *"16. I am far from persuaded that there is a need for full and exhaustive description. But sufficient circumstances must be set out in order for there to be compliance with Article 8 to enable the requested state and the requested person to be able to ensure that any barriers to extradition, whether compulsory or optional, do or do not apply...In principle there is no material difference between what is required in an accusation or conviction case.*
>
> ...
>
> *22. I do not believe that the particulars required whether for an accusation or a conviction warrant need great detail. As I have said, provided they give sufficient information to enable any available point on a bar to be taken and the ability to judge whether the offence is properly listed in the framework list and dual criminality can be shown if that should be needed, they will suffice whether for accusation or conviction cases."*

Following the Divisional Court's judgment in *Alexander v The Public Prosecutor's Office, Marseille District Court of First Instance, France* [2017] EWHC 1392 (Admin), [2018] QB 408, it is accepted that the appropriate Judge at the extradition hearing may admit further information to supplement the contents of a Part 1 warrant or Part 2 extradition request. However, a request must be made in the prescribed form to be so supplemented. The Court emphasised that extradition could not be achieved on the basis of a "*bit of paper*"[70], and *"[t]he question in a given case whether the court is faced with lacunae or a wholesale failure to provide the necessary particulars can only be decided on the specific facts."*

Identity (Part 2)

Provided the requirements of section 78(2) are met, the judge will then go on to consider the requirements of section 78(4). This requires, first, that the judge be satisfied on the balance of probabilities that the person appearing before them is the person whose extradition is requested by virtue of s.74(5). The cases of *Lumenica v Albania* [2012] EWHC 3802 (Admin), *Riza Vatoci v Albania* [2011] EWHC 1295 (Admin), *Stefan v Albania* [2007] EWHC 3267 (Admin), [2008] Extradition L.R. 49 and *Prendi v Albania* [2015] EWHC 1809 (Admin) and *Prendi v Albania (No.2)* [2021] EWHC 2625 (Admin) consider the sorts of evidence that the Court may admit when deciding if identity has been proven to the requisite standard.

In Part 1 cases, the Judge will have already resolved the issue of identity under section 7 at the initial hearing.

Whether the warrant was issued by a Judicial Authority (Part 1)

Under the 2002 Framework Decision it was a legitimate ground of challenge to an EAW to argue that the authority that had issued the EAW was not a 'judicial' authority for the purposes of section 2 of the 2003 Act or as a matter of EU law.

The Supreme Court considered this issue in detail by reference to issuing prosecutorial authorities in *Assange v The Swedish Prosecution Authority* [2012] UKSC 22, [2012] AC 471 and Ministries of Justice in *Bucnys v Ministry of Justice, Lithuania* [2013] UKSC 71, [2014] AC 480. The CJEU has also considered the question in a number of cases, most recently in Criminal proceedings against PI C-648/20. Under the Trade and Co-Operation Agreement 'Judicial Authority' is defined in article

---

70 *Alexander*, at [75]

598(b) as being an authority which is a Judge, a Court or a public prosecutor under the domestic law of the issuing state. Therefore the scope for challenges of this nature to such warrants appeared limited. However, this basis of challenge has also been used to argue that the Judiciary of the issuing territory lack sufficient independence to properly be considered as a Judicial Authority competent to issue an arrest warrant, see: *Lis & Ors v Regional Court In Warsaw, Poland & Ors* [2018] EWHC 2848 (Admin) and *Bogdan v Judge of Law Enforcement at Veszprem Regional Court, Hungary* [2022] EWHC 1149 (Admin).

Extradition Offence

Provided identity is established, the Judge must decide whether the conduct in the extradition request amounts to an extradition offence. That requires consideration of sections 64 or 137 (for accused persons) and 65 or 138 (for convicted and sentenced persons) of the 2003 Act.

Sections 64 and 137 provide a number of gateways for conduct to constitute an extradition offence for a person who has not been sentenced for the offence or offences for which they are sought.

The first gateway is that of dual criminality. Under section 64(3) conduct will be an extradition offence if it occurs in the category 1 territory requesting extradition, in like circumstances would constitute an offence in the UK and the conduct is punishable with at least 12 months imprisonment in the requesting territory.

In relation to section 137(3), conduct will constitute an extradition offence if it occurs in the category 2 territory requesting extradition, in like circumstances would constitute an offence punishable with imprisonment for 12 months or more in the UK and the conduct is punishable with at least 12 months imprisonment in the requesting territory.

In *El Khouri v Government of the USA* [2025] UKSC 3 the Supreme Court discharged an extradition request where very little of the conduct occurred In the territory of the requesting state. It disapproved of the *obiter* remarks of Lord Hope *Kings Prosecutor Brussels v Cando Armas* [2005] UKHL 67; [2006] 2 AC 1 that conduct should be understood as occurring in a territory if its effects were intentionally felt there, even if the requested person was not physically present in that jurisdiction. The Supreme Court held at [37] that the Court must focus on where the requested person's acts were done. The Court concluded at [137]:

> *"(1) Subsections 137(3) and (4) are mutually exclusive. In applying section 137, it is therefore necessary to decide at the outset whether the conduct of the person whose extradition is sought occurred "in" or "outside" the territory of the requesting state.*
>
> *(2) For this purpose the court is concerned, and concerned only, with where the person's acts specified in the extradition request were physically done, ignoring in the case of both provisions mere narrative background and focusing on the substance of the alleged criminality. The court is not concerned with where any consequences of those acts occurred or were felt.*
>
> *(3) It is not a requirement of subsection (3) or (4) that the relevant conduct occurred exclusively in, or outside, the territory of the requesting state (as the case may be)."*

Section 64(4) allows for conduct occurring outside the territory of the Requesting State, which would be an extra-territorial offence under UK law and is punishable with at least 12 months imprisonment in the Requesting State, to constitute an extradition offence.

Section 137(4) allows for conduct occurring outside the territory of the Requesting State, which would be an extra-territorial offence under UK law punishable with at least 12 months imprisonment in both the UK and in the Requesting State to constitute an extradition offence. The Supreme Court analysed these requirements in *El Khouri* at [40]-[48] and [68]-[73].

Finally, for Part 2 requests only, section 137(5) allows conduct outside the category 2 territory, in which no part occurs in the UK, and is punishable with imprisonment for 12 months or more in the Requesting State, to constitute an extradition offence if it falls within the offences specified in section 137(6). These include: genocide, crimes against humanity, war crimes and related conduct. Section 137(7A) provides that references to conduct in that section are to the conduct specified in the extradition request.

Sections 65 and 138 make provision for conduct committed by persons who have been sentenced to constitute extradition offences in near identical terms to sections 64 and 137, save that the conduct must have resulted in a sentence of at least 4 months' imprisonment in the Part 1 or Part 2 territory. For Part 2 requests the conduct must be an offence which is punishable with at least 12 months imprisonment, had it occurred in the UK.

In *Norris v The Government of the United States of America* [2008] UKHL 16, [2008] 1 AC 920, the House of Lords confirmed that the Court should look to the conduct alleged (within the extradition request and not confined simply to that alleged in the indictment), ignoring mere narrative background, rather than seeking to match the ingredients of the foreign offence with those of an offence known to English law. At [91], the Court held:

> *"The committee has reached the conclusion that the wider construction should prevail. In short, the conduct test should be applied consistently throughout the 2003 Act, the conduct relevant under Part 2 of the Act being that described in the documents constituting the request (the equivalent of the arrest warrant under Part 1), ignoring in both cases mere narrative background but taking account of such allegations as are relevant to the description of the corresponding United Kingdom offence. Had Mr Norris's appeal failed on the first issue the extradition order on count 1 would have stood."*

In *Mauro v Government of the United States of America* [2009] EWHC 150 (Admin), [2009] Extradition LR 140, the High Court emphasised that the extradition court must consider the position as if the conduct alleged in the extradition request was proved, rather than whether there is sufficient material or evidence before the court to actually prove the guilt of the Requested Person. Maurice Kay LJ held at [9] (with emphasis in the original):

> *"It is the language of the statute that matters. The court has to be satisfied (to the criminal standard: section 206) that "the conduct would constitute an offence" under the law of England and Wales: section 137(2)(b). This does not mean that the requesting state must prove the guilt of the person in English law. That would be absurd and*

> *would be a higher test than the prima facie case which had to be established under earlier legislation. The words "would constitute an offence" simply mean "would, if proved, constitute" the English offence."*

Service (Part 2 cases)

The final requirement of section 78(4) is that the Requested Person has been served with a copy of the extradition request. This is routinely done on arrest where a request has been certified beforehand or after service of papers in a provisional arrest case. However, failure to serve the certified request by the extradition hearing is a ground for discharge under the statute.

Provided all the requirements of section 78 have been met, the Judge will turn to consider whether any bars to extradition are made out. These are considered in detail in the next chapter in this book.

Prima facie case (selected Part 2 countries)

In a Part 2 'accusation' case, where no bars to extradition are raised or made out under sections 79-83 of the 2003 Act, the judge must consider the requirements of section 84 of the 2003 Act.

Provided the Requesting State is not designated under section 84(7), the Judge is required to consider whether there is evidence in this case which would be sufficient to make a case requiring an answer by the Requested Person if the proceedings were the summary trial of an information against them. In *Devani v Kenya* [2015] EWHC 3535 (Admin) the Divisional Court described the test at [49] as requiring the District Judge to:

> "*determine whether, on one possible view of the facts, he is satisfied that there is evidence upon which the requested person could be convicted at a summary trial of an information against him, upon the basis of the notional English charges.*"

By virtue of s. 84(4) a summary in a document of a statement made by a person must be treated as a statement made by that person for the purposes of s.84(2). Section 84(2) itself permits statements made to police officers and others investigating offences to be treated as admissible evidence, if direct oral evidence of those facts would be admissible. The Judge must consider the criteria in section 84(3) when deciding whether to treat a statement made by a person in a document as admissible evidence of a fact.

Section 84 of the 2003 Act provides its own code for the admissibility or exclusion of evidence. Evidence that might not be admissible in a domestic criminal trial may be admitted under section 84, including evidence which might otherwise not be admissible under normal English rules of evidence and procedure.[71] The fact that the sole or decisive evidence against the Requested Person is hearsay does not mean that a case to answer cannot be made out.[72] There is no requirement that evidence in support of an extradition request be accompanied by a statement of truth, in contrast to the previous requirements under the Extradition Act 1989. *Patel v the Government of India* [2013] EWHC 819 (Admin), [2013] ACD 90, confirms that sections 84(2)-(4) of the 2003 Act extend the scope of admissible evidence in line with the modern domestic approach to the admissibility of hearsay evidence.[73] However, multiple hearsay Is unlikely to be admissible: *India v Singh* [2021] EWHC 3333 (Admin).

Section 86 imposes the same requirements as section 84, and is applicable where a person has been found to have been convicted in their (non-deliberate) absence.

---

71 *Tudor v United Arab Emirates* [2012] EWHC 1098, at [16]-[29] *and Patel v Government of India & Anor* [2013] EWHC 819 (Admin), [2013] ACD 90, at [31-46]).

72 *Tudor*, at [28] for a contrary example of a single hearsay statement not being sufficient to establish a case to answer see *Shankaran v Government of India* [2014] EWHC 957 (Admin)

73 *Patel*, at [45] and *Government of Ghana v Gambrah* [2014] EWHC 1569 (Admin), [2014] 1 WLR 4464, at [51].

Receivable evidence

Under section 202 of the 2003 Act a judge may receive in evidence a document issued in a category 1 or 2 territory that is duly authenticated. Section 202(4) sets out the requirements for authentication, namely that it purports to be signed by a judge, magistrate or officer of the category 1 or 2 territory; it purports to be certified, whether by seal or otherwise, by the Ministry or Department of the territory responsible for justice or for foreign affairs; or it purports to be authenticated by the oath or affirmation of a witness. Section 202(5) provides that a document that is not duly authenticated may still be received in evidence. However, simply because a document is 'receivable' under section 202, does not automatically mean that the judge should admit it into evidence. For a discussion of the relevant principles, see *Prendi v Albania* [2015] EWHC 1809 (Admin), [2015] ACD 148. Nor does Section 202 create an alternative gateway for evidence to be admitted when considering whether there Is admissible evidence of a case to answer under sections 84 and 86 of the 2003 Act: *India v Singh* [2021] EWHC 3333 (Admin).

Section 206 of the 2003 Act provides that where a question arises as to the burden or standard of proof in extradition proceedings, the question must be decided as if the person whose extradition is sought were accused of the offence and the Requesting State were the prosecution, namely that the burden is on the Requesting State to prove the matter in issue to the criminal standard. There are exceptions to this requirement, most notably on the question of identity, which needs only to be proved to the civil standard under section 78(5).

Disclosure

The rules governing disclosure in extradition proceedings are significantly different from those which apply in domestic criminal or civil proceedings. Although the proceedings are governed by the Criminal Procedure Rules, the Criminal Procedure and Investigation Act 1986 does not apply to extradition proceedings. There is no general duty of disclosure on the Requesting State. Instead it will provide material on which it relies in support of the extradition case. However, the Requesting State, and the CPS acting on its behalf, are subject to a duty of candour and good faith. They are required to disclose material which seriously destroys or undermines the Requesting State's case.[74]

There is no duty on the CPS in extradition cases to make enquiries of other UK Government bodies or agencies (the police, prisons etc) to gather evidence to assist the defence.[75]

In *VB & Ors v Westminster Magistrates Court* [2014] UKSC 59, [2015] AC 1195 the Supreme Court held that extradition proceedings, being governed by statute, could not include a 'closed material procedure' or orders for evidence to be disclosed to the court but not the CPS acting on behalf of the Requesting State. However, in limited circumstances the court could receive evidence from anonymous witnesses or witnesses whose identity was withheld from the Requesting State because of the risk of harm that would result from their identity being revealed.

Asylum Claims

Where the competent UK authorities have granted the Requested Person asylum from the Requesting State they cannot be extradited to that jurisdiction.[76]

Following *District Court in Ostroleka v Dytlow* [2009] EWHC 1009 (Admin) the High Court has made it clear that, in any case in which asylum has not been determined, extradition proceedings should not be adjourned to await asylum proceedings. In *Kozlowski v District Court of Torun, Poland* [2012] EWHC 1706 (Admin) Ouseley J stated, at [13]

> *"...the thrust of what Keene LJ is saying [in Dytlow] is that adjournments to test someone's refugee status should be rare rather than routine...it is a discouragement to adjournments..."*

74 (*Raissi v SSHD* [2008] EWCA Civ 72, [2008] QB 836 at [140] and *Knowles v USA* [2006] UKPC 38, [2007] 1 WLR 47, at [35].

75 *Gambrah*, at [10]

76 *District Court in Ostroleka v Dytlow* [2009] EWHC 1009 (Admin), [2009] Extradition LR 238, at [10-31].

Recognising the evidential disadvantages that surround immigration decision-making, the authorities make clear that Requested Persons are expected to raise and litigate any and all issues of political persecution and the like during the extradition proceedings, and that such proceedings should not be adjourned to await asylum proceedings. In *R (Troitino) v NCA* [2017] EWHC 931 (Admin), [2017] EWHC 931 Ouseley J held, at [56]:

> *"…The Magistrates' Court and Divisional Court must be kept fully informed as to the precise position with any actual or purported asylum claim. The human rights bars in ss21 and 21A, and the extraneous consideration bar in s13 of the 2003 Act should be fully presented and resolved in the extradition proceedings. They should not be reserved for any asylum claim nor should the extradition proceedings be adjourned to await the outcome of the asylum proceedings, unless very good reason to the contrary is shown…"*

While the Court of Appeal (Civil Division) expressed the view that extradition proceedings could be adjourned to await the determination of an asylum claim in *R. (Chichvarkin) v SSHD* [2011] EWCA Civ 91, at [61], the High Court has subsequently expressed caution regarding that judgment, see Ouseley J's judgment in *Kozlowski* at [21]:

> *"…I would express a word of caution about what Richards LJ said in Chichvarkin. Of course, there may be circumstances in which it is possible to demonstrate that the nature of the claim and the nature of the extradition mean that the intertwining of the extradition appeal grounds and the asylum claim grounds make it appropriate for the asylum claim be considered before the other. But I do not accept as a universally applicable statement the notion that because there is something that an asylum claimant wishes the requesting state not to know, the extradition appeal should be adjourned. It is after all envisaged by Sections 13, 21 and 25 that a person whose extradition is requested will be making statements for the purposes of his appeal which are critical of the country to which he is to be extradited. The state against whom those allegations are made is entitled and empowered by the Extradition Act to respond to them. One would need to think very carefully before opting for a procedure with the deliberate aim of preventing a state from responding to those points which could*

be raised in an extradition appeal. It might be thought that that was a reason why those matters could be dealt with in the extradition appeal should be dealt with in that appeal, rather than dealt with in such a way as to prevent the requesting state from being able to answer them…"

Procedure at the Extradition Hearing

The normal procedure at a substantive extradition hearing is as follows:

(a) The advocate appearing for the Requesting State will open the facts and take the court through the relevant documents at a length commensurate with the complexity of the case and the issues. This may include presenting "draft charges".[77]

(b) The defence may make a short opening statement if merited in a complex or lengthy case;

(c) Live evidence will be called, ordinarily by the Requested Person, but there is no bar on the Requesting State calling live evidence on any issue in dispute if it wishes to do so;

(d) The judge will receive closing submissions orally and/or in writing;

(e) If necessary a case will be part-heard over a number of consecutive or non-consecutive days;

(f) After hearing evidence and submissions the judge will remand the Requested Person in custody or on bail;

(g) At the close of the hearing the judge will either give an extempore judgment or hand down a reserved judgment. In general, judgment will be reserved.

(h) Following judgment the Requested Person will again be remanded in custody or on bail.

---

77 *Biri v High Court in Miskolc, Hungary* [2018] EWHC 50 (Admin), [2018] 4 WLR 50 and Criminal Procedure Rule 50.4(5)(b).

The general rule is that the Magistrates' court must exercise its powers at a hearing in public, but that is subject to the court's powers to: impose reporting restrictions; withhold information from the public; or order a hearing in private (see r.50.3 Criminal Procedure Rules 2020/759 as amended).

Under section 206A of the 2003 Act the Judge may give a live link If satisfied that it is in the Interests of justice to do so. A Live Link is defined in section 206C as being an arrangement by which a person Is able to see and hear all other persons taking part In the hearing who are not at their location and to be seen and heard by them. A requested person, advocate or witness may apply to the Court to appear at a hearing by live link. A prescribed form to make such an application under Criminal Procedure Rule 3.36 is available on the Criminal Procedure Rules Forms website. Where a party wishes to call a witness located outside of the UK to give evidence by a live link, that party must satisfy themselves and the Court that an International Letter of Request or Mutual Legal Assistance request Is not required before inviting the Court to grant permission to use the Cloud Video Platform to give evidence. Some jurisdictions including Poland and Italy require the completion of a request for Mutual Legal Assistance or an International Letter of Request submitted via Westminster Magistrates' Court to the appropriate authority of the territory where the witness is located. Others, such as the USA, do not object to witnesses in their territory giving evidence at extradition proceedings by video-link. Practitioners may need to consult with a witness abroad to confirm whether Mutual Legal Assistance is required and to make any such application in ample time before the Extradition Hearing as some jurisdictions may take In excess of two months to respond and to make the practical arrangements. Failure to do so could result In the hearing being adjourned or the witness abroad not being permitted to give live evidence.

Order of Issues at the extradition hearing

The 2003 Act provides a staged process whereby the Judge at the extradition hearing will consider first the requirements of section 10 or section 78, then whether there are any bars to extradition. If relevant, the Judge will consider whether a prima facie case is demonstrated on the evidence, whether the Requested Person was convicted in their presence, before considering convention rights and whether extradition would be unjust or oppressive by reason of the Requested Person's physical or mental condition. Ordinarily all of the relevant evidence and issues will be dealt with in a single hearing.[78]

Sending a case to the SSHD (Part 2)

Provided the Judge is satisfied that the requirements of section 78 are met, that there are no bars to extradition under sections 79-83, (and where relevant the requirements of sections 84 or 85 and 86 are met) and that extradition is compatible with the Requested Person's convention rights, the judge must send the Requested Person's case to the Secretary of State under section 87(3) for their decision on whether to order extradition. When doing so, the Judge must explain to the Requested Person 'in ordinary language' that they have a right to seek permission to appeal to the High Court but that any appeal will not be heard until after the Secretary of State has made their decision. The Requested Person will be remanded in custody or on bail to wait for the Secretary of State's decision.

Bail pending prosecution appeal

Where the judge orders a Requested Person's discharge, the Requesting State may seek permission to appeal the judge's decision. By virtue of sections 30/107 of the 2003 Act, where the representative of the Requesting State indicates an intention to appeal the decision immediately after discharge is ordered the judge must remand the Requested Person in custody or on bail while the appeal is pending.

Costs

Where a Requested Person's extradition is ordered or the High Court or Supreme Court dismisses an application for permission to appeal or a substantive appeal brought by the Requested Person, the Requesting State may seek its costs under section 60 (in a Part 1 case) and 133 (in

---

78 *Romania v Bohm* [2013] EWHC 1171 (Admin), [2013] ACD 89, *Demspey v USA* [2020] EWHC 603 (Admin) at [28]-[31] and *Romania v Gurau* [2023] EWHC 439 (Admin) [2023] WLR 2813.

Part 2) of the 2003 Act. Any order for costs must be just and reasonable. The jurisdiction to make an order for costs against the requested person under section 133(2) of the 2003 Act only arises when the Secretary of State orders the person's extradition which necessarily will not be at the same time that the case Is sent to the Secretary of State.

A Requested Person whose discharge is ordered by the Magistrates' Court, High Court or Supreme Court or who successfully resists an appeal against an order for discharge in the High Court or Supreme Court may seek their costs under sections 61 or 134 respectively.

Re-opening the extradition hearing

After the Judge has made a decision to order a Requested Person's extradition, discharge, or to send the matter to the Secretary of State, they have no jurisdiction to re-open the case under section 142 of the Magistrates' Court Act 1980 i.e. to correct an error.[79] In those circumstances, a statutory appeal is likely to be the only available remedy.

---

79 Zubkovs v Latvia [2012] EWHC 3331 (Admin), Klimeto v City of Westminster Magistrates' Court [2012] EWHC 2051 (Admin) [2013] 1 W.L.R. 420 and R (on the application of Berners) v Westminster Magistrates' Court, Berners v Council of The Criminal Matters Court Regional Court of Riga Latvia [2010] EWHC 1010 (Admin).

CHAPTER THREE

BARS TO EXTRADITION

This chapter deals with the 'bars' to extradition contained in the 2003 Act. Additionally, whilst they do not formally constitute 'bars', 'abuse of process' and 'Physical or Mental condition' are also covered herein.

Double Jeopardy

Section 12 of the 2003 Act creates the bar of double jeopardy for requests made under part 1. It provides:

> *'A person's extradition to a category 1 territory is barred by reason of the rule against double jeopardy if (and only if) it appears that he would be entitled to be discharged under any rule of law relating to previous acquittal or conviction on the assumption—*
>
> *(a) that the conduct constituting the extradition offence constituted an offence in the part of the United Kingdom where the judge exercises jurisdiction;*
>
> *(b) that the person were charged with the extradition offence in that part of the United Kingdom.'*

Section 80 of the 2003 Act makes similar, but not identical, provision for extradition requests made under Part 2 of the Act. It provides:

> *'A person's extradition to a category 2 territory is barred by reason of the rule against double jeopardy if (and only if) it appears that he would be entitled to be discharged under any rule of law relating to previous acquittal or conviction if he were charged with the extradition offence in the part of the United Kingdom where the judge exercises his jurisdiction.'*

The bar of double jeopardy reflects the long established legal principles of *ne bis in idem.*[80]

Article 600 of the TCA, titled 'Grounds for mandatory non-execution of the arrest warrant' provides:

> *'The execution of the arrest warrant shall be refused:*
>
> ...
>
> *(b) if the executing judicial authority is informed that the requested person has been finally judged by a State in respect of the same acts, provided that, if a penalty has been imposed, it has been enforced, is in the process of being enforced or can no longer be enforced under the law of the sentencing State;*
>
> ...'

The TCA also includes Article 601, albeit as a discretionary ground for refusal, which provides, so far as is relevant:

> *'1. The execution of the arrest warrant may be refused:*
>
> *(a) ....*
>
> *(b) if the person who is the subject of the arrest warrant is being prosecuted in the executing State for the same act as that on which the arrest warrant is based;*

80 In Heathfield v Staatsanwaltschaft Würzberg, Germany [2017] EWHC 2602 (Admin), Mr Justice Julian Knowles stated, at [17]: "The doctrine of ne bis in idem – that no person should be tried twice for the same crime - is a fundamental principle of law whose origins can be traced back to 355BC, when Demosthenes reasoned that 'the laws forbid the same man to be tried twice on the same issue' (Hunter, The Rule Against Double Jeopardy, (1984) Journal of Legal History 5). In the United States the rule is enshrined in the Double Jeopardy Clause of the Fifth Amendment to the Constitution:

"...nor shall any person be subject for the same offense to be twice put in jeopardy of life or limb ..."

(c) if the judicial authorities of the executing State have decided either not to prosecute for the offence on which the arrest warrant is based or to halt proceedings, or if a final judgment which prevents further proceedings has been passed upon the requested person in a State in respect of the same acts;

(d) if the criminal prosecution or punishment of the requested person is statute-barred under the law of the executing State and the acts fall within the jurisdiction of that State under its own criminal law;

(e) if the executing judicial authority is informed that the requested person has been finally judged by a third country in respect of the same acts provided that, if a penalty has been imposed, it has been enforced, is in the process of being enforced or can no longer be enforced under the law of the sentencing country;

(f) if the arrest warrant has been issued for the purposes of execution of a custodial sentence or detention order and the requested person is staying in, or is a national or a resident of the executing State and that State undertakes to execute the sentence or detention order in accordance with its domestic law; if consent of the requested person to the transfer of the sentence or detention order to the executing State is required, the executing State may refuse to execute the arrest warrant only after the requested person consents to the transfer of the sentence or detention order;

(g)....'

The bar in sections 12 and 80 of the 2003 Act applies where, in like circumstances, an English court would stay criminal proceedings as barred by *autrefois convict* and *autrefois acquit*. However, the bar has been interpreted as having a broader application, and includes circumstances in which domestic proceedings would be stayed as an abuse of process, as explained by the Divisional Court in *Fofana v Deputy Prosecutor Thubin Tribunal de Grande Instance de Meaux, France* [2006] EWHC 744 (Admin), [2006] Extradition LR 102 where Auld LJ held at [18]:

"18. In summary the authorities establish two circumstances in English law that offend the principle of double jeopardy:

> *i) Following an acquittal or conviction for an offence, which is the same in fact and law — autrefois acquit or convict; and*
>
> *ii) following a trial for any offence which was founded on "the same or substantially the same facts", where the court would normally consider it right to stay the prosecution as an abuse of process and/or unless the prosecution can show "special circumstances" why another trial should take place."*

The court explained at [21] that the bar applies "*where, even though the charge is different, it is founded on the same or substantially the same facts as an earlier trial.*"

The fact that a Requested Person has been convicted of like offences which are relied on as a particular of conduct making out a wider conspiracy does not engage the bar of double jeopardy. It is necessary to compare the content of the conduct, its scale and the time period over which the offences occurred[81]. Where a person has been involved in multiple offences committed by a trans-national criminal organisation, the bar of double jeopardy in its wider sense will not prevent extradition in circumstances where there was no cross-over between the criminality prosecuted in two different states and no agreement that one state should take responsibility for prosecuting all the criminality alleged. In *Zada v Italy* [2017] EWHC 513 (Admin) the Requested Person had been extradited to France[82] for his involvement in people trafficking. He was prosecuted and convicted there and then returned to the UK where he faced a second request for his extradition, this time from Italy, for his involvement in the same criminal organisation, but for its actions in Italy. In those circumstances the High Court held that a second extradition to face trial was not necessarily unfair. Holroyde LJ held, at [64]:

> "*To assume unfairness, regardless of the circumstances of the case, would be to put something of a premium on offending which is so well-organised and extensive that it is able to cross state boundaries.*"

---

81 *John v USA* [2006] EWHC 3512 (Admin), [2007] ACD 55

82 See *Hosseini & Ors v Courts of Higher Instance, Paris, France* [2006] EWHC 1333 (Admin), [2006] Extradition LR 176

The court will pay careful attention to the conduct which is alleged to constitute the extradition offence. The fact that a person has been convicted of legally different offences but based on the same facts did not prevent the bar of double jeopardy from applying. In *Zdinjak v Croatia* [2012] EWHC 1554 (Admin), [2012] ACD 95 the High Court held that the District Judge had erred by finding that the bar did not apply in such circumstances.

Whilst the 2002 Framework Decision and TCA's mandatory ground for refusal refers to the requirement that a Requested Person has been finally judged in a "Member State", our Courts have construed section 12 as also applying to convictions in third countries. Hence, in *Hamburg Public Prosecutor's Office, Germany* v *Altun* [2011] EWHC 397 (Admin), the fact that the Requested Person had been convicted and sentenced in Turkey prior to being granted an amnesty (thereby dispensing with the need for him to serve the full sentence) meant that his extradition to Germany was barred under section 12. Although, in *Ristea v Prosecutor's Office, Court of Bologna, Italy* [2018] EWHC 1876 (Admin), [2018] ACD 93, Mrs Justice Laing adopted a narrow approach to the bar, concluding that, although the Requested Person had served 74% of the total sentence in Romania, because the sentence had not been transferred in conformity with EU law (the 2002 Framework Decision) the bar did not apply. However, recognising that this was not the fault of the Requested Person, she held that it would be an abuse of process to order his extradition.

In the *Government of Rwanda v Emmanuel Nteziryayo and others* [2017] EWHC 1912 (Admin) the High Court considered the question of whether a requested person who had been convicted by a particular type of local customary Court called a 'gacaca' court, set up to hear cases of genocide that had occurred in Rwanda, but whose conviction had been quashed by an appeal court acting beyond its powers was entitled to rely on the bar of double jeopardy. The High Court found that the trial "gacaca" court had jurisdiction to acquit the requested person under Rwandan law in force at the time and that the Rwandan court of appeal had erred in declaring the acquittal a nullity. Therefore, it concluded that the Requested Person's extradition was barred as to try him again would be an abuse of process and barred by double jeopardy under s.80[83].

Absence of prosecution decision

Section 12A provides:

> *'(1) A person's extradition to a category 1 territory is barred by reason of absence of prosecution decision if (and only if)—*
>
> *(a) it appears to the appropriate judge that there are reasonable grounds for believing that—*
>
> > *(i) the competent authorities in the category 1 territory have not made a decision to charge or have not made a decision to try (or have made neither of those decisions), and*
> >
> > *(ii) the person's absence from the category 1 territory is not the sole reason for that failure,*
>
> *and*
>
> *(b) those representing the category 1 territory do not prove that—*
>
> > *(i) the competent authorities in the category 1 territory have made a decision to charge and a decision to try, or*
> >
> > *(ii) in a case where one of those decisions has not been made (or neither of them has been made), the person's absence from the category 1 territory is the sole reason for that failure.*
>
> *(2) In this section "to charge" and "to try", in relation to a person and an extradition offence, mean—*
>
> > *(a) to charge the person with the offence in the category 1 territory, and*
> >
> > *(b) to try the person for the offence in the category 1 territory.'*

83 Judgment at [431]-[445]

This provision was inserted by the Anti-Social Behaviour, Crime and Policing Act 2014. The explanatory notes state the bar is intended to "*ensure that a case is sufficiently advanced in the issuing State (that is, there is a clear intention to bring the person to trial) before extradition can occur, so that people do not spend potentially long periods in pre-trial detention following their extradition, whilst the issuing State continues to investigate the offence*".

The explanatory memorandum also notes that courts have interpreted the provisions of the 2003 Act in a "cosmopolitan" way, mindful of the differences in criminal procedure in other Member States, and it is anticipated that the courts will apply the same approach to the interpretation of section 12A and, in particular, the concepts *"decision to charge"* and *"decision to try"*.

The bar, is not replicated in Part 2 of the Act, has no basis in the 2002 Framework Decision and has not been included in the TCA. The introduction of the TCA is therefore not expected to have a significant impact on the development of this bar, save perhaps that the high level of mutual trust and confidence that underpinned the 2002 Framework Decision may become less relevant.

The bar has not proved fertile ground for the discharge of extradition requests. Perhaps because the view of the Divisional Court is that since the majority of persons subject to arrest warrants are sought by the prosecuting authorities of their own nation state, "*it cannot have been intended by Parliament to make it easier for such persons to continue to reside in the UK or to make the task of progressing a prosecution more difficult*" *Puceviciene v The Prosecutor General's Office of the Republic of Lithuania* [2016] EWHC 1862, [2016] 1 WLR 4937, at [50].

The First Stage

The first stage of the section 12A inquiry is determining whether there are reasonable grounds for believing that one or more of the relevant decisions have not been made. The burden is on the Requested Person[84].

---

84 Kandola v Generalstaatwaltschaft Frankfurt, Germany [2015] EWHC 619, [2015] 1 WLR 5097 at [30]

The phrase *"reasonable grounds for believing"* involves something less than proof on balance of probabilities, but more than simple assertion, or a fanciful view or "feeling"[85].

If the arrest warrant, read as a whole, is clear that the decisions have been taken, the District Judge should look no further in relation to that point.[86] However, if further information is provided by the issuing judicial authority, it is to be treated as part and parcel of the warrant.[87]

If the issue is unclear, then the District Judge is entitled to consider extraneous evidence. However, the Requested Person should not be permitted to introduce extraneous evidence to cast doubt on a clear statement in the warrant,[88] unless there is evidence which demonstrates that the Judicial Authority has acted in bad faith or with impropriety[89].

"Elaborate" expert evidence, especially at the "reasonable grounds" stage is to be discouraged. Additionally, is not appropriate to direct inquiries of the Judicial Authority at the first stage, as the onus is on the Requested Person to satisfy the District Judge that there are reasonable grounds for believing that one of the two decisions has not been taken, or that the failure to take the decision is not solely due to the Requested Person's absence from the Requesting State.[90]

However, the bar is not intended to prevent extradition where the case is not 'trial ready' *Killoran v Belgium* [2021] EWHC 2290 (Admin) at [36].

---

85 *Kandola,* at [30].

86 *Kandola,* at [31]

87 Litwinczuk v The Circuit Court in Szczecin, Poland [2019] EWHC 2745, at [23]

88 *Kandola,* at [32]

89 *Puceviciene,* at [58]

90 *Kandola,* at [32]

The Second Stage

If the Requested Person satisfies the District Judge that there are reasonable grounds to believe one or more of the decisions has not been taken, the burden then falls on the Requesting State to prove, to the criminal standard, that the two decisions have been made, or that the sole reason for them not being taken is the Requested Person's absence from the territory.[91]

In *Puceviciene,* the Divisional Court disapproved of the approach taken by Aikens LJ in *Kandola* as to how information from the Requesting State should be obtained to satisfy the burden imposed at the second stage, as well as the role of mutual legal assistance in the operation of the bar. In *Puceviciene,* Lord Thomas LCJ held that the requesting Judicial Authority must be provided with some explanation of what is meant by the terms *"decision to charge"* and *"decision to try"*. The use of the terms *"decision to charge"* and *"decision to try"* did not imply that the case must be trial ready. In explaining the requirements, it will be necessary to deal with the issue of formality and contingent or conditional decisions. No formality is required in the making of a decision, unless the procedural law of the Requesting State prevents informality. A decision to try is still a decision to try even if it is conditional or subject to review[92].

The boundaries between investigation, prosecution and trial are not necessarily precise and activities generally attributable to one stage can be carried out in the course of another stage. Decisions are often informal, and do not require a high evidential threshold in some jurisdictions. They may also be taken by police, prosecutors or judges[93]. The decision must, however, be taken by the person who has the institutional competence to take it.[94]

---

91 *Kandola*, at [34]

92 *Puceviciene*, at [54]

93 *Puceviciene*, at [40]

94 *Doci v Court of Brescia, Italy* [2016] EWHC 2100 (Admin), [2017] ACD 21, at [33].

The decision to charge is the decision which is made when there is sufficient evidence under the relevant procedural system to make an allegation that the defendant has committed the crime alleged.[95] A decision to try is the decision by the relevant decision maker (who may be the police, prosecutor or judge) to go ahead with the process of taking to trial the defendant against whom the allegation is made, even if it is conditional or contingent upon other matters. However, an intention to make a decision to charge or try is not sufficient.[96]

The real focus of section 12A is always on whether there has been a decision to try. If such a decision has been taken, inevitably a decision to charge will have been taken earlier or at the same time[97].

Should further information be required, it should be obtained in one exchange of questions and answers, even though section 12A contemplates two difference stages.[98]

The failure to employ mutual legal assistance to further a prosecution is not a relevant consideration when determining whether the Requested Person's absence is the sole reason for the failure to take the required decisions.[99]

Extraneous Considerations

In relation to the *"extraneous considerations"* bar to extradition, sections 13 and 81 are drafted in the same terms and there is no substantive difference in the case law that has developed in relation to the two sections.

Section 13 of the 2003 Act provides that:

---

95 Puceviciene, at [55]

96 *Doci*, at [3]

97 Puceviciene, at [50]

98 Puceviciene, at [35]

99 Puceviciene at [68-81].

'A person's extradition to a category 1 territory is barred by reason of extraneous considerations if (and only if) it appears that-

(a) The Part 1 warrant issued in respect of him (though purporting to be issued on account of the extradition offence) is in fact issued for the purpose of prosecuting or punishing him on account of his race, religion, nationality, gender, sexual orientation or political opinions, or

(b) If extradited he might be prejudiced at his trial or punished, detained or restricted in his personal liberty by reason of his race, religion, nationality, gender, sexual orientation or political opinions.'

The bar is in similar terms to the discretionary ground of refusal contained in Article 601(h) of the TCA, which provides:

'if there are reasons to believe on the basis of objective elements that the arrest warrant has been issued for the purpose of prosecuting or punishing a person on the grounds the person's sex, race, religion, ethnic origin, nationality, language, political opinions or sexual orientation, or that that person's position may be prejudiced for any of those reasons;'

There are two different ways to show that a Requested Person's extradition should be barred as a result of extraneous considerations:

Section 13(a)/ 81(a) – Ulterior Motive

Subsection (a) is concerned with the motivation behind the request for extradition. It is concerned with something that has already happened.[100] It prevents extradition, if the real reason for the request is not to seek the Requested Person's return for prosecution, or to serve a sentence of imprisonment, but rather to punish them on account of their race,

100 *Antonov v Prosecutor General's Office Lithuania* [2015] EWHC 1243 (Admin), [2015] A.C.D. 109 at [20].

religion, nationality, gender[101], sexual orientation, or political opinions[102].

The Requested Person bears the burden of showing the causal link between the issue of the request and the particular circumstances relied upon. [103] The court must assess the state of mind of the Requesting State at the time of the request, so as to establish whether its purpose was in fact to prosecute or punish the Requested Person for one of the extraneous reasons.[104] The Requested Person must persuade the court that, on the balance of probabilities, it *"appears"* that the reason for the request was for the purpose of prosecuting or punishing them for one of the extraneous reasons.[105] In doing so, the judge is not limited to considering the precise moment of issue of the warrant, but must have regard to the underlying process which led to that decision and whether it was driven by one of the 'extraneous' reasons.[106]

Section 13(b)/81(b) – Risk of Prejudice in Detention, Prosecution or Punishment

---

101 Including transgender identity: *Prusianu v Romania* [2022] EWHC 1929 (Admin)

102 There is a distinction between extradition for the purpose of prosecuting the Requested Person on account of their political opinions – which is precluded by the 2003 Act – and extradition on the basis of a political offence; Parliament has legislated to cover the former, not the latter: *Assange v United States* [2024] EWHC 700 (Admin) at [92].

103 Hilali v Central Court of Criminal Proceedings No. 5, Madrid [2006] EWHC 1239 (Admin), [2007] 1 W.L.R. 768 at [62]; Antonov at [20].

104 *Slepcik v Governor of HMP Brixton* [2004] EWHC 1224 (QB) at [23]; *Antonov v Prosecutor General's Office Lithuania* [2015] EWHC 1243 (Admin), [2015] A.C.D. 109 at [20].

105 In Antonov at [21], Aitkens LJ stated that "[t]his burden on the requested person must be one on the balance of probabilities, to enable the court to find that "it appears" that the reason for the issue of the EAW was for the purpose of punishing him on account of one of the "extraneous considerations" that are identified in section 13(a)".

106 *Adamescu v Romania* [2020] EWHC 2709 (Admin) at [66]

Subsection (b) is concerned with what might happen to the Requested Person if extradited. It calls on the court *"to prophesy what will happen to the fugitive in the future if he is returned"*. [107] It prevents extradition, where it can be shown that if extradited, the Requested Person will suffer prejudice at trial, or be punished or detained, as a result of their race, religion, nationality, gender, sexual orientation or political opinions. The Requested Person does not need to prove the risk of prejudice on the balance of probabilities.[108] Rather, the Requested Person must show that there is a *"reasonable chance"* or *"reasonable grounds for thinking"* or a *"serious possibility"* that such events will occur.[109]

In respect of prejudice at trial, s.81(b) does not require precise particularisation by the court of how the prejudice would arise or become manifest.[110] However, where the claim of future prejudice is grounded in a factual allegation of past corruption, the court "*would expect to see the allegation proved before considering the likelihood that some future action might be taken based on it*".[111]

There is a clear overlap between this bar and a number of the human rights challenges. Despite the lower threshold under (b), the bar remains very difficult to establish. However, in establishing a case under section 13/81 the Requested Person is not bound by the ordinary rules of

---

107 Lord Diplock in *Fernandez v Government of Singapore* [1971] 1 WLR 987 at 994.

108 Lord Diplock in Fernandez at 993-994: "For my part I think it only leads to confusion to speak of "balance of probabilities" in the context of what the court has to decide under section 4 (1) (c) of the Act. It is a convenient and trite phrase to indicate the degree of certitude which the evidence must have induced in the mind of the court as to the existence of facts, so as to entitle the court to treat them as data capable of giving rise to legal consequences. But the phrase is inappropriate when applied not to ascertaining what has already happened but to prophesying what, if it happens at all, can only happen in the future...". See also Hilali at [62].

109 *Antonov* at [27], referring to Lord Diplock in *Fernandez* (993-994) and *Hilali* at [62].

110 *Turkey v Tanis* [2021] EWHC 1675 (Admin) at [45]-[47]

111 *Kaderli v Turkey* [2021] EWHC 1096 (Admin) at [65]

evidence.[112] In addition, the court can invite assurances from the Requesting State that the Requested Person will not be prejudiced in the manner alleged.[113]

Passage of time

Under section 14/82 of the Act a person's extradition is barred by reason of the passage of time, if it appears that it would be unjust or oppressive for them to be surrendered. The bar does not appear in the TCA as a ground for non-execution of an arrest warrant. Section 14[114] provides:

> *'A person's extradition to a category 1 territory is barred by reason of the passage of time if (and only if) it appears that it would be unjust or oppressive to extradite him by reason of the passage of time since he is alleged to have*
>
> *(a) committed the extradition offence (where he is accused of its commission), or*
>
> *(b) become unlawfully at large (where he is alleged to have been convicted of it)'*

In terms of the meaning of "unjust or oppressive", Lord Diplock observed in *Kakis v Government of the Republic of Cyprus* [1978] 1 WLR 779, 782H–783A:

> "*'Unjust' I regard as directed primarily to the risk of prejudice to the accused in the conduct of the trial* itself, *'oppressive' as directed to hardship to the accused resulting from changes in his circumstances that have occurred during the period to be taken into consideration; but*

112 *Hilali* at [63]; *Antonov* at [21].

113 See. *Assange v United States* [2024] EWHC 700 (Admin) after which assurances were provided to the appeal court that Mr Assange would not be prejudiced by reason of his nationality. These were insufficient to prevent permission to appeal being granted. However, ultimately, the appeal proceedings went no further as Mr Assange reached a plea deal with US prosecutors which allowed him to return to Australia.

114 Section 82 is in materially identical terms.

> *there is room for overlapping, and between them they would cover all cases where to return him would not be fair."*

This is an oft-raised bar to extradition, and the burden lies on the Requested Person to show that, on the balance of probabilities, the passage of time is such as to make an extradition unjust and oppressive[115]. It is fact-dependent. Lawyers representing Requested Persons who raise this bar will therefore need to ensure that the evidence addresses matters including what they knew before they left the country, the reasons they left, and events since they arrived in the UK (with a focus on major life events and changes). Expert evidence as to the law of the Requesting State may be required to establish "injustice".

Injustice

The key authority remains *Gomes v Trinidad and Tobago* [2009] UKHL 21, [2009] 1 WLR 1038 at [30-34] itself citing *Knowles v Government of the United States of America* [2006] UKPC 38, [2007] 1 WLR 47 at [31] and *Woodcock v Government of New Zealand* [2003] EWHC 2668 (Admin), [2004] 1 WLR 1979. The essential question is whether, in any particular case, a fair trial is impossible. In considering this, the court will have regard to the domestic legal safeguards in the Requesting State.

In *Gomes*, the House of Lords, at [35], thought that signatories to the ECHR should be assumed to have the necessary protections:

> "*What, however, of extradition to countries of whose judicial systems we know less and in which, it is submitted, we should have less confidence? Council of Europe countries in our view present no problem. All are subject to article 6 of the Convention and should readily be assumed capable of protecting an accused against an unjust trial—whether by an abuse of process jurisdiction like ours or in some other way.*"

115 *Guven v HM Prison Brixton* [2005] EWHC 1391 (Admin), [2005] Extradition LR 86 at [18] and *Khan v Central Trial Court No.3 National High Court, Spain* [2012] EWHC 3231 (Admin) at [24]

Even outside this group, a lack of safeguards would almost certainly "*be apparent from widely available international reports.*"[116] The House of Lords emphasised, at [36], that:

> "*The extradition process, it must be remembered, is only available for returning suspects to friendly foreign states with whom this country has entered into multilateral or bilateral treaty obligations involving mutually agreed and reciprocal commitments. The arrangements are founded on mutual trust and respect. There is a strong public interest in respecting such treaty obligations. As has repeatedly been stated, international co-operation in this field is ever more important to bring to justice those accused of serious cross-border crimes and to ensure that fugitives cannot find safe havens abroad.*"

The governing principles were summarised by Leggatt LJ in *Eason v Government of the United States of America* [2020] EWHC 604 (Admin) at [27], [2020] ACD 54:

> "*i) If, because of the passage of time, a fair trial is now impossible, it would clearly be unjust to order extradition;*
>
> *ii) A court should, however, be very slow to come to such a conclusion where the state making the request is one that is shown to have, or may be presumed to have, appropriate safeguards to protect the defendant against unfairness resulting from the passage of time in the trial process;*
>
> *iii) The possibility or otherwise of a fair trial is not the only relevant consideration, as the question is not whether it would be unjust or oppressive to try the accused but whether it would be unjust or oppressive to extradite him.*"

The test of injustice is not exceptionality, and is not "*limited to cases where there is "evidence" of prejudice*"; the question in such cases is whether there

116 *Gomes at [36]*

is a risk of prejudice. It requires judgment "*reflecting shades of grey rather than black or white*", and considering all the circumstances.[117]

Delay by itself can cause injustice, particularly where such delay is culpable (on the principle of which, see more below).[118]

Oppression

In order to decide whether extradition would be oppressive, a court considers the "*hardship to the accused resulting from changes in his circumstances that have occurred during the period to be taken into consideration*".[119] However, it "*goes beyond mere or ordinary hardship, which is a comparatively common consequence of an order for extradition, and will not easily be satisfied*".[120] Relevant factors may include culpable delay on the part of the Requesting State, the seriousness of the offence, and the impact of extradition on other family members.

As with challenges brought under Article 8 of the ECHR, reported cases are highly fact-sensitive and little is to be gained by excessive citation of numerous authorities. However, it is important to stress that "oppression" may include ordinary events in one's life. In *Antochi v Germany* [2020] EWHC 3092 (Admin), [2021] ACD 15, Mr Justice Fordham stated, at [45]:

> "*What the case-law makes clear is that developments in an individual's life arising from familiar changes in circumstances occurring during the relevant period – marriage, birth of children, relocation, onset of ill-health – can support a conclusion of relevant hardship supporting a conclusion that extradition, in light of the passage of time, would*

---

117 *United States of America v Tollman & Tollman* [2008] EWHC 184 (Admin), [2008] 3 All ER 150 at [47] and [50]

118 See, for example, *Sagman v the Government of Turkey* [2001] EWHC Admin 474, at [27] and *Oncel v the Governor of HM Prison Brixton and Turkey* [2001] EWHC Admin 1142, [2002] ACD 17

119 *Kakis* at p. 782

120 *Eason v Government of the United States of America* [2020] EWHC 604 (Admin) at [28], [2020] ACD 54

> *involve oppression. Oppression is not excluded, simply because developments in a life are commonplace occurrences in human lives."*

Whilst the seriousness of the offence is relevant to the issue of oppression, it is not an overwhelming factor or a trump card.[121]

There is an *"exceptionally high test for establishing oppression"*.[122] Knowles J's dicta in the context of a bail application is of relevance; he observed that *"one gets somewhat hardened to the passage of time, but 21 years is a striking period of time on any view."*[123] By contrast, in *Scott v Commonwealth of Australia* [2020] EWHC 2924 (Admin) an order for extradition was upheld for 4 sexual offences that were alleged to have occurred over 40 years earlier.

Accusation versus conviction warrants

In the case of accusation warrants, time will run from the date of the alleged offence.

In the case of conviction warrants, a person is "unlawfully at large" if they are at large in contravention of a lawful and immediate sentence of imprisonment under the applicable legal system. It is an objective test, unaffected by the Requested Person's state of knowledge or understanding[124]. It is important, however, not to confuse whether (and when) a person is unlawfully at large, with whether that person is a fugitive.[125] In *Wisniewski v Poland* [2016] EWHC 386 (Admin), [2016] 1 WLR 3750, the appellant left the jurisdiction while subject to a suspended sentence. Whilst he may have been in breach of the terms of the sentence it had not yet been activated. He was therefore not unlawfully at large at the point that he left the jurisdiction. Instead, he

---

121 *Hasani v UK Central Authority* [2018] EWHC 1772 (Admin) at [20]

122 *Lord Advocate v M (R)* [2021] 12 WLUK 117 at [15]

123 *Surmaj v Presov District Court (Slovakia)* [2020] EWHC 3956 (Admin) at [10]

124 *Wisniewski v Poland* [2016] EWHC 386 (Admin), [2016] 1 WLR 3750 at [54]

125 *Wisniewski,* at [50].

became unlawfully at large later – when the suspended sentence was activated.

Section 14(b) suggests that the passage of time which the Requested Person can rely upon starts at the point the individual becomes unlawfully at large. In *Wisniewski*, the court opined, at [56], that a Requested Person could not rely on the passage of time before they became unlawfully at large. In *Konecny v District Court in Brno-Venkov, Czech Republic* [2019] UKSC 8, [2019] 1 WLR 1586, Lord Lloyd-Jones identified that this wording could operate to the disadvantage of a person who had been convicted in their absence, as they could only rely on the passage of time from the date of conviction. He suggested that the current wording ought to be re-considered by the legislature[126].

Until the legislation is amended, both the High Court in *Wisniewski* and the Supreme Court in *Konecny* identified the same solution: "*article 8 provides an appropriate and effective alternative means of addressing passage of time resulting in injustice or oppression in cases where the defendant has been convicted in absentia*"[127]. The appropriate test under Article 8 is one of proportionality rather than injustice or oppression. Furthermore, the relevant period of time would commence from the date of the offence.[128]

The period of time to be taken into account does not necessarily end at the date of the extradition hearing and may continue throughout the proceedings. However, additional time accrued during extradition proceedings will not be counted if the Requested Person has deliberately spun out proceedings.[129]

---

126 *Konecny,* at [54]

127 *Konecny,* at [57]

128 H (H) v Deputy Prosecutor of the Italian Republic, Genoa (Official Solicitor intervening), [2012] UKSC 25,[2013] 1 AC 338, at [8]

129 *Gomes v Trinidad and Tobago* [2009] UKHL 21, [2009] 1 WLR 1038 at [38]

Fugitive status

A Requested Person cannot usually rely on any passage of time while they are a fugitive. The House of Lords in *Gomes v Trinidad and Tobago* [2009] UKHL 21, [2009] 1 WLR 1038 held at [27]:

> "*Generally it will be clear one way or the other whether the accused has deliberately fled the country and in any event, as was held in Krzyzowski [2007] EWHC 2754 , given that flight will in all save the most exceptional circumstances operate as an almost automatic bar to reliance on delay, it will have to be proved beyond reasonable doubt (just as the issue whether a defendant has deliberately absented himself from trial in an inquiry under section 85(3) of the Act)*".

For those Requested Persons who have been convicted, it is particularly challenging to rely on any difficulties caused by deliberate flight:

> "*Given, however, that in these cases he will by flight have brought upon himself such difficulties as may then ensue from the passage of time, we see no reason why he should not be required to accept them—again, save in the most exceptional circumstances. He, after all, will not merely be accused of the crime but will actually have been convicted of it.*"[130]

It is for the Requesting State to prove fugitive status beyond all reasonable doubt. It is a subjective test: whether the Requested Person had deliberately and knowingly placed themselves beyond the reach of a legal process[131].

The case of *De Zorzi v France* [2019] EWHC 2062 (Admin), [2019] 1 WLR 6249 is an illustration of the principle set out in *Pillar-Neumann v Austria* [2017] EWHC 3371 (Admin) at [65-73], that a Requested Person who is legally resident in another country does not become a fugitive simply by failing to surrender themselves upon receipt of a document from a foreign court informing them of their conviction, nor

130 *Gomes*, at [30]

131 *De Zorzi v France* [2019] EWHC 2062 (Admin), [2019] 1 WLR 6249 at [48]

by appealing their conviction via lawyers, nor by resisting extradition. *Pillar-Neumann,* at [70], draws a distinction between a Requested Person placing themselves beyond the reach of a legal process, and a Requested Person who does not take positive steps to place themselves within the reach of a legal process instituted in another country. See also *Maris v Romania* [2019] EWHC 2013 (Admin) at [22-29].

Culpable delay

Culpable delay on the part of the Requesting State may be taken into account, although there is a dichotomy amongst the jurisprudence as to whether culpability can only be considered in "borderline" cases,[132] or whether all relevant circumstances should be taken into account.[133] In *Nika v The Douai County Court, France* [2020] EWHC 3335 (Admin), Mrs Justice Farbey stated, at [18], that "*Culpable delay on the part of the requesting state can weigh more heavily in the balance and may sometimes be decisive, especially in a borderline case*". It is worth noting that recent cases have taken the approach that it is only in borderline cases, where the accused is not to blame, that culpable delay by the Requesting State might tip the balance against extradition (see, for example, *Michalak v Poland* [2022] EWHC 342 (Admin) and *Soszynski v Poland* [2022] EWHC 3666 (Admin)).

Culpable delay can include long periods of unexplained delay: such as 6 years in *Eason v Government of the United States of America* [2020] EWHC 604 (Admin), [2020] ACD 54, 15 years in *Jindrich Kovac v The Regional Court in Prague* [2010] EWHC 1959 (Admin), and 9 years in *Antochi v Germany* [2020] EWHC 3092 (Admin), [2021] ACD 15. In some cases the (culpable) inaction of the Requesting State over a very

[132] *Gomes* at [28] and *Khan* [2012] EWHC 3231 (Admin) at [23]

[133] *Kakis v Government of the Republic of Cyprus* [1978] 1 WLR 779 at pp.782 to 785, *La Torre v Italy* [2007] EWHC 1370 (Admin), [2007] Extradition LR 185 at [37], and *Baksalry v Regional Court Warsaw, Poland* [2013] EWHC 372 (Admin) at [15]

long period may engender a false sense of security in the Requested Person.[134]

The delay will not be culpable if the Requesting State is actively seeking the individual, but does not know their whereabouts. It is not required to undertake 'detective work' to find them.[135]

Age

Section 15 of the Act creates a bar to extradition, solely in relation to Part 1 requests, on grounds of age:

> *'A person's extradition to a category 1 territory is barred by reason of his age if (and only if) it would be conclusively presumed because of his age that he could not be guilty of the extradition offence on the assumption-*
>
> *(a) that the conduct constituting the extradition offence constituted an offence in the part of the United Kingdom where the judge exercised jurisdiction;*
>
> *(b) that the person carried out the conduct when the extradition offence was committed (or alleged to be committed);*
>
> *(c) that the person carried out the conduct in the part of the United Kingdom where the judge exercised jurisdiction.'*

Applying these assumptions, the question is whether the Requested Person would be conclusively presumed to be not guilty on grounds of their age. In England and Wales there is a conclusive presumption that no one under the age of 10 can be guilty of any offence.[136]

The High Court recently considered the availability of the defence of *doli incapax* in the case of *Short v Falkland Islands* [2020] EWHC 438

---

134 Jindrich Kovac v The Regional Court in Prague [2010] EWHC 1959 (Admin) at [15]

135 Lopes v Comarca DI Braga Guimaraes (Portugal) [2021] EWHC 515 (Admin) at [23-24].

136 Section 50 of the Children and Young Persons Act 1933.

(Admin), [2020] 1 WLR 1644. Whilst the defence was available at the material time in the Falkland Islands, it had been abolished in England and Wales. The court held that the District Judge was not obliged to consider this potential defence under section 84 of the Act, as they were only concerned with whether "*there would be sufficient evidence to establish that there was a case to answer if the offence had been committed in England and Wales*".[137]

Section 15 had a basis in the 2002 Framework Decision as a mandatory ground to refuse surrender.[138] This provision has been retained in identical terms in the TCA. Article 600(c) provides that surrender shall be refused '*if the person who is the subject of the arrest warrant may not, owing to the person's age, be held criminally responsible for the acts on which the arrest warrant is based under the law of the executing State*'.

Practitioners are, however, unlikely to have recourse to this bar to extradition, given that England and Wales has the lowest age for criminal responsibility in Europe.

Hostage Taking considerations

Section 83 of the 2003 Act provides:

'(1) *A person's extradition to a category 2 territory is barred by reason of hostage-taking considerations if (and only if) the territory is a party to the Hostage-taking Convention and it appears that—*

(a). if extradited he might be prejudiced at his trial because communication between him and the appropriate authorities would not be possible, and

(b). the act or omission constituting the extradition offence also constitutes an offence under section 1 of the Taking of Hostages Act 1982 (c. 28) or an attempt to commit such an offence.

---

137 See [34]. Extradition was refused in relation to one of the offences, as it had allegedly occurred when the defence was available under domestic law.

138 Article 3(3)

(2) *The appropriate authorities are the authorities of the territory which are entitled to exercise rights of protection in relation to him*

(3) *A certificate issued by the Secretary of State that a territory is a party to the Hostage-taking Convention is conclusive evidence of that fact for the purposes of subsection (1).*

(4) *The Hostage-taking Convention is the International Convention against the Taking of Hostages opened for signature at New York on 18 December 1979.'*

Whilst the bar was also incorporated into Part 1 of the 2003 Act, at section 16, it was repealed on 21st July 2014 by section 158(1) of the Anti-social Behaviour, Crime and Policing Act 2014.

Section 83 applies where the Requesting State is a party to the Hostage-taking Convention, the extradition offence is hostage taking or attempted hostage taking, as defined in section 1 of the Taking of Hostages Act 1982, the Requested Person would be unable to communicate with the relevant protective authorities, and this might prejudice their trial.

Unsurprisingly, there is no reported case where section 83 has been discussed, let alone applied. Nor is there any reported judicial consideration of either its predecessor (section 25 of the Extradition Act 1989) or of its now repealed Part 1 counterpart.

In the unlikely event that section 83 is of relevance to a future case, the drafting of section 83(1)(a) is not particularly clear but it seems more likely that it is intended to set a low bar i.e. that there is a possibility of being prejudiced at trial because (of a possibility that) communication with the appropriate authorities would not be possible, rather than requiring the Requested Person to demonstrate first with certainty that such communication "would not be possible" and second that this might prejudice them at their trial.

Specialty

This bar to extradition was pithily summarised by a Divisional Court (Holroyde LJ and Swift J) in *Enasoaie v Bacau Court, Romania* [2021] EWHC 69 (Admin), [2021] ACD 37, at [38]:

> *"The principle of speciality (also referred to as "specialty") requires that an extradited person may only be dealt with for offences for which he is extradited to the requesting state, and may not be dealt with for any other offence allegedly committed prior to his extradition, unless he is first given a reasonable opportunity to leave the requesting state."*

In *Mihaylov v Bulgaria* [2022] EWHC 908 (Admin) the Divisional Court (Coulson LJ and Holgate J) at [18] explained that specialty can be infringed in two ways: *"where the individual is extradited and then subjected to unrelated charges or proceedings; or where the individual is prosecuted for enhanced charges based upon the conduct which gave rise to the EAW in the first place"*.

In Part 1 cases it is for the District Judge to consider. Under Part 2, it is a matter for the Secretary of State.[139] Section 17 provides:

> *'17 Speciality*
>
> *(1) A person's extradition to a category 1 territory is barred by reason of speciality if (and only if) there are no speciality arrangements with the category 1 territory.*
>
> *(2) There are speciality arrangements with a category 1 territory if, under the law of that territory or arrangements made between it and the United Kingdom, a person who is extradited to the territory from the United Kingdom may be dealt with in the territory for an offence committed before his extradition only if—*
>
> *(a) the offence is one falling within subsection (3), or*
>
> *(b) the condition in subsection (4) is satisfied.*
>
> *(3) The offences are—*
>
> *(a) the offence in respect of which the person is extradited;*

[139] In relation to Part 2, please see the chapter on the Secretary of State's role.

(b) an extradition offence disclosed by the same facts as that offence;

(c) an extradition offence in respect of which the appropriate judge gives his consent under section 55 to the person being dealt with;

(d) an offence which is not punishable with imprisonment or another form of detention;

(e) an offence in respect of which the person will not be detained in connection with his trial, sentence or appeal;

(f) an offence in respect of which the person waives the right that he would have (but for this paragraph) not to be dealt with for the offence.

(4) The condition is that the person is given an opportunity to leave the category 1 territory and—

(a) he does not do so before the end of the permitted period, or

(b) if he does so before the end of the permitted period, he returns there.

(5) The permitted period is 45 days starting with the day on which the person arrives in the category 1 territory.

(6) Arrangements made with a category 1 territory which is a Commonwealth country or a British overseas territory may be made for a particular case or more generally.

(7) A certificate issued by or under the authority of the Secretary of State confirming the existence of arrangements with a category 1 territory which is a Commonwealth country or a British overseas territory and stating the terms of the arrangements is conclusive evidence of those matters.'

The protection is additionally provided for in the European Convention on Extradition 1957[140], the 2002 Framework Decision[141] and the TCA.[142]

In practice the specialty bar is hard to deploy. The principles established by the case law in relation to specialty were summarised by Coulson LJ in *Mihaylov* at [18] as follows:

(a) There is a strong presumption that EU Members States will respect specialty rights in accordance with their international obligations;

(b) Accordingly, the Administrative Court will presume that the State in question will act in compliance with those obligations unless there is compelling evidence to the contrary;

(c) The court must be satisfied that there are practical and effective arrangements in the requesting territory to ensure that specialty will not be infringed;

(d) The basic question is whether the rule of specialty is catered for in the law of the requesting territory.

(e) The burden of proof is on the requested person to show that the presumption has been rebutted in the particular case and that appropriate specialty arrangements were not in place.

In Mihaylov the Divisional Court observed that it was common ground that the principle of specialty was provided for in Bulgarian law. The Court found that where an expert witness had referred to five cases over several years in which there had been an initial breach of specialty, but which once raised had been corrected, that this did not amount to "compelling evidence" that Bulgaria would not comply with specialty.[143]

---

140 Article 14

141 Article 27

142 Article 625(1). The UK has not provided notification under Article 625(1).

143 *Mihaylov* at [20] - [25]

A Divisional Court (Holroyde LJ delivering the judgment) in *Romania v Gurau* [2023] EWHC 439 (Admin) agreed with the observations of Coulson LJ in *Mihaylov*, noting that "the burden will not necessarily be discharged by pointing to some instances where the requesting state may have breached the specialty rule" [41]. In that case, the Divisional Court overturned a decision in which at first instance the District Judge had discharged the requested person because of specialty. The requested person's extradition was sought on an EAW containing five offences. However, there was an additional live indictment in Romania for a further offence, in relation to which the Romanian judicial authority had not issued an EAW, but had sought mutual legal assistance from the UK in relation to whether the requested person wanted to plead guilty or to be "judged in absentia" [4 - 9]. In allowing the appeal on behalf of the Romanian judicial authority, the Divisional Court observed that the relevant provision concerning specialty in the Romanian Criminal Code had not been before the District Judge at first instance and that significantly there had been no evidence before that Romania had breached the specialty rule in relation to any other requested person.[144] The Divisional Court found that the District Judge had fallen into error, first by disregarding the possibility that a request for consent could be made pursuant to section 54 of the Act, and secondly, by regarding the fact that proceedings were ongoing as providing compelling evidence of a likely breach of specialty and thereby displacing the presumption of confidence [44].

In Part 1 cases, specialty is most commonly raised where a Requested Person has been sentenced to an aggregate/composite sentence in relation to a number of offences, some of which do not constitute extradition offences, and there is a concern that the sentence cannot be dis-aggregated in the Requesting State. This arose before a Divisional Court in *Brodziak and ors v Polish Judicial Authorities* [2013] EWHC 3394

[144] *Romania v Gurau* [2023] EWHC 439 (Admin) at [41] –[42]

(Admin), [2014] ACD 59. The Divisional Court set out the relevant principles and explained that in this situation:

i) A Requested Person should be formally discharged in relation to any offence which fails to satisfy the dual criminality criteria[145];

ii) The burden is on a Requested Person to demonstrate, on the balance of probabilities, that appropriate speciality arrangements are not in place in the Requesting State[146]. There is a requirement for "compelling evidence"[147];

iii) There is a strong presumption that Member States will act in accordance with their international obligations in respect of specialty[148];

iv) There is no distinction between the test applicable to 'sentence' cases and that applied to 'accusation' cases[149];

The court found that, whilst the further information regarding the prospects of a dis-aggregation of the composite sentence had caused them a "*degree of anxiety*", it was not sufficiently compelling to displace the presumption that the Requesting State would act in accordance with its international obligations. Two factors led the court to this outcome. Firstly, it relied on the clear terms of the Polish Criminal Procedure Code, as opposed to how it is applied in practice. Secondly, the court relied on the lack of evidence to show that, notwithstanding numerous extraditions from the UK to Poland, there was nothing to demonstrate that an extraditee had been compelled to serve a sentence relating to a non-extraditable offence. The issue of disaggregation in relation to

---

145 Brodziak, at [33]

146 Brodziak, at [42]

147 *Brodziak*, at [46]

148 *Brodziak*, at [49]

149 *Brodziak*, at [48]

requests from Portugal is the subject of ongoing litigation: *Nobre v Portugal* [2024] EWHC 417 (Admin)

In order to ensure that the courts in the Requesting State are accurately informed of the offences for which extradition has been ordered (and those for which it has not), Westminster Magistrates' Court must make the position clear in its Judgment and Order. Furthermore, the CPS, in its capacity as the representative for the Judicial Authority must explicitly inform its client of the outcome. Additionally, a copy of the court's determination should accompany the Requested Person.[150]

Earlier extradition to the United Kingdom

Section 18 of the Act provides that:

> *'A person's extradition to a category 1 territory is barred by reason of his earlier extradition to the United Kingdom from another category 1 territory if (and only if) –*
>
> *(a) The person was extradited to the United Kingdom from another category 1 territory (the extraditing territory);*
>
> *(b) Under arrangements between the United Kingdom and the extraditing territory, that territory's consent is required to the person's extradition from the United Kingdom to the category 1 territory in respect of the extradition offence under consideration;*
>
> *(c) That consent has not been given on behalf of the extraditing territory'.*

Section 19 is in materially identical terms, save that it refers to the Requested Person's extradition to the UK from a non-category 1 territory.

Section 19A of the Act provides that:

[150] *Kortas v Regional Court in Bydgoszcz, Poland* [2017] EWHC 1356 (Admin), [2017] ACD 88, at [28]-[29].

'(1) *A person's extradition to a category 1 territory is barred by reason of his earlier transfer by the International Criminal Court if (and only if)-*

(a) *The person was transferred to the United Kingdom to serve a sentence imposed by the Court;*

(b) *Under arrangements between the United Kingdom and the Court, the consent of the Presidency of the Court is required to the person's extradition from the United Kingdom to the category 1 territory in respect of the extradition offence under consideration;*

(c) *That consent has not been given.*

(2) *Subsection (1) does not apply if the person has served the sentence imposed by the Court and has subsequently-*

(a) *remained voluntarily in the United Kingdom for more than 30 days, or*

(b) *left the United Kingdom and returned to it'.*

Sections 18 and 19 of the 2003 Act address the situation where an extradition request is received in circumstances where the Requested Person is present in the United Kingdom because they have been extradited here from another category 1 territory (section 18), or a non-category 1 territory (section 19). Where the country that originally extradited the Requested Person to the United Kingdom is required to give consent to onwards extradition but does not do so, extradition will be barred. Section 19A addresses the situation where an extradition request is received from another country and the Requested Person is present in the United Kingdom because they have been extradited here by the International Criminal Court to serve a sentence of imprisonment imposed by that court. In Part 1 cases this is considered by a judge at the extradition hearing. In Part 2 cases the equivalent provisions are sections 96 and 96A and this will be considered by the Secretary of State.

Forum

Under sections 19B (in Part 1) and 83A (in Part 2) of the 2003 Act extradition is barred by reason of forum if the judge decides that extradition would not be in the interests of justice, as defined in that section. Section 19B provides:

> *'(1) The extradition of a person ("D") to a category 1 territory is barred by reason of forum if the extradition would not be in the interests of justice.*
>
> *(2) For the purposes of this section, the extradition would not be in the interests of justice if the judge—*
>
> > *(a) decides that a substantial measure of D's relevant activity was performed in the United Kingdom; and*
> >
> > *(b) decides, having regard to the specified matters relating to the interests of justice (and only those matters), that the extradition should not take place.*
>
> *(3) These are the specified matters relating to the interests of justice—*
>
> > *(a) the place where most of the loss or harm resulting from the extradition offence occurred or was intended to occur;*
> >
> > *(b) the interests of any victims of the extradition offence;*
> >
> > *(c) any belief of a prosecutor that the United Kingdom, or a particular part of the United Kingdom, is not the most appropriate jurisdiction in which to prosecute D in respect of the conduct constituting the extradition offence;*
> >
> > *(d) were D to be prosecuted in a part of the United Kingdom for an offence that corresponds to the extradition offence, whether evidence necessary to prove the offence is or could be made available in the United Kingdom;*
> >
> > *(e) any delay that might result from proceeding in one jurisdiction rather than another;*

(f) the desirability and practicability of all prosecutions relating to the extradition offence taking place in one jurisdiction, having regard (in particular) to—

(i) the jurisdictions in which witnesses, co—defendants and other suspects are located, and

(ii) the practicability of the evidence of such persons being given in the United Kingdom or in jurisdictions outside the United Kingdom;

(g) D's connections with the United Kingdom.

(4) In deciding whether the extradition would not be in the interests of justice, the judge must have regard to the desirability of not requiring the disclosure of material which is subject to restrictions on disclosure in the category 1 territory concerned.

(5) If, on an application by a prosecutor, it appears to the judge that the prosecutor has considered the offences for which D could be prosecuted in the United Kingdom, or a part of the United Kingdom, in respect of the conduct constituting the extradition offence, the judge must make that prosecutor a party to the proceedings on the question of whether D's extradition is barred by reason of forum.

(6) In this section "D's relevant activity" means activity which is material to the commission of the extradition offence and which is alleged to have been performed by D.'

The forum bar was introduced by the Crime and Courts Act 2013. Prior to the amendment of the 2003 Act, the English courts considered arguments that a person should be tried in the UK under Article 8 ECHR.[151] The Police and Justice Act 2006 proposed the introduction of a simply drafted forum bar that would have prevented extradition if a significant part of the conduct had occurred in the UK and it appeared to the judge that it would not be in the interests of justice for the person

151 See, for example, *Bermingham v Director of the SFO and ors* [2006] EWHC 200 (Admin), [2007] QB 727, and *Norris v USA* [2010] UKSC 9, [2010] 2 AC 487, Lord Philips at [67]

to be tried in the Requesting State. However, that amendment was never brought into force. The Scott Baker review into the UK's extradition arrangements recommended that the forum bar provisions not be brought into force, but in 2013 the Government ignored that recommendation and introduced the bar.

The forum bar, as enacted, provides that the extradition of a person to either a category 1 or category 2 territory is barred by reason of forum if the extradition would not be in the interests of justice.

The bar contains a threshold condition, that the person must be accused of the offence or offences for which their extradition is sought[152]. It does not apply to cases where a person is sought to serve a sentence, even following conviction in absence with a right to a retrial[153].

The forum bar prevents extradition where the judge determines that it is not in the interests of justice as defined by the specified matters contained in sections 19B(3) or 83A(3). Before considering those factors the judge must determine that a substantial measure of the Requested Person's relevant activity was performed in the United Kingdom. If it wasn't, then the bar of forum cannot apply[154]. *'Relevant activity'* is defined in sections 19B(6) and 83A(6) as activity which is material to the commission of the extradition offence and which is alleged to have been performed by the Requested Person.

The only matters that the judge is permitted to consider when deciding whether or not extradition would be in the interests of justice are set out in sections 19B(3) and 83A(3). In making that decision the judge must also *'have regard'* to the desirability of not requiring the disclosure of material which is subject to restrictions on disclosure in the category 2 territory concerned (ss. 19B(4) and 83A(4)).

---

152 S.19B(2)(a) and s.83A(2)(a)

153 See *Bagri v France* [2014] EWHC 4066 (Admin) and *Belbin v France* [2015] EWHC 149 (Admin), [2015] ACD 58. This approach is consistent with the Supreme Court's judgment in *Konecny.*

154 See *Pham v USA* [2014] EWHC 4167 (Admin), [2015] ACD 62 at [83-89]

The relative importance of each of the specified matters, and the weight to be given to them, will vary from case to case.[155] The place where most of the harm took place will usually be a *"very weighty factor"*.[156] Whilst the forum bar is aimed at preventing extradition where offences can *"fairly and effectively"* be tried in the United Kingdom, the statutory test is not whether the Requested Person should be tried in the Requesting State or in the United Kingdom, but rather whether, in the interests of justice, there should not be an extradition to the Requesting State.[157]

One of the more unusual aspects of the forum bar is the potential for a domestic prosecutor to issue a *"prosecutor's certificate"*. Where such a certificate is issued, the judge considering the extradition request is prohibited from concluding that extradition would not be in the interests of justice by virtue of sections 19C(1) or 83B(1), provided that the judge has not already determined whether the bar applies.

A prosecutor's certificate is a certificate issued by a designated prosecutor[158] certifying that a responsible prosecutor has considered the offences for which the Requested Person could be prosecuted in the United Kingdom, or a part of the United Kingdom, in respect of the conduct constituting the extradition offence and that the responsible prosecutor has decided that there are one or more offences that correspond to the extradition offence.[159] Sections 19D(4) and 83C(4) provide that the certificate must also certify that the responsible prosecutor has either:

---

155 *Shaw v USA* [2014] EWHC 4654 (Admin), [2015] ACD 63, at [40]

156 *Love v USA* [2018] EWHC 172 (Admin), [2018] 1 WLR 2889 at [28], approved in *Scott v USA* [2018] EWHC 2021 (Admin), [2019] 1 WLR 774, at [37].

157 *Shaw,* at [41]

158 A designated prosecutor is defined in section 19F(2)/ 83E(2) as either a member of the Crown Prosecution Service or, any other person who is a prosecutor designated for the purposes of the Section by order made by the Secretary of State or is within a description of prosecutors so designated.

159 Sections 19D and 83C.

a) made a formal decision that the Requested Person should not be prosecuted for the corresponding offences and that the reason for that decision is a belief that (i) there would be insufficient admissible evidence for the prosecution or (ii) that the prosecution would not be in the public interest;

or

b) That the responsible prosecutor believes that the Requested Person should not be prosecuted for the corresponding offences because there are concerns about the disclosure of sensitive material in the prosecution of D for the corresponding offences or any other proceedings.

Sections 19D(7) and 83C(7) defines *'sensitive material'* as including material which appears to be sensitive on grounds relating to national security, international relations, or the prevention or detection of crime.

Under sections 19E and 83D respectively, a prosecutor's certificate can only be questioned on an appeal under section 26 (in Part 1) and sections 103 or 108 (in Part 2) of the 2003 Act. The High Court must apply the principles that apply to an application for judicial review[160]. Where the High Court quashes a prosecutor's certificate it must decide the question of whether extradition is barred by reason of forum for itself[161].

Under sections 19C(3)-(5) or 83B(3)-(5) a designated prosecutor may apply for the judge's consideration of the forum bar to be adjourned for the purpose of assisting themselves or any other designated prosecutor in considering whether to give a prosecutor's certificate, in giving such a certificate or in sending such a certificate to the judge.

In practice, the issue of prosecutor's certificates is rare to the point of being nearly unheard of; it is more common for a domestic prosecutor to express a statement of belief rather than to issue a certificate under section 19B or section 83C.

160 Sections 19E(1)-(3) and 83D(1)-(3).

161 Sections 19E(4) and 83D(4)

Sections 19B(5) and 83A(5) provide that the Judge must order that a domestic prosecutor be joined as a party to the proceedings on the question of whether D's extradition is barred by reason of forum if the prosecutor applies to be joined and it appears to the judge that the prosecutor has considered the offences for which D could be prosecuted in the United Kingdom, in respect of the conduct constituting the extradition offence. As with the issuance of prosecutor's certificates, it is also rare for a domestic prosecutor to apply to be joined as a party to the extradition proceedings.

One of the first cases in which the High Court considered the forum bar was *Dibden v France* [2014] EWHC 3074 (Admin). Simon J set out the correct approach to the interpretation of the bar, at [18]:

> "*18. Five initial points may be noted:*
>
> *First, the ultimate test is whether the extradition would not be in the interests of justice (see section 19(B)(1) . Secondly, there is a threshold or qualifying condition that a substantial measure of a defendant's relevant activity was performed in the United Kingdom (see section 19B(2)(a). Thirdly, the section is not concerned with a case where a defendant has been charged with an offence in the United Kingdom. That situation is covered by section 22 of the Act which requires the adjournment of an extradition hearing, ... Section 19B is concerned with a case where there is a possibility of a prosecution in this country. Fourthly, where the court finds that the threshold or qualifying condition is satisfied, the court must go on to consider the six specified matters which relate to the interests of justice, which are set out in sub-section 3(a) to (g) and "only those matters" see (2)(b). Fifthly, the terms of section 19B contain no further guidance as to the weight to be given to the specified matters which should be taken into account. The relative importance of each matter will vary from case to case, and the weight to be accorded to the specified matters may also vary. The court will be engaged in a fact-specific exercise in order to determine whether the particular extradition would not be in the interests of justice.*"

As to the correct standard of review of a 'prosecutor's belief' under section 19B(3)(c) (and section 83A(3)(c)) the court held:

> *"35. … Section 19B(3)(c) was not intended to invite a review of the prosecutor's belief as to the more appropriate jurisdiction on grounds short of irrationality. It was certainly not intended to invite a debate with demands for documents justifying the belief."*

In *Atraskevic v Lithuania* [2015] EWHC 131 (Admin), [2016] 1 WLR 2762, Aikens LJ and Nicola Davies J reviewed and approved the decision in *Dibden*[162]. They held that the parties and the Court could not take steps to create a belief on the part of a domestic prosecutor as to whether the jurisdiction in which the extradition hearing was taking place or the Requesting State was the more appropriate venue for prosecution. At [37], Aikens LJ held:

> *"37. In our view, the use of the words "any belief of a prosecutor" is important. The "prosecutor" in question here is a domestic prosecutor, that is someone in the domestic CPS. Such a prosecutor may or may not have formed any such belief at the time of the extradition hearing. If none has been formed or expressed, the statutory wording does not require that any party or the court should demand that a prosecutor must then take steps to create a "belief" on the part of the prosecutor. The initiative to declare "a belief" or not lies with the domestic CPS. There is no statutory mechanism that enables the court to compel further investigation by the CPS so as to put it in a position to have a "belief". That view of the construction of this factor is consistent with the rule, applicable in extradition cases, that a decision by domestic authorities not to investigate whether there should be a criminal prosecution in the UK is not susceptible to judicial review except in wholly exceptional circumstances such as bad faith: R(Bermingham) v DPP [2007] QB 207 at [64]; R(McKinnon) v Secretary of State for Home Affairs [2009] EWHC 2021 at [53]."*

One of the first cases in which a Requested Person relied on the forum bar successfully was *Love v USA* [2018] EWHC 172 (Admin), [2018] 1 WLR 2889. The Divisional Court held that the Requested Person's connections to the UK under section 83A(3)(g) were sufficiently strong to outweigh the other factors favouring extradition in section 83A(3), in

---

[162] Judgment at [14]

light of Mr Love's state of physical and mental health, the prison conditions that he would face in the USA and the deleterious effect extradition would have on his mental health (even if those factors would not in and of themselves have led to discharge under sections 87 or 91 of the 2003 Act). The court held, at [22] and [26]:

> *"In our judgment, section 83A is clearly intended to provide a safeguard for Requested Persons, not distinctly to be found in any of the other bars to extradition or grounds for discharge, including section 87 and the wide scope of article 8 ECHR. The safeguard is not confined to British nationals, but it is to be borne in mind that the United Kingdom is one of those countries which is prepared to extradite its own nationals. Its underlying aim is to prevent extradition where the offences can be fairly and effectively tried here, and it is not in the interests of justice that the Requested Person should be extradited. But close attention has to be paid to the wording of the statute rather than to short summaries of its purpose or to general Parliamentary statements. The forum bar only arises if extradition would not be in the interests of justice; section 83A(1). The matters relevant to an evaluation of "the interests of justice" for these purposes are found in section 83A(2)(b). They do not leave to the court the task of some vague or broader evaluation of what is just. Nor is the bar a general provision requiring the court to form a view directly on which is the more suitable forum, let alone having regard to sentencing policy or the potential for prisoner transfer, save to the extent that one of the listed factors might in any particular case require consideration of it.*
>
> ...
>
> *26. The true approach is more simply expressed by requiring the appellate court to decide whether the decision of the district judge was wrong. What was said in Celinski*[163] *and Re B (A Child)*[164] *are apposite, even if decided in the context of article 8. In effect, the test is the same here. The appellate court is entitled to stand back and say that a question ought to have been decided differently because the overall*

163 [2015] EWHC 1274

164 [2013] UKSC 33

evaluation was wrong: crucial factors should have been weighed so significantly differently as to make the decision wrong, such that the appeal in consequence should be allowed."

As to the meaning of 'connections' in section 83A(3)(g) the Court held that it was wider than simply being a UK citizen or having a right of residence:

> " *40.... In our judgment, "connection" goes rather wider than that, without being so elastic that it replicates the full scope of article 8 ECHR. No exhaustive definition can be attempted judicially, but "connection" is closer to the notion of ties for the purposes of bail decisions. It would cover family ties, their nature and strength, employment and studies, property, duration and status of residence, and nationality. It would not usually cover health conditions or medical treatment, unless there was something particular about the nature of the medical condition or the treatment it required, that connected the individual to treatment in the United Kingdom."*

Love was followed by *Scott v USA* [2018] EWHC 2021 (Admin), [2019] 1 WLR 774 in which the Divisional Court (Lord Burnett LCJ and Males J) held that a prosecutor's letter stating that there would be no investigation in the UK of the offences contained in the extradition request, which did not address the question of where it would be more appropriate for the Requested Person to be tried, was not a prosecutor's statement of belief under section 83A(3)(c). That there was no possibility of a trial in the United Kingdom was relevant to the other factors in section 83A(3). The Court held that the fact that most of the harm took place in the UK and the appellant's strong connection with the United Kingdom and absence of any significant connection with the United States outweighed the other factors in favour of extradition in section 83A(3) and that extradition was therefore not in the interests of justice.

In *Wyatt v USA* [2019] EWHC 2978 (Admin) the Divisional Court (Lord Burnett LCJ and May J) considered a challenge to extradition based on reference to the factors in section 83A(3) in a prosecutor's statement of belief. The Court held:

> *"18. The judge deciding an issue under section 83A of the 2003 Act is obliged to have regard exclusively to the statutory lexicon when determining where the interests of justice lie. One of those factors is a belief of the prosecutor that the United Kingdom is not the most appropriate place in which a prosecution should proceed. The statute requires her to have regard to such a statement of belief but the weight to be attached to it is a matter for the judge. The more reasoned or explained the belief, the more likely it is to carry substantial weight. It is almost inevitable that a prosecutor will take into account the statutory factors found in section 83A(3) in forming a belief. It would be very odd not to do so. Factors such as the interests of the victims, the availability of evidence, the location of harm, delay, the defendant's connections with the United Kingdom and the prospect of multiple prosecutions could be influential in forming a belief. The prosecutor is not, however, limited by the statutory factors in the same way that the judge is. He may take anything that rationally bears on the question into account. Obvious examples would include the dynamics of a trial and the practical implications of having to investigate alleged offences and prosecute them here, including resource implications. There may also be differences between the legal regimes in the requesting state and England and Wales which could have an impact on admissibility of evidence or raise other legal issues.*
>
> *19. Thus, the judge is required to have regard to the prosecutor's belief; and that may be based largely on the statutory factors or may extend well beyond them. Yet the prosecutor's belief is an independent factor that weights in the balance. It may be, for example, that the judge's provisional view having regard to all factors except the prosecutor's belief would be not to favour extradition. Then, taking into account the prosecutor's belief the balance may tip the other way. Whether or not that is the case, the belief must weigh in the balance, but weight is for the judge.*
>
> *20. The prosecutor's belief is not diminished or undermined for the purposes of the 2003 Act simply because it takes into account factors found in section 83A..."*

The weight to be attached to the factors in sections 19B(3) and 83A(3) is for the judge to determine on the facts of each case. It is not a matter of simply totting up the number of factors in favour of extradition and those against, but requires appropriate weight to be attached to each factor. In *USA v McDaid* [2020] EWHC 1527 (Admin) Holroyde LJ and William Davis J upheld a District Judge's decision to discharge an extradition request as being barred by forum. The compelling factors that were in the Requested Person's favour in making out the bar were that the evidence necessary to prove the offences could be made available in the UK, that a prosecution in the UK would be unlikely to result in delay, the fact that a co-defendant had been convicted and sentenced and there was no prospect of a joint trial, and the Requested Person's very close ties to the UK including his family whose support he would lose if extradited. The court held that section 83A does not require a court to decide in a general way, which of the UK and the Requesting State is the more suitable, or preferable, forum. Assuming that a substantial measure of the Requested Person's relevant activity was performed in the UK, it requires an evaluation of the specified matters in order to decide whether extradition would not be in the interests of justice and should not take place. That evaluation is necessarily fact-specific, because the importance of each of the matters specified in sections 19B(3) and 83A(3), and the weight to be given to each of them, will vary according to the circumstances of the case[165].

In *Hamilton v USA* [2023] EWHC 2893 (Admin) the Divisional Court (Dame Sharp P. and Johnson J) ("*Hamilton*") disagreed with the District Judge's finding that a Crown Prosecutor's belief that the United Kingdom was the most appropriate jurisdiction for a prosecution was a factor that weighed in favour of extradition [68]. At [86] Dame Sharp P. explained that:

> *"[The Crown Prosecutor] expresses the clear view that the UK is not the most appropriate jurisdiction in which to prosecute the appellant. That is a factor that weighs heavily in the balance, if the view is sound. Conversely, if it is based on flimsy material, or is ill-considered or even irrational then it will carry no weight at all. Similarly, the mere assertion the UK is the most appropriate jurisdiction in which to prosecute a requested person does not, in itself, carry any significant*

165 Judgment at [43]

> *weight: Shaw at [51]-[53], Dibden at [35], Love at [54] and Wyatt at [18] - [20]".*

The Divisional Court observed that the Crown Prosecutor had not merely asserted a belief but had provided a detailed analysis covering the background, the investigation, the current position, and the statutory factors. However, the Court identified *"a number of difficulties with her analysis"* [87]. It was significant that since the Prosecutor had expressed her belief, (a) the requested person's co-accused had been discharged from the extradition proceedings, so the only place a trial could take place against the co-accused was in the UK and not the USA, and that (b) additional evidence had been identified by the US authorities which related to the requested person and his (discharged) co-accused and which had not previously been available to the CPS [88] - [89]. The Crown Prosecutor's analysis of the statutory factors was found to be flawed, which included her failure to recognise that "*the requested persons conduct took place in the UK and that most of the harm directly occasioned by his activities was in the UK*" [90]. The Divisional Court decided that *"no weight"* should be attached to the statement of belief made by the Crown Prosecutor [91].

The Divisional Court allowed the requested persons appeal in *Hamilton*, concluding that extradition would not be in the interests of justice. The requested person was a British national, who had lived his entire life in the UK and was dependent on doctors in the UK for his medical treatment. His conduct took place in the UK. The greatest share of the harm that he had allegedly caused occurred in the UK rather than the US. US victims had *"secured a measure of vindication"* though prosecutions in the US but there were also UK victims and there had been no prosecution in the UK. All the evidence necessary for the prosecution could be made available in the UK. The co-defendant had been discharged from the extradition proceedings, so could be prosecuted in the UK but not the USA. It was "*highly desirable and practicable, that they be tried in the same jurisdiction*". Whilst proceedings in the USA would conclude more quickly than in the UK, *"it was not possible to quantify how much more quickly"* and that factor was not sufficient to change the overall interests of justice assessment. The Court's view was that the most appropriate location for a prosecution was the UK, and the judge should have decided, having regard to the statutory matters relating to the interests of justice, that extradition should not take place.[166]

Convictions in absence

Domestic legal framework:

Sections 20 (in Part 1) and 85 (in Part 2) prevent extradition to serve a sentence imposed in the requested person's absence in breach of the Requested Person's rights of defence, where there is no entitlement to a retrial.

In deciding whether this bar applies, the judge must answer a series of questions, set out in s.20 as follows:

> *'(1) If the judge is required to proceed under this section (by virtue of section 11) he must decide whether the person was convicted in his presence.*
>
> *(2) If the judge decides the question in subsection (1) in the affirmative he must proceed under section 21.*
>
> *(3) If the judge decides that question in the negative he must decide whether the person deliberately absented himself from his trial.*
>
> *(4) If the judge decides the question in subsection (3) in the affirmative he must proceed under section 21.*
>
> *(5) If the judge decides that question in the negative he must decide whether the person would be entitled to a retrial or (on appeal) to a review amounting to a retrial.*
>
> *(6) If the judge decides the question in subsection (5) in the affirmative he must proceed under section 21.*
>
> *(7) If the judge decides that question in the negative he must order the person's discharge.*

166 *Hamilton* at [108]

> *(8) The judge must not decide the question in subsection (5) in the affirmative unless, in any proceedings that it is alleged would constitute a retrial or a review amounting to a retrial, the person would have these rights—*
>
> *(a) the right to defend himself in person or through legal assistance of his own choosing or, if he had not sufficient means to pay for legal assistance, to be given it free when the interests of justice so required;*
>
> *(b) the right to examine or have examined witnesses against him and to obtain the attendance and examination of witnesses on his behalf under the same conditions as witnesses against him.'*

Section 85 is in materially identical terms. The effect of both sections is to require the judge to determine whether the Requested Person was convicted *in absentia*, if so whether this was in breach of their fair trial rights because they did not deliberately absent themselves from their trial, and if so whether they are entitled to a retrial on return. Sections 20 and 85 were enacted to safeguard a Requested Person's rights of defence,[167] since "*conviction in absentia with no possibility subsequently to obtain a fresh determination of the merits of the charge*" is one of the few types of unfairness which the ECtHR has consistently held constitutes a "*flagrant*" breach of Art 6 ECHR.[168]

The European legal framework:

Although ss.20 and 85 are domestic in origin, similar provisions were enacted in relation to the EAW scheme by Council Framework Decision

---

167 See for example *Szatkowski v Poland* [2019] EWHC 883 (Admin), [2019] 1 WLR 4528 at [33]; *Koc v Turkey* [2021] EWHC 1234 (Admin) at [13].

168 See for example *Willcox and Hurford v United Kingdom* (2013) 57 EHRR SE16, at [95]. However, it should be remembered that where ss.20 or 85 bite, the court is to consider and apply the statutory tests those provisions lay down, and is not directly concerned with Arts 5 or 6 ECHR; cf. *Barci v The Government of Albania* [2017] EWHC 369 (Admin); *Foster Taylor v Italy* [2019] EWHC 2938 (Admin), [80]-[82].

2009/299/JHA of 26 February 2009 ('the 2009 Framework Decision'). This amended the 2002 Framework Decision so as to introduce a new Article 4a(1), establishing an optional ground for non-surrender where the Requested Person was convicted *in absentia*, subject to four exceptions. If the EAW stated that one of the exceptions applied, the executing court was obliged to proceed with extradition.[169] The four exceptions were that the Requested Person:

> *(a) in due time:*
>
> > *(i) either was summoned in person and thereby informed of the scheduled date and place of the trial which resulted in the decision, or by other means actually received official information of the scheduled date and place of that trial in such a manner that it was unequivocally established that he or she was aware of the scheduled trial;*
> >
> > *and*
> >
> > *(ii) was informed that a decision may be handed down if he or she does not appear for the trial;*
>
> *or*
>
> *(b) being aware of the scheduled trial, had given a mandate to a legal counsellor, who was either appointed by the person concerned or by the State, to defend him or her at the trial, and was indeed defended by that counsellor at the trial;*
>
> *or*
>
> *(c) after being served with the decision and being expressly informed about the right to a retrial, or an appeal, in which the person has the right to participate and which allows the merits of the case, including fresh evidence, to be re-examined, and which may lead to the original decision being reversed:*

169 Stefano Melloni v Ministerio Fiscal [2013] QB 1067.

(i) expressly stated that he or she does not contest the decision;

or

(ii) did not request a retrial or appeal within the applicable time frame;

or

(d) was not personally served with the decision but:

(i) will be personally served with it without delay after the surrender and will be expressly informed of his or her right to a retrial, or an appeal, in which the person has the right to participate and which allows the merits of the case, including fresh evidence, to be re-examined, and which may lead to the original decision being reversed;

and

(ii) will be informed of the time frame within which he or she has to request such a retrial or appeal, as mentioned in the relevant European arrest warrant.'

Under the EAW scheme, Article 4a(1) had a profound influence on our domestic jurisprudence. Following *Cretu v Local Court of Suceava, Romania*,[170] the English courts were obliged to interpret s.20 as far as possible in conformity with the Framework Decisions[171] (although this obligation could not serve as a basis for interpreting national law *contra legem*).[172] Further, although the Framework Decisions were not directly

170 *Cretu v Local Court of Suceava, Romania* [2016] EWHC 353 (Admin), [2016] 1 WLR 3344.

171 Cf. *Criminal proceedings against Pupino* [2006] QB 83. The *Pupino* principle is the corollary of the *Marleasing* principle which applies to domestic provisions implementing Directives.

172 Criminal proceedings against Lopes Da Silva Jorge [2013] QB 283, at [55].

relevant to s.85, the caselaw decided in accordance with them was consistently treated as highly persuasive in Part 2 cases.

Although the UK is no longer party to the Framework Decisions following the end of the transition period, caselaw based on it will continue to apply in this area. There are four principal reasons for this. First, the language and effect of Art 4a(1) of the 2009 Framework Decision[173] is similar to that of ss.20 and 85. This is unsurprising; the UK was one of the main architects of the 2009 Framework Decision and it was largely based on our domestic legislation. Second, the terms of Article 4a(1) have been, in essence, replicated in Article 601(1)(i), suggesting that the drafters of the TCA intended there to be continuity of approach in relation to convictions *in absentia.* Third, Parliament has evidently not thought it necessary to amend s.20 in light of the TCA. Fourth, as noted above, s.20, s.85, Article 4a and Article 601(1)(i) all share a common objective, namely to safeguard a Requested Person's Article 6 ECHR rights in circumstances where they have been proceeded against *in absentia.*

It is therefore necessary to consider how the courts have so far approached the questions under subsections (1), (3) and (5) of ss.20 and 85. Practitioners should note that these provisions have proved to be among the most difficult and controversial in the 2003 Act. They should therefore take extra care to ensure that they are familiar with the latest caselaw.

Subsection (1): presence at trial:

Under ss.20(1) and 85(1) the court must consider whether a Requested Person was "*convicted in his presence*". If so, it may proceed straight to s.21 (or s.87, as the case may be).

A Requested Person will have been "*convicted in his presence*" if they appeared at the "*trial which resulted in the decision*", as envisaged in Article 4a(1). Often, what hearing constituted the 'trial resulting in the decision'

---

173 And now Art 601(1)(i) of the TCA.

will be uncontroversial.[174] But the position may be less straightforward where there were one or more appeal stages, giving rise to successive decisions, some of which were given *in absentia*. For the avoidance of doubt, appellate proceedings can in principle constitute 'the trial resulting in the decision'.[175] In such circumstances, the relevant hearing is the one which resulted in the final decision, as long as that ruling followed a factual and legal assessment of the evidence.[176]

Where, in addition to the original conviction and sentencing decision, there was a later decision which affected the sentence the Requested Person has to serve, they may have been entitled to attend the hearing resulting in the later decision, as well as the trial resulting in the original decision.[177] Thus, for example, activation, aggregation, and resentencing hearings which were conducted *in absentia* may fall within the scope of Art 4a(1). Here, the litmus test is whether the hearing in question was "*not a purely formal and arithmetic exercise but [entailed] a margin of discretion in the determination of the level of the sentence*".[178] Where a Requested Person is subject to a suspended sentence or is released on license subject to conditions, a later decision to activate the sentence will not fall within Art 4a(1) if that decision "*does not change the nature or the level of the sentence initially imposed*".[179]

174 For example, in *Niziol v Poland* [2023] EWHC 3252 (Admin), [2023] 12 WLUK 240 at [93], an appellate challenge relating to bias of a lower court was a "far cry from the re-examination of the substance of the charges and from any determination of the [Requested Person's] guilt or innocence which would require his or her lawyer's presence."

175 See, for example, *Doga v France* [2022] EWHC 3342 (Admin), [2022] 11 WLUK 555 at [76] – [77]

176 *Criminal proceedings against Tupikas* [2017] 4 WLR 188. Thus, a cassation procedure may not amount to the 'trial resulting in the decision', even if it was the last stage of the stage of the process chronologically: *Foster Taylor v Italy* [2019] EWHC 2938 (Admin).

177 Criminal proceedings against Zdziaszek [2017] 4 WLR 189.

178 *Zdziaszek* at [88].

179 Criminal Proceedings Against Samet Ardic (Case C-571/17 PPU).

A Requested Person will have been 'present' at the 'trial resulting in the decision' not only where they were physically present, but also where they instructed a lawyer to represent them at it, as envisaged by Art 601(1)(i)(ii) of the TCA.

Subsection (3): deliberate absence:

A Requested Person who was absent from their trial need not be entitled to a retrial if they were "*deliberately absent*" from it: ss.20(3) and 85(3).

The key issue here is whether, in view of the Requested Person's conduct, the decision to proceed in their absence did not offend against Article 6 ECHR.

Article 601(1)(i)(i) outlines two of the situations in which a Requested Person will have been "*deliberately absent*": where they were personally summoned to their trial, or it was unequivocally established that they were actually notified of the trial by other means, and they chose not to attend despite being warned that a decision could be handed down in their absence.

A Requested Person could also be regarded as "*deliberately absent*" for the purposes of ss.20(3) and 85(3) if by their conduct they knowingly and unequivocally waived their right to appear at trial.

The Divisional Court in *Cretu* gave the following guidance on 'deliberate absence':

> "*i) 'Trial' in section 20(3) of the 2003 Act must be read as meaning 'trial which resulted in the decision' in conformity with article 4a paragraph 1(a)(i). That suggests an event with a 'scheduled date and place' and is not referring to a general prosecution process, Mitting J was right to foreshadow this in <u>Bicioc</u>;*
>
> *ii) An accused must be taken to be deliberately absent from his trial if he has been summoned as envisaged by article 4a paragraph 1(a)(i) in a manner which, even though he may have been unaware of the scheduled date and place, does not violate article 6 ECHR;*
>
> ...

v) Whilst, by virtue of section 206 of the 2003 Act, it remains for the requesting state to satisfy the court conducting the extradition hearing in the United Kingdom to the criminal standard that one (or more) of the four exceptions found in article 4a applies, the burden of proof will be discharged to the requisite standard if the information required by article 4a is set out in the EAW."

Post *Cretu*, Hickinbottom J sought to provide an overview of the relevant principles. In *Stryjecki v District Court in Lublin, Poland* [2016] EWHC 3309 (Admin), at [50] he held:

"i) It is for the requesting judicial authority to prove, to the criminal standard, that the requested person has 'deliberately absented himself from his trial'.

ii) 'Trial' is not a reference to the general prosecution process, but rather the trial as an event with a scheduled time and venue which resulted in the decision.

iii) The EAW system is based on trust and confidence as between territories. Consequently, where the EAW contains a statement from the requesting judicial authority as required by paragraph 4A(1)(a) of the Framework Decision, that will be respected and accepted by the court considering the extradition request, unless the statement is ambiguous (or, possibly, if there is an argument that the warrant is an abuse of process). If the statement is unambiguous, the court will not conduct its own examination into those matters, nor will it press the requesting authority for further information.

iv) If the statement in the EAW is ambiguous or confused (a fortiori , if there is no statement at all), then it is open to the court considering the request to conduct its own assessment of whether the requested person was summoned in person or, by other means, actually received official information of the scheduled date and place of that trial, on the evidence before it, the burden being born by the requesting authority to the criminal standard.

v) 'Summoned in person' means personally served with the relevant information. If there has not been such service, generally the requesting authority must unequivocally establish to the criminal standard that

> *the person actually received the relevant information as to time and place. It is insufficient for the requesting authority to show merely that the domestic rules as to service of such a summons were satisfied, if it is not established that the person actually received the trial information.*
>
> *vi) Establishment of the fact that the requested person has taken steps which make it difficult or impossible for the requesting state to serve the requested person with documents which would have notified him of the fact, date and place of the trial is not in itself proof that the requested person has deliberately absented himself from his trial.*
>
> *vii) However, where the requesting authority cannot establish that the person actually received that information because of 'a manifest lack of diligence' on the part of the requested person, notably where the person concerned has sought to avoid service of the information so that his own fault led the person to be unaware of the time and place of his trial, the court may nevertheless be satisfied that the surrender of the person concerned would not breach his rights of defence".*

It is of note that points (vi) and (vii) have not commanded complete support.[180] However, in *Oprea v The Constanta Tribunal, Romania* [2021] EWHC 223 (Admin) Sir Ross Cranston noted *Tyrakowski* and *Dziel*, but stated that all seven of Hickinbottom J's propositions "*must be regarded as authoritative*" as they were approved by a Divisional Court in *Szatkowski v Poland.*[181]

The Supreme Court recently considered the test for deliberate absence in *Bertino v Public Prosecutor's Office* [2024] UKSC 9. The Court endorsed the conclusions in *Cretu* (but did not explicitly reference *Stryjecki*).[182] It reiterated that *"the phrase 'deliberately absented himself from his trial' should be understood as being synonymous with the concept in Strasbourg*

180 Tyrakowski v Regional Court in Poznan, Poland [2017] EWHC 2675 (Admin), at [30], and Dziel v District Court in Bydgoszcz, Poland [2019] EWHC 351 (Admin), at [17]

181 *Szatkowski v Poland* [2019] EWHC 883 (Admin), [2019] 1 WLR 4528 at [22].

182 *Bertino v Italy* [2024] UKSC 9, [2024] 1 WLR 1483 at [26]

jurisprudence that an accused has unequivocally waived his right to be present at the trial."183 It reviewed that Strasbourg jurisprudence and held that it was apparent from *"...[those] cases that the standard imposed by the Strasbourg Court is that for a waiver to be unequivocal and effective, knowing and intelligent, ordinarily the accused must be shown to have appreciated the consequences of his or her behaviour. That will usually require the defendant to be warned in one way or another"*.184

This may be the case where they deliberately avoided the summons to their trial, or where a "*manifest lack of diligence*" on their part led to them being unaware of it. However, the Supreme Court in *Bertino* explicitly considered the import of the term 'manifest lack of diligence'. It clarified that a *"general manifest lack of diligence which results in ignorance of criminal proceedings"*185 is not in itself sufficient for a conclusion of deliberate absence and that the Divisional Court *"...in Zagrean v Romania [2016] EWHC 2786 (Admin) put the point too widely at para 81 in saying "a requested person will be taken to have deliberately absented himself from his trial where the fault was his own conduct in leading him to be unaware of the date and time of trial.""186*

Put differently, the term 'manifest lack of diligence' does not displace the underlying test i.e. that the individual has knowingly and unequivocally waived the right to a trial. As the Administrative Court observed in *JK v Poland* [2018] EWHC 197 (Admin): *"what is required is ultimately an answer to the question whether the requested person has knowingly waived his right to a trial. Questions of manifest lack of diligence, for example, can be taken into account, but are evidential matters which go to answering that ultimate question."*[187]

---

183 Ibid at [45]

184 Ibid at [54]

185 Ibid at [54]

186 Ibid at [55]

187 *JK v Poland* [2018] EWHC 197 (Admin), [2018] 1 WLUK 259 at [49]; cited with approval in *Oprea v Constanta Tribunal* [2021] EWHC 223 (Admin), [2020] 7 WLUK 725 at [19].

The Supreme Court in *Bertino* did observe that *"behaviour of an extreme enough form might support a finding of unequivocal waiver even if an accused cannot be shown to have had actual knowledge that the trial would proceed in absence."*[188]

As to whether an individual case gives rise to a sufficient evidence of waiver remains dependent on the facts. Swift J observed as follows in the recent case of *Gisca v Italy* [2024] EWHC 1980 (Admin) at [22]: *"What is clear from Bertino is that the facts of each case matter. Whether it is possible to draw the inference that a person deliberately absented himself from the proceedings must be measured in specifics."*

It is not enough to be a fugitive in general terms.189The test for fugitivity and deliberate absence is not the same.190

Subsection (5): retrial rights:

If the appropriate Judge proceeds to ss.20(5) or 85(5) (as the case may be), the Requested Person must be "*entitled to a retrial or (on appeal) to a review amounting to a retrial*". Any such retrial must carry with it the procedural entitlements set out in subsection (8), which correspond to those in Article 6(3)(c) and (d) ECHR.

The equivalent right under Article 601(1)(i)(iv) is to "*a retrial, or an appeal ... which allows the merits of the case, including fresh evidence, to be re-examined, and which may lead to the original decision being reversed*". In *Cretu*, the court held that "*[t]he question whether an accused is entitled to a retrial or a review amounting to a retrial for the purposes of section 20(5), is to be determined by reference to [this paragraph]*".[191]

188 *Paiva v Portugal* [2024] EWHC 980 (Admin) at [22], citing *Bertino v Italy* at [58].

189 *Lord Advocate v Daja* [2021] SLT (Sh Ct) 139, [2021] 3 WLUK 128 at [39].

190 *Stafi v Romania* [2023] EWHC 429 (Admin), [2023] 2 WLUK 459 at [27].

191 *Cretu* at [34(iv)].

What is required is that the Requested Person has a right to a retrial, not merely a right to apply for a retrial.[192]

However, it is permissible for there to be procedural formalities (such as a requirement to file a request for a retrial, or time limits) with which they have to comply.[193] However, any such requirements must be possible to discharge in practice.[194]

The Supreme Court considered in *Merticariu v Romania* [2024] UKSC 10, [2024] 1 WLR 1506 whether there was an entitlement to a retrial where that retrial was contingent on the Requested Person's attendance (or deliberate absence) at their trial. The Court relevantly held at [51] - [52]:

> *"51. We consider that the natural and ordinary meaning of the words in section 20(5) are plain. The judge must decide whether the requested person is "entitled" to a retrial or (on appeal) to a review amounting to a retrial. Section 20(5) does not require the judge to decide a different question, namely whether the requested person is entitled to apply for a retrial. Furthermore, the answer to the question in section 20(5) cannot be "perhaps" or "in certain circumstances" the appellant is entitled to a retral or (on appeal) to a review*

192 *Bohm v Romanian Judicial Authority* [2011] EWHC 2671 (Admin), [2013] ACD 89 at [5]; *Kotsev v Bulgaria* [2018] EWHC 3087 (Admin), [2019] 1 WLR 2353 at [53].

193 *Nastase v Italy* [2012] EWHC 3671 (Admin), [2013] ACD 30 at [45] cited with approval in *Taranenco v Romania* [2020] EWHC 1198 Admin, [2020] 5 WLUK 153; see also *Lord Advocate v Daja* [2021] HCJAC 31, 2021 SLT 873..

194 Albeit obiter, see the dicta of Bean LJ at *Galusca v Italy* [2021] EWHC 3345 (Admin), [2022] 1WLR 1615 at [25]: "I would not so far as to endorse with what appears to have been the provisional view of Carr LJ at paragraph 83 of *Dumitrache* that any burden of proof imposed on the applicant for a retrial by the law of the requesting state is irrelevant. If that law were to place on the applicant a burden impossible to discharge in practice (such as, arguably, a requirement to prove lack of knowledge of the hearing beyond reasonable doubt), it would be difficult to say that the requested person is in reality "entitled to a retrial"."

amounting to a retrial: see Bohm v Romania [2011] EWHC 2671 (Admin), at para 5. Accordingly, an entitlement to a retrial cannot be continent on the court in the requesting state making a factual finding that the requested person was not present at or was not deliberately absent from their trial. Accordingly, we consider that the Divisional Court in B P v Romania [2015] EWHC 3417 (Admin), at para 44 , incorrectly construed section 20(5) of the 2003 Act and in Zeqaj v Albania [2013] EWHC 261 (Admin), at para 12 , incorrectly construed the equivalent provision in section 85(5) of the 2003 Act.

52. We agree that a requested person may have the right to a retrial even if the domestic law of the requesting state requires him to take "procedural steps" to invoke the right. But if the entitlement to a retrial is contingent on a finding that the requested person was not deliberately absent from his trial, the proceedings leading to that finding would not naturally be referred to as a "procedural step". Rather, those proceedings in the requesting state should be regarded as involving a decision on a substantive issue. We consider that the Divisional Court in BP v Romania , at para 44, incorrectly characterised as a procedural step an application for a retrial which was contingent on the court in the requesting state determining whether the requested person had or had not instructed a lawyer to represent her at her trial."

It is worth noting that, in principle, a Requested Person can be extradited where they have already chosen to exercise their right to a retrial once they have already arrived in the UK, have had an EAW issued against them, and know that they are facing the prospect of extradition. That would be so even if the outcome of that hearing were adverse to them such that their guaranteed entitlement to any further and future retrial were already extinguished at the point of any subsequent extradition.[195]

[195] *Konczos v Hungary* [2021] EWHC 3287 (Admin), [2021] 12 WLUK 81 at [13]

Burden and standard of proof:

It is also necessary to briefly consider the court's approach to the burden and standard of proof under ss.20 and 85. It is for the Requesting State to prove to the criminal standard that at least one of subsections (1), (3) or (5) are to be answered in the affirmative: s.206.

In Part 1 cases, under the EAW scheme, it was said that "*the burden of proof will be discharged to the requisite standard if the information required by article 4a is set out in the EAW*"[196] or further information.[197]

Consequently, if, taken together, the warrant and further information set out the required information, "*the court will not conduct its own examination into those matters, nor will it press the requesting authority for further information*".[198] The court would only "*conduct its own assessment*" of whether the relevant subsection was satisfied if the information given by the EAW and further information was incomplete, ambiguous or confused.[199]

<u>Section 21 - Person unlawfully at large: human rights</u>

Section 21 of the 2003 Act provides:

> *'(1) If the judge is required to proceed under this section (by virtue of [section 20]) he must decide whether the person's extradition would be compatible with the Convention rights within the meaning of the Human Rights Act 1998 (c. 42).*
>
> *(2) If the judge decides the question in subsection (1) in the negative he must order the person's discharge.*

---

196 *Cretu* at [34(v)].

197 *Ticu v Romania* [2018] EWHC 269 (Admin), [2018] ACD 44 at [17].

198 *Stryjecki* at [50], as approved in *Szatkowski v Poland* [2019] EWHC 883 (Admin), [2019] 1 WLR 4528 at [22].

199 *Stryjecki* at [50], as approved in *Szatkowski* at [22] The same test was recently reiterated in *Poland v Pultorak* [2023] EWHC 2777 (Admin), [2023] 11 WLUK 250 at [35] and *Merticariu* at [27].

> *(3) If the judge decides that question in the affirmative he must order the person to be extradited to the category 1 territory in which the warrant was issued.*
>
> *(4) If the judge makes an order under subsection (3) he must remand the person in custody or on bail to wait for his extradition to the category 1 territory.*
>
> *(5) If the person is remanded in custody, the appropriate judge may later grant bail.'*

Where a person is deemed to be unlawfully at large, any Convention rights that they seek to enforce will be argued under section 21. The most common challenges are considered in greater detail in the next chapter.

Section 21A, Person not convicted: human rights and proportionality

If none of the bars to extradition in section 11(1) apply, and the Requested Person is accused of the commission of the extradition offence, but is not alleged to be unlawfully at large after conviction of it, section 11(5) requires the judge to proceed under section 21A. This section directs the judge to consider the compatibility of extradition with human rights, and whether extradition would be disproportionate. This section was inserted into the Act by s.157(2) of the Anti-social Behaviour, Crime and Policing Act 2014, and provides for a free-standing proportionality test.

Section 21A provides:

> *'(1) If the judge is required to proceed under this section (by virtue of section 11), the judge must decide both of the following questions in respect of the extradition of the person ("D")—*
>
> > *(a) whether the extradition would be compatible with the Convention rights within the meaning of the Human Rights Act 1998;*
> >
> > *(b) whether the extradition would be disproportionate.*
>
> *(2) In deciding whether the extradition would be disproportionate, the judge must take into account the specified matters relating to*

proportionality (so far as the judge thinks it appropriate to do so); but the judge must not take any other matters into account.

(3) These are the specified matters relating to proportionality—

(a) the seriousness of the conduct alleged to constitute the extradition offence;

(b) the likely penalty that would be imposed if D was found guilty of the extradition offence;

(c) the possibility of the relevant foreign authorities taking measures that would be less coercive than the extradition of D.

(4) The judge must order D's discharge if the judge makes one or both of these decisions—

(a) that the extradition would not be compatible with the Convention rights;

(b) that the extradition would be disproportionate.

(5) The judge must order D to be extradited to the category 1 territory in which the warrant was issued if the judge makes both of these decisions—

(a) that the extradition would be compatible with the Convention rights;

(b) that the extradition would not be disproportionate.

(6) If the judge makes an order under subsection (5) he must remand the person in custody or on bail to wait for extradition to the category 1 territory.

(7) If the person is remanded in custody, the appropriate judge may later grant bail.

(8) In this section "relevant foreign authorities" means the authorities in the territory to which D would be extradited if the extradition went ahead.'

This freestanding "proportionality" bar is only available to Part 1 territories and is only applicable to accusation warrants. The "proportionality safeguard" in respect of conviction warrants is the requirement under section 65(3) that the Requested Person must have been sentenced to a term of imprisonment of 4 months or more.[200]

The leading case in respect of s.21A is *Miraszewski v District Court in Torun, Poland* [2014] EWHC 4261 (Admin), [2015] 1 WLR 3929:

> "*The court may, depending on its evaluation of factors, conclude that extradition would be disproportionate if (i) the conduct is not serious and/or (ii) a custodial penalty is unlikely and/or (iii) less coercive measures to ensure attendance are reasonably available to the requesting state in the circumstances*". [31]

The "*scope for judgment is comparatively broad*" against a "*background of mutual respect between the UK court and the issuing authority*". The statutorily specified matters are not listed in order of importance and the seriousness of the offences is not a trump card[201]. Reasons must be given by a judge, either for the weight given to a factor or for the judicial exercise of discretion not to take into account one or more of the specified factors.[202]

There can be no other free-standing factors in the proportionality judgment besides those three specified in s. 21A. If delay is of relevance, it is only to the extent that it informs the factors contained at a) to c).[203]

The seriousness of the conduct

Judged in the first instance against domestic standards, "*the main components of the seriousness of conduct are the nature and quality of the acts*

200 *Saptelei v Romania* [2021] EWHC 506 (Admin) at [34-36]

201 *Osso v Germany* [2023] EWHC 1728 (Admin) at [112]

202 *Miraszewski* at [31-33].

203 *Miraszewski*, at [34]

alleged, the requested person's culpability for those acts and the harm caused to the victim".[204]

Criminal Practice Directions 2023, paragraph 12.2.1 provides that when considering "*the seriousness of the conduct alleged to constitute the extradition offence, the judge will determine the issue on the facts of each case as set out in the warrant, subject to paragraph 12.2.2 below*". If the offence falls within the table at paragraph 12.2.4 (minor theft, minor financial offences, minor road traffic, driving and related offences, and minor public order offences – subject to considerations set out in the table), then the court should generally determine that extradition would be disproportionate.

However, if any "exceptional circumstances" apply, that conclusion will not follow.[205] The exceptional circumstances are listed at paragraph 12.2.23: a vulnerable victim; crime committed against someone because of their disability, gender-identity, race, religion or belief, or sexual orientation; significant premeditation; multiple counts; extradition also sought for another offence; and previous offending history.

The table identifies a floor not a ceiling: a judge may consider other offences outside those categories to not be serious offences.[206]

The burden rests with the Judicial Authority, "*where an issue under s.21A is raised, to show that the offence is not excluded by virtue of s.21A.*"[207]

The likely penalty

The principal focus is whether it would be proportionate to order the extradition of a person who is not likely to receive a custodial sentence, giving appropriate respect to the Requesting State's sentencing regime

---

204 Miraszewski at [36].

205 The existence of an 'exceptional circumstance' does not preclude the District Judge from finding that extradition would be disproportionate (*Miraszewski*, at [28]);

206 *Miraszewski* at [27–28].

207 Rinkevicius v Prosecutor General's Office, Lithuania [2018] EWHC 145 (Admin), [2018] ACD 22, at [11].

which may impose more severe penalties than that of the UK (though in an "*extremely rare case when a particular penalty would be offensive to a domestic court in the circumstances of particular criminal conduct*" the judge may give this factor less weight in the overall judgment of proportionality).[208]

The statutory question is the 'likely penalty that would be imposed' – not whether a custodial sentence is a 'realistic possibility'.[209]

The assessment is based on the information provided by the Judicial Authority, though in the absence of information about the likely penalty in the Requesting State, courts may draw inferences from the contents of the warrant and also apply domestic sentencing practice as a measure of likelihood.[210] However, judges are not required to embark on a detailed analysis of domestic sentencing guidelines.[211]

A suspended custodial sentence is to be regarded as falling on the 'non-custodial' side of the line, for the purposes of applying the guidance in *Miraszewski*.[212] If the Requesting State would have to deduct time spent on remand during the extradition proceedings from a custodial penalty, then that deduction is taken into account for the purposes of s. 21A.[213]

A finding that a non-custodial penalty is likely does not automatically lead to the conclusion that extradition would be disproportionate: sufficiently or particularly weighty considerations that fall within the other two statutorily prescribed matters may mean extradition is still proportionate.[214] Illustrative examples given in *Miraszewski* at [39] are a

---

208 Miraszewski at [37].

209 *Antochi v Germany* [2020] EWHC 3092 (Admin), [2021] ACD 15 at [19].

210 *Miraszewski* at [38], and *Antochi* at [18].

211 *Swiatek v Poland* [2024] EWHC 726 (Admin) at [24]

212 *Antochi* at [21], applied by Murray J in *Slovak Republic v Macko* [2024] EWHC 2564 (Admin) at [45].

213 *H v Hungary* [2018] EWHC 2667 (Admin) at [43].

214 *Antochi* at [24].

serious offence against the environment, and a fugitive with a history of disobeying court orders.

The possibility of the relevant foreign authorities taking measures that would be less coercive

It is possible that s.21A(3)(c) was intended "*to cover cases where the supposed "accused" was no more than wanted for questioning as a mere suspect*".[215] It is "*a reasonable assumption in most cases that the requesting state has, pursuant to its obligation under article 5.3 of the ECHR, already considered the taking of less coercive measures*", and the evidential burden is on the Requested Person to show otherwise.[216] Less coercive measures than extradition to achieve the Requested Person's attendance at court include appearance by videolink or telephone. If the Requested Person left the Requesting State in breach of their obligations, it is unlikely that a less coercive measure than extradition will be appropriate.

Although *Miraszewski* refers to mutual legal assistance at [40], as does *Kandola v Germany* [2015] EWHC 619 (Admin), [2015] 1 WLR 5097; the later case of *Puceviciene v Lithuania* [2016] EWHC 1862 (Admin), [2016] 1 WLR 4937 at [76-81] considered the correct interpretation of *Miraszewski* and found that *Kandola* was wrongly decided. In *Sutas v Lithuania* [2017] EWHC 156 (Admin) at [30-31] the court found that an interview via mutual legal assistance was not a less coercive measure.

If the Requested Person can only evidence that the possibility of a less coercive measure was discussed, not that it had materialised, this will not assist them because "*this issue of proportionality must not be judged against simply some bare possibility of something happening, but the extent of that possibility*".[217]

The approach of the parties to any s. 21B request will be relevant to whether there is a possibility of less coercive measures, though where a Requesting State refuses a s.21B invitation for incoherent reasons that

---

215 Puceviciene at [81]

216 Miraszewski at [41].

217 *Matusiak v Poland* [2017] EWHC 3026 (Admin) at [26-29].

will carry less weight.[218] Where less coercive measures are raised and are reasonably applicable, the Requesting State should consider them and, if they are rejected, give some explanation, however brief, for rejecting them.[219] If the Requested Person offers to cooperate with the prosecution by returning on a voluntary basis, but the Requesting State refuses the offer without giving any reasons, the court can conclude that the prosecution is able to proceed without the need for extradition which significantly erodes the public interest in extradition.[220]

As with each of the three statutory factors, a failure by the Requesting State to adopt less coercive measures is not necessarily decisive of the overall judgment on proportionality.[221]

Whilst s.21A had no basis in the 2002 Framework Decision, it has been incorporated into the TCA. Article 597 provides:

> *'Cooperation through the arrest warrant shall be necessary and proportionate, taking into account the rights of the requested person and the interests of the victims, and having regard to the seriousness of the act, the likely penalty that would be imposed and the possibility of a State taking measures less coercive than the surrender of the requested person particularly with a view to avoiding unnecessarily long periods of pre-trial detention.'*

This Article must be read in conjunction with the Joint Political Declaration on Title VII [Surrender] of Part Three [Law enforcement and Judicial cooperation in criminal matters], which provides:

> *"Article LAW.SURR.77*[222] *[Principle of proportionality] of Title VII [Surrender][of Part Three [Law enforcement and judicial cooperation in criminal matters] provides that cooperation on surrender must be necessary and proportionate, taking into account the rights of the*

218 *Antochi* at [28-30].

219 *Komar v Poland* [2015] EWHC 2547 (Admin) at [31]

220 *Milewska v Poland* [2024] EWHC 2760 (Admin) at [46]

221 *Powney v Slovenia* [2015] EWHC 2543 (Admin) at [40].

222 This has since been re-numbered to Article 597.

requested person and the interests of the victims, and having regard to the seriousness of the act, the likely penalty that would be imposed and the possibility of a State taking measures less coercive than the surrender of the requested person, particularly with a view to avoiding unnecessarily long periods of pre-trial detention.

The principle of proportionality is relevant throughout the process leading to the surrender decision set out in Title VII [Surrender]. Where the executing judicial authority has concerns about the principle of proportionality, it shall request the necessary supplementary information to enable the issuing judicial authority to set out its views on the application of the principle of proportionality.

Both Parties note that Articles LAW.SURR 77[223] *[Principle of proportionality] and 93 [Surrender decision] enable the competent judicial authorities of the States to consider proportionality and the possible duration of pre-trial detention when implementing Title VII [Surrender], and note that this is consistent with their respective domestic laws."*

It is envisaged that the higher courts will need to re-visit section 21A in light of the TCA in order to determine how District Judges should address the issue of lengthy pre-trial detention and a failure to provide supplementary information.

Whilst there has been some suggestion that concern with proportionality has been enhanced following Brexit[224], Swift J in *Vascenkovs v Latvia* [2023] EWHC 2830 (Admin) confirmed that *Miraszewski* remains good law in relation to the proper interpretation of the section 21A(1)(b) proportionality test.[225] Swift J concluded that the TCA does not require a new approach to be taken to section 21A(1)(b) proportionality and

223 This has since been re-numbered to Article 597.

224 *Dujka v Czech Republic* [2023] EWHC 1842 (Admin) at [22]

225 *Vascenkovs* at [16-20], applied by Murray J in *Slovak Republic v Macko* [2024] EWHC 2564 (Admin) at [22]

"*there is nothing in [the Joint Political Declaration] that is inconsistent with any of the points set out by Pitchford LJ in his judgment in Miraszewski*".[226]

Section 21B requests

This section applies only to accusation warrants under Part 1 of the 2003 Act. This section provides a process by which a Judicial Authority or a Requested Person may make a request for temporary transfer of the person to the Requesting State, or that arrangements be made to enable the Requested Person to speak to the authorities of the Requesting State.

Section 21B provides:

> '*(1) This section applies if—*
>
> > *(a) a Part 1 warrant is issued which contains the statement referred to in section 2(3) (warrant issued for purposes of prosecution for offence in category 1 territory), and*
> >
> > *(b) at any time before or in the extradition hearing, the appropriate judge is informed that a request under subsection (2) or (3) has been made.*
>
> *(2) A request under this subsection is a request by a judicial authority of the category 1 territory in which the warrant is issued ("the requesting territory")—*
>
> > *(a) that the person in respect of whom the warrant is issued be temporarily transferred to the requesting territory, or*
> >
> > *(b) that arrangements be made to enable the person to speak with representatives of an authority in the requesting territory responsible for investigating, prosecuting or trying the offence specified in the warrant.*
>
> *(3) A request under this subsection is a request by the person in respect of whom the warrant is issued—*

226 *Vascenkovs* at [20]

(a) to be temporarily transferred to the requesting territory, or

(b) that arrangements be made to enable the person to speak with representatives of an authority in the requesting territory responsible for investigating, prosecuting or trying the offence specified in the warrant.

(4) The judge must order further proceedings in respect of the extradition to be adjourned if the judge thinks it necessary to do so to enable the person (in the case of a request under subsection (2)) or the authority by which the warrant is issued (in the case of a request under subsection (3)) to consider whether to consent to the request. An adjournment under this subsection must not be for more than 7 days.

(5) If the person or authority consents to the request, the judge must—

(a) make whatever orders and directions seem appropriate for giving effect to the request;

(b) order further proceedings in respect of the extradition to be adjourned for however long seems necessary to enable the orders and directions to be carried out.

(6) If the request, or consent to the request, is withdrawn before effect (or full effect) has been given to it—

(a) no steps (or further steps) may be taken to give effect to the request;

(b) the judge may make whatever further orders and directions seem appropriate (including an order superseding one made under subsection (5)(b)).

(7) A person may not make a request under paragraph (a) or (b) of subsection (3) in respect of a warrant if the person has already given consent to a request under the corresponding paragraph of subsection (2) in respect of that warrant (even if that consent has been withdrawn).

(8) A person may not make a further request under paragraph (a) or (b) of subsection (3) in respect of a warrant if the person has already

made a request under that paragraph in respect of that warrant (even if that request has been withdrawn).

(9) If—

(a) a request under subsection (2) or (3) is made before a date has been fixed on which the extradition hearing is to begin, and

(b) the proceedings are adjourned under this section, the permitted period for the purposes of fixing that date (see section 8(4)) is extended by the number of days for which the proceedings are so adjourned.'

The process to be followed

The process set out in s. 21B is strict. When an application is made, the judge must consider whether it is necessary to adjourn the extradition proceedings for up to 7 days to enable the other party to decide whether to consent to the request. If consent is given the court will continue the adjournment of proceedings in respect of the extradition and will make directions to give effect to the request.

The request may be made at any time, including at the final extradition hearing. It must be clearly expressed and particularised and, though the statute does not require it to be made in writing, in practice this will be the case. A request will need to set out the nature of the request, the reasoning behind it, and in particular if made late in the extradition proceedings, should be accompanied by reasons for the time taken to make the request.[227]

The court may at the case management stage of proceedings require any request to be made by a certain date.[228]

The judge has a discretion under s. 21B(4) and may refuse to adjourn – the discretion must be exercised judicially and the judge has a duty to give reasons. Whether it is 'necessary' to order an adjournment is affected

[227] *Duncan v Spain* [2015] EWHC 3466 (Admin), [2016] 1 WLR 1351 at [27-29, 30].

[228] *Duncan* at [28].

by the timing and appropriateness of the request. The court may take into account the parties' obligation under the Criminal Procedure Rules 2020 r.1.2(1)(a).[229]

If, before the request has been given full effect, the consenting party withdraws their consent then no further steps may be taken to give effect to the request and the court will give directions accordingly. There are no requirements for there to be any particular reasons for the withdrawal of consent. In *Duncan v Spain* [2015] EWHC 3446 (Admin) the High Court held that failure to adjourn for a s.21B request did not give rise to a basis to order discharge'.

Section 21B is "*the route to the use of MLA to advance the criminal process through interview before extradition so as to reduce pre-trial delay after extradition, or perhaps as a means of changing the mind of the requesting judicial authority on the decision which has already been made to charge and try*".[230] It is important to note that section 21B does not require the UK to co-operate with providing mutual legal assistance, and a failure to do so would require challenge in separate legal proceedings.

Physical or Mental condition

Section 25 of the 2003 Act provides:

> '*(1) This section applies if at any time in the extradition hearing it appears to the judge that the condition in subsection (2) is satisfied.*
>
> *(2) The condition is that the physical or mental condition of the person in respect of whom the Part 1 warrant is issued is such that it would be unjust or oppressive to extradite him.*
>
> *(3) The judge must—*
>
> > *(a) order the person's discharge, or*

229 *Duncan* at [26, 29].

230 *Puceviciene* at [81], and *Sutas v Republic of Lithuania* [2017] EWHC 156 (Admin) at [32].

> *(b) adjourn the extradition hearing until it appears to him that the condition in subsection (2) is no longer satisfied.'*

Section 91, drafted in materially identical terms. confers the same protection under Part 2 of the Act.

The provision was introduced under the 2003 Act to give the court (as opposed to the Home Secretary) the power to either adjourn proceedings or discharge the Requested Person where extradition would be *'unjust or oppressive'*. Whilst the test bears resemblance to Article 23(4) of the 2002 Framework Decision and Article 621 of the TCA, by using the terms ('unjust' or 'oppressive') it is clear that Parliament intended to impose its own test. Whilst the test imposes a high threshold,[231] it is less demanding than that imposed under Article 3 ECHR.[232] Were it otherwise, its inclusion in the 2003 Act would have been otiose.[233] Furthermore, whilst the 2002 Framework Decision and the TCA only permit the court to postpone the surrender "*for serious humanitarian reasons*", section 91 permits the District Judge to discharge the Requested Person, recognising that some conditions or illnesses may never improve.[234]

---

231 Al-Awa v Czech Republic [2021] EWHC 1297 (Admin) at [56]: "It is noteworthy that, despite what was said in Dewani, the Divisional Court in both Turner and, most recently, Love had no problem in stating that oppression "requires a high threshold, not readily surmounted". It seems, therefore, that there can be no objection to a court expressly recognising the nature of the threshold, so long as the court remains focused on all the relevant facts of the case before it."

232 However, the extent of the difference between the two tests has yet to be examined since the Supreme Court's decision in the immigration case of *AM (Zimbabwe) v Secretary of State for the Home Department* [2020] UKSC 17, [2020] 2 WLR 1152

233 *Pesut v Republic of Croatia* [2015] EWHC 46 (Admin), at [38].

234 Although it remains open to the Requesting State to make a further request for extradition, should the Requested Person's circumstances, or those in the Requesting State, improve in the future per *Auzins v Prosecutor General's Office of the Republic of Latvia* [2016] EWHC 802 (Admin), [2016] 4 WLR 75 and *Kieronski v Regional Court in Tarnow, Poland* [2014] EWHC 2666 (Admin), [2015] ACD 32.

The terms 'unjust' and 'oppressive' were explained by Lord Diplock in *Kakis v Government of the Republic of Cyprus* [1978] 1 WLR 799, at pages 782-783

> *"Unjust" I regard as directed primarily to the risk of prejudice to the accused in the conduct of the trial itself, "oppressive" as directed to hardship to the accused resulting from changes in his circumstances that have occurred during the period to be taken into consideration; but there is room for overlapping, and between them they would cover all cases where to return him would not be fair. Delay in the commencement or conduct of extradition proceedings which is brought about by the accused himself by fleeing the country, concealing his whereabouts or evading arrest cannot, in my view, be relied upon as a ground for holding it to be either unjust or oppressive to return him. Any difficulties that he may encounter in the conduct of his defence in consequence of the delay due to such causes are of his own choice and making. Save in the most exceptional circumstances it would be neither unjust nor oppressive that he should be required to accept them."*

Whilst the case of *Kakis* dealt with the 'passage of time' bar, Lord Diplock's exposition is equally applicable to sections 25/91 of the Act[235].

The cases that engage sections 25/91 tend to fall into three, often overlapping, categories. Firstly, "suicide" cases, where there is a real risk that extradition will result in the Requested Person attempting to take their own life. Secondly, fitness to stand trial, where, as a result of their condition, it is argued that the Requested Person would lack the capacity to take part in any trial in the Requesting State. Thirdly, physical health conditions, where it is argued that treatment is either unavailable, inadequate or regardless of the treatment available, their condition will deteriorate.

Suicide cases

With regards to the first category, "suicide" cases, the applicable principles can be found in *Turner v Government of the United States of*

---

[235] *Government of South Africa v Dewani* [2012] EWHC 842 (Admin), [2013] 1 WLR 82, at [74].

America[236] and *Polish Judicial Authority v Wolkowicz*[237]. It will rarely be necessary to look outside those two authorities. The factors that the court will consider were summarised in *Turner*:

> *"28. There have been a number of cases in which the courts have considered what has to be established under section 91 of the Act (or the equivalent section in respect of an application for surrender under Part 1 of the Act, which is section 25) in order that a court may be satisfied that it would be unjust or oppressive to return a person to the state requesting extradition, because of the risk of suicide if the order to return were made. The relevant cases, which were recently examined with care by Bean J in Marius Wrobel v Poland [2011] EWHC 374 at [17] establish the following propositions: (1) the court has to form an overall judgment on the facts of the particular case: United States v Tollman [2008] 3 All ER 150 at [50] per Moses LJ. (2) A high threshold has to be reached in order to satisfy the court that a requested person's physical or mental condition is such that it would be unjust or oppressive to extradite him: Howes v HM's Advocate [2009] SCL 341 and the cases there cited by Lord Reed in a judgment of the Inner House. (3) The court must assess the mental condition of the person threatened with extradition and determine if it is linked to a risk of a suicide attempt if the extradition order were to be made. There has to be a "substantial risk that [the appellant] will commit suicide". The question is whether, on the evidence the risk of the appellant succeeding in committing suicide, whatever steps are taken is sufficiently great to result in a finding of oppression: see Jansons v Latvia [2009] EWHC 1845 at [24] and [29]. (4) The mental condition of the person must be such that it removes his capacity to resist the impulse to commit suicide, otherwise it will not be his mental condition but his own voluntary act which puts him at risk of dying and if that is the case there is no oppression in ordering extradition: Rot v District Court of Lubin, Poland [2010] EWHC 1820 at [13] per Mitting J. (5) On the evidence, is the risk that the person will succeed in committing*

236 Turner v Government of the United States of America [2012] EWHC 2426 (Admin).

237 Polish Judicial Authority v Wolkowicz [2013] EWHC 102.

> *suicide, whatever steps are taken, sufficiently great to result in a finding of oppression: ibid . (6) Are there appropriate arrangements in place in the prison system of the country to which extradition is sought so that those authorities can cope properly with the person's mental condition and the risk of suicide: ibid at [26]. (7) There is a public interest in giving effect to treaty obligations and this is an important factor to have in mind: Norris v Government of the USA (No 2) [2010] 2 AC 487 ."* (emphasis added)

The key issue in almost every case will be the measures in place to prevent an attempt at suicide by a Requested Person with a mental illness.[238] In *Modi v Government of India*[239], the Divisional Court gave further guidance on the *Turner* propositions:

> *[116] There will be cases where the requested person's medical condition is not severe enough, and the risk of suicide not high enough, to engage section 91 at all. In our view, the clause "whatever steps are taken" in propositions (3) and (5) are really addressing opposite sides of the coin. If the risk is too low, the meaning and effect of proposition (3) is that it is unnecessary to consider the adequacy of the preventative arrangements referred to under proposition (6) because the requested person's case has already failed. In this context, therefore, "whatever steps are taken" in proposition (3) may be understood to mean, "ignoring any steps taken". The primary submission of Ms Malcolm was, on our understanding, that the present case falls into this category. On the other hand, proposition (5) recognises that there may also be cases where the risk of suicide is so great that, whatever steps may be taken, they will not reduce the risk to an acceptable level. Examples of cases falling into this category are Jansons and, subject to the qualification we make below, Fletcher v Government of India [2021] EWHC 610 (Admin).*
>
> *[117] Between these two poles there will be cases where the risk of suicide may be moderate or even high – too high to be discounted,*

---

238 Polish Judicial Authority v Wolkowicz [2013] EWHC 102 at [10].

239 *Modi v Government of India* [2022] EWHC 2829 (Admin) at [116]-[117].

> *but not so high that nothing can be done to address it that will render the risk acceptable. By risk of suicide we mean the risk that, in the absence of preventative measures, an attempt at suicide will be made and succeed. In such circumstances, the proposition (5) issue (level of risk) must be considered in conjunction with proposition (6) (steps taken to ameliorate the risk and reduce it to an acceptable level). In practice, most cases will fall into this category, which explains the emphasis in Wolkowicz on proposition (6). This reflects the practical realities including the fact that even in relatively weak cases it will be appropriate, out of an abundance of caution, to have regard to the system in the relevant prison.*

The concept of oppression entails a value judgment[240]: the focus is not solely on the nature and severity of the Requested Person's condition and the risk of suicide but also the public interest in extraditing those who may have committed serious offences. The reduction of the risk to an acceptable level does not impose an absolute standard on Requesting States.[241]

The Divisional Court in *Modi* also considered some of the difficulties with the terms 'impulse' and 'capacity' as used in *Turner*, as these can have technical meanings in law or when used by clinicians:[242]

> *[128] In our judgment, to the extent that Turner proposition (4) adds anything to propositions (3) and (5), its function is to indicate that in situations where the decision to commit suicide is voluntary, in the sense of being rational and thought-through, a finding of oppression should not be made. We heed Ms Malcolm's warning that it would be unwise to gloss Turner proposition (4) with some additional or alternative form of words which imports a specific causation test: the verb "linked" already appears in proposition (3). In particular, we would deprecate any attempt to introduce concepts of causation as are routinely applied in tort or contract: the fact that (in conventional causation terms) a person's depression would be*

240 *Modi v Government of India* [2022] EWHC 2829 (Admin) at [120].

241 *Modi v Government of India* [2022] EWHC 2829 (Admin) at [120].

242 *Modi v Government of India* [2022] EWHC 2829 (Admin) at [125-129].

> *either a cause or even the dominant cause of a person's decision to commit suicide does not mean or necessarily suggest that the act was not voluntary within the meaning of Turner proposition (4).*
>
> *[129] It is always to be remembered that the Turner propositions form part of a judgment that attempted to set out general principles. It is not to be treated in the same way as if it were embodied in a statute. In our judgment, Turner proposition (4) should be read in a common-sense, broad-brush way giving full effect to the question whether the act of suicide would be the person's voluntary act. This approach does not demand proof of "impulse" as that term is used by clinicians. "Compulsion", "wish", "desire" or "intentions", as terms familiar to lay persons, are suitable synonyms; but none should be given particular precedence after being press-ganged into service. In Assange, the evidence was that the requested person had a "single-minded determination" to commit suicide. Consistently with this approach, "capacity" in proposition (4) is synonymous with "ability" or "capability". It does not import the provisions or workings of the Mental Capacity Act 2005.*

The Court will analyse this risk in three stages: i) the risk to the Requested Person whilst they are in the United Kingdom; ii) whilst they are being transported to the Requesting State; and iii) at the custodial institution in which they are likely to be held.

In relation to ii), a Divisional Court in *Bobbe v Regional Court in Bydgoszcz, Poland* [2017] EWHC 3161 (Admin), [2018] ACD 11, applied CJEU jurisprudence regarding transfers under the Dublin III Regulation to extradition law[243]. Accordingly, extradition may be "unjust or oppressive" where the transfer of a Requested Person "*with a particularly serious mental or physical illness would result in a real and proven risk of a significant and permanent deterioration in his state of health, that transfer would constitute inhuman and degrading treatment*"[244] The initial burden rests with the Requested Person to demonstrate "... *the particular seriousness of his mental health and the significant and irreversible*

243 *CK v Slovenia* (C-578/16 PPU) [2017] 3 CMLR 10

244 *CK*, at [74].

consequences to which his transfer might lead". If that burden is satisfied, it is for the authorities to assess the risk and "*eliminate any serious doubts concerning the impact of the transfer*".[245]

With regard to iii), where the Requesting State is a Member of the European Union[246], it will be presumed that they will discharge their responsibilities to prevent the Requested Person from committing suicide. Accordingly, "*In the absence of evidence to the necessary standard that calls into question the ability of the receiving state to discharge its responsibilities or a special matter that gives cause for concern, it should not be necessary to require any assurances from requesting states within the European Union. It will therefore ordinarily be sufficient to rely on the presumption....*"[247] However, the measures used to prevent suicide in the Requesting State i.e. lengthy periods of being subjected to segregation and constant monitoring, may of themselves satisfy the test of 'oppression'.[248]

Appeals in "suicide" cases should be heard expeditiously. In *Wolkowicz*, Lord Thomas envisaged that they be listed within 2-3 weeks of the Appellant's notice having been filed. The court's hope was that it should not be necessary to obtain fresh reports pending the appeal. However, where a lengthy period of time has elapsed, and new reports are available, it could be considered an "*exercise in artificiality*" if the court refused to consider the most up to date evidence.[249]

Fitness to stand trial

The issue of whether a Requested Person is fit to stand trial is ordinarily one for the courts in the Requesting State. The only circumstance in which a court would be likely to determine that it would be 'unjust' or

---

245 *Bobbe*, at [62].

246 And, arguably the Council of Europe.

247 *Wolkowicz v Regional Court at Bialystok, Poland* [2013] EWHC 102 (Admin), [2013] 1 WLR 2402, at [10].

248 Love v Government of the United States of America (Liberty intervening) [2018] EWHC 172 (Admin), [2018] 1 WLR 2889, at [115].

249 *Bobbe*, at [28].

'oppressive' to order a Requested Person's extradition would be where it was clear that the courts in the Requesting State would reach this conclusion.[250] However, in *R. (Warren) v Secretary of State for the Home Department* [2003] EWHC 1177 (Admin), Lady Justice Hale held that, even in cases where a finding of unfitness was inevitable, there may be countervailing considerations e.g. to ascertain whether the Requested Person had done the act. Although, should this situation arise, it is likely to be challenged on the basis that the Requested Person is being sought for the purposes of civil detention.[251]

Where an individual is currently unfit to plead, the Court may seek assurances to the effect that, should they not regain capacity within a reasonable period of time, the Requested Person be free to return to the United Kingdom[252]. However, whether there is a need for such assurances is fact sensitive, there being no absolute obligation to do so where a Requested Person was currently unfit.[253]

Physical health

The threshold under sections 25/91 is a high one and the exercise is inherently fact-specific. The court will take into account all relevant circumstances, including the seriousness of the offence.[254] Consequently, the courts deprecate the citing of numerous authorities which do little more than apply the well-established principles to the facts of those cases[255].

There is a rebuttable presumption that Member States will be able to provide adequate medical treatment to prisoners. Whilst, not seeking to

250 *Republic of South Africa v Dewani (No 2)* [2014] EWHC 153 (Admin), [2014] 1 WLR 3220, at [51].

251 *Bobbe*, at [47].

252 Dewani (No 2), at [60].

253 *Bobbe*, at [37].

254 *Pesut*, at [40].

255 Dewani (No 1), at [73].

lay down a general rule, in *Magiera v District Court of Krakow, Poland* [2017] EWHC 2757 (Admin), Mr Justice Julian Knowles held, at [34]:

> *"However, in other cases, where the treatment or management of the illness or condition is more complex, more detail may be required before the court considering matters under Part 1 of the EA 2003 can be satisfied that concerns arising from the defendant's medical condition have been met such that there are no bars to extradition".*

The treatment in the Requesting State need not be of equivalent quality to that available in the United Kingdom. Instead, it must be shown that it is seriously inadequate, by reference to accepted medical standards. In all cases the court is required to undertake an intensely fact specific approach, which may require information from the Requesting State dealing with the specific concerns and needs of the individual, as a general discussion of the available facilities may not be fact specific enough: *Giana v Court of Roman, Romania*[256] where McGowan J held:

> *39. When s.25 is raised as a potential bar to extradition the court must establish what precisely the individual requires to achieve a basic standard of health and wellbeing. Only then can the provision offered be assessed to see if it adequately meets the need. ... As is clear from Magiera the requesting state should not be expected to provide a detailed care plan or similar but information about the special measures available must be part of the Judge's assessment.*

Accordingly, the court should assess what the effect of extradition would be on the Requested Person and his or her medical condition and the extent to which any adverse effects or hardship can be met by the Requesting State providing medical care or other arrangements.[257] The Requesting State does not necessarily have to show that the adverse effects or hardship would be eliminated, but the more complex or challenging the medical condition, the more detailed the information that may need

256 *Giana v Court of Roman, Romania* [2024] EWHC 1613 (Admin) [38]-[39].

257 *Al-Awa v Czech Republic* [2021] EWHC 1297 (Admin) at [51], citing *Magiera v District Court of Krakow, Poland* [2017] EWHC 2757 (Admin) at [32].

to be to show how it proposes to deal with the person concerned during their imprisonment.[258]

In some cases, judicial authorities have proposed that the Requested Person will have the assistance of a 'supporting convict'.[259] However, the reliance on often unqualified fellow prisoners or other such measures may not be sufficient to demonstrate that the Requesting State has adequate measures in place to accommodate a Requested Person's condition.[260]

Abuse of Process

Despite not being enshrined in statute, the availability of the abuse of process jurisdiction in extradition proceedings in England and Wales[261] is now beyond dispute.[262] Whilst Magistrates were previously precluded from considering such a challenge (it being a matter for the Secretary of State or, to a limited extent, the High Court), this approach did not survive the introduction of the Human Rights Act 1998.[263]

The abuse of process jurisdiction is residual in nature. It applies only when the issues raised cannot be addressed by the statutory

258 *Al-Awa* at [51] citing *Magiera* at [32]

259 See for example, *Giana v Court of Roman, Romania* [2024] EWHC 1613 (Admin) [30]-[41], which refers to leading cases on the subject from the European Court of Human Rights: *Rooman v Belgium*, 18052/11/31, January 2019; *Potoroc v Romania,* 37772/17, September 2020; and *Epure v Romania*, 73731/17, May 2021.

260 *Giana v Court of Roman, Romania* [2024] EWHC 1613 (Admin) at [34]-[43].

261 According to *Mirza v Lord Advocate* [2015] SLT (Sh Ct) 89, the protection does not extend to Scotland.

262 R (Bermingham & Ors) v Director of the Serious Fraud Office [2006] EWHC 200 (Admin), [2007] QB 727, at [97].

263 R (Kashamu) v Governor of Brixton Prison [2001] EWHC Admin 980, [2002] QB 887

protections.[264] Consequently, whilst certain challenges e.g. delay[265], could constitute an abuse of process, one would expect the argument to be pursued under sections 14/82 of the Act. With regard to the order in which a District Judge should consider challenges to extradition, any abuse of process argument should be dealt with last.[266]

In setting out the scope of the protection, Aikens LJ held in *Belbin v The Regional Court in Lille, France* [2015] EWHC 149 (Admin), [2015] ACD 58, at [59]:

> *"We wish to emphasise that the circumstances in which the court will consider exercising its implied "abuse of process" jurisdiction in extradition cases are very limited. It will not do so if, first, other bars to extradition are available, because it is a residual, implied jurisdiction. Secondly, the court will only exercise the jurisdiction if it is satisfied, on cogent evidence, that the Judicial Authority concerned has acted in such a way as to "usurp" the statutory regime of the EA or its integrity has been impugned. We say "cogent evidence" because, in the context of the European Arrest Warrant, the UK courts will start from the premise, as set out in the Framework Decision of 2002, that there must be mutual trust between Judicial Authorities, although we accept that when the emanation of the Judicial Authority concerned is a prosecuting authority, the UK court is entitled to examine its actions with "rigorous scrutiny". Thirdly, the court has to be satisfied that the abuse of process will cause prejudice to the requested person, either in the extradition process in this country or in the requesting state if he is surrendered."*

In *Malarz v Regional Court of Opole, Poland* [2018] EWHC 28 (Admin), at [54], Lord Justice Simon summarised it as follows:

---

264 Mehtab Khan v Government of the United States of America [2010] EWHC 1127 (Admin), at [11]

265 *Fuller v The Attorney General of Belize* [2011] UKPC 23, 32 BHRC 394, at [76].

266 *Belbin* at [59]

"54. It is important to keep in mind what the concept of abuse of process involves in the context of extradition. In its most obvious form it involves the use of an established process for illegitimate ends; or, to use the words of Lord Sumption in Zakrzewski v Regional Court in Lodz, Poland [2013] 1 WLR 324 at [11], where the foreign authority 'has manipulated the process of the executing court for a collateral and improper purpose.' Mistakes made in extradition proceedings may invalidate them but mistakes as such are not abuses of the process, not even egregious mistakes, unless the abuse undermines the very nature of the extradition jurisdiction. The court will only exercise the jurisdiction to stay the extradition proceedings as abuse of process if satisfied on (a) cogent evidence that (b) the requesting authority has acted in a way that subverts or impugns (the word 'usurped' is sometimes used) the integrity of the domestic process, acting in breach of the mutual trust that exists between Judicial Authorities. The need for cogent evidence in the context of European Arrest Warrants is that the domestic courts start from the premise that there must be mutual trust between Judicial Authorities, see Belbin v France [2015] EWHC 149 (Admin) Aikens LJ at [59]. This will be particularly so, where a foreign court is seeking to invoke the assistance of the executing court in extraditing someone to serve a sentence that has been evaded. So far as the application of Henderson v Henderson is concerned, I agree with the observations of Ouseley J in Camaras (see above) at [27] that it does not apply as such to extradition case, although the principles may feed into an abuse argument."

It has been stressed that the court has an implied jurisdiction to consider whether there has been an abuse of process committed by a *"requesting judicial authority"*[267] or the *"requesting authorities"*[268] It does not, however, extend to considering misconduct or bad faith by the Police[269]

[267] *Belbin*, at [43].

[268] Symeou v Public Prosecutor's Office at the Court of Appeals, Patras, Greece [2009] EWHC 897 (Admin), [2009] 1 WLR 2384, at [33].

[269] *Symeou*, at [34].

or others responsible for the investigation, save in exceptional circumstances[270].

This distinction is premised on the fact that it is the exclusive function of the courts in the Requesting State to determine guilt or innocence, and for them to assess the admissibility of evidence and whether their own domestic rules have been breached.

Whilst it is incumbent upon the court to satisfy itself that its process is not being abused, the challenge will ordinarily be raised by the Requested Person. In such circumstances, the approach to be taken by a District Judge was set out by the court in *R (Government of the United States of America) v Bow Street Magistrates Court (Tollman & Tollman)* [2006] EWHC 2256 (Admin), [2007] 1 WLR 1157. At [84], Lord Phillips CJ held:

> *"The judge should be alert to the possibility of allegations of abuse of process being made by way of delaying tactics. No steps should be taken to investigate an alleged abuse of process unless the judge is satisfied that there is reason to believe that an abuse may have taken place. Where an allegation of an abuse of process is made, the first step must be to insist on the conduct alleged to constitute the abuse being identified with particularity. The judge must then consider whether the conduct, if established, is capable of amounting to an abuse of process. If it is, he must next consider whether there are reasonable grounds for believing that such conduct may have occurred. If there are, then the judge should not accede to the request for extradition unless he has satisfied himself that such abuse has not occurred".*

The approach to establishing an abuse of process remains as set out in *Tollman* (cited above) and *Haynes v Malta:*[271]

---

270 See e.g. *Sofia City Court, Bulgaria v Atanasova-Kalaidzhieva* [2011] EWHC 2335 (Admin), [2011] 155(36) SJLB 35, at [36] and *Jasvins v General Prosecutor's Office Latvia* [2017] EWHC (Admin) 1606, [2020] ACD 59

271 *Argeseanu v Romania* [2023] EWHC 513 (Admin) at [60-62]: the quote is from *Haynes v Malta* [2009] EWHC 880 (Admin) at [6].

> *"To sustain an allegation of abuse of process in relation to proceedings under the Act, it is necessary, first, to identify with specificity what is alleged to constitute the abuse; secondly, to satisfy the court that the matter complained of is capable to amounting to an abuse; and thirdly, to satisfy the court that there are reasonable grounds for believing that such conduct has occurred. If the matter gets that far, then the court should require the judicial authority to provide an explanation. The court should not order extradition unless satisfied that no such abuse has taken place (see R (on the application of The Government of the United States of America) v Bow Street Magistrates' Court and Tollman [2007] 1 WLR 1157, in particular at paragraphs 84 to 89)."*

In *Rymarski v Regional Court of Szczecin, Poland,*[272] the following examples were given of circumstances where it was unlikely to be abusive to seek extradition[273]:

> *(1) where the new extradition request is based on an entirely new underlying offence, particularly where that offence post-dates the previous proceedings.*
>
> *(2) where there has been a fundamental change in the underlying facts since the previous proceedings. An example may be where the extradition was refused on the grounds that it would be incompatible with the right to respect for his private or family life and where factors that were critical to the Article 8 balance have since ceased to apply.*
>
> *(3) where the requested authority takes steps to address concerns that led to the refusal of an extradition request, for example by giving an assurance as to prison conditions. Giese is such a case as Fordham J explained in Konczos v Hungary [2021] EWHC 3287 Admin at [30].*
>
> *(4) where new evidence comes to light after the proceedings and after the time for an appeal has expired in circumstances where the judicial*

[272] Rymarski v Regional Court of Szczecin, Poland [2023] EWHC 3389 (Admin) at [35].

[273] ibid

authority could not have obtained such evidence at any earlier stage. Conversely, it is more likely to be an abuse if extradition is sought for the same offence and on the same evidence as in previous proceedings which resulted in the requested person's discharge. Such proceedings, in substance if not in form, are almost inevitably a collateral attack on the previous decision.

Although it is beyond the scope of this book to set out all the different circumstances in which the court may find that its process has been abused, some examples are illustrative.

Enticement

Evidently, abducting an individual in order that they may stand trial in the Requesting State would be abusive[274]. However, deceiving a fugitive into travelling to another jurisdiction is unlikely to constitute an abuse of process. In *Somchai Liangsiriprasert v Government of the United States of America* [1991] 1 AC 225, a drug dealer was persuaded by a United States DEA agent to travel from Thailand to Hong Kong to receive payment for drugs. There was, at the time, no extradition treaty between Thailand and the USA covering drugs offences. Upon arrival in Hong Kong the applicant was arrested in relation to an extradition request from the USA. The applicant argued that it would be an abuse of process for a government agency to entice a criminal to a jurisdiction from which extradition was available. In answer to this submission Lord Griffiths held, at pp. 242-243:

"As to the suggestion that it was oppressive or an abuse of process the short answer is that international crime has to be fought by international co-operation between law enforcement agencies. It is notoriously difficult to apprehend those at the centre of the drug trade; it is only their couriers who are usually caught. If the courts were to regard the penetration of a drug dealing organisation by the agents of a law enforcement agency and a plan to tempt the criminals into a jurisdiction from which they could be extradited as an abuse of process it would indeed be a red letter day for the drug barons. . . . In the

[274] R. v Horseferry Road Magistrates Court Ex p. Bennett (No.1) [1994] 1 AC 42, [1993] 3 WLR 90

present case the applicant and S.C. came to Hong Kong of their own free will to collect, as they thought, the illicit profits of their heroin trade. They were present in Hong Kong not because of any unlawful conduct of the authorities but because of their own criminality and greed. The proper extradition procedures have been observed and their Lordships reject without hesitation that it is in the circumstances of this case oppressive or an abuse of the judicial process for the United States to seek their extradition."

Subsequent requests for extradition

Whilst issue estoppel is said to have no application to extradition proceedings, the issuance of a subsequent request following the Requested Person's discharge can, in certain circumstances, amount to an abuse of process[275]. In *Jasvins v General Prosecutor's Office, Latvia* [2020] EWHC 602 (Admin), [2020] ACD 59, a Divisional Court (Davis LJ and Swift J held, at [20]:

> *"Mr Jones's submission in this case is that wherever proceedings on a subsequent EAW amount to collateral attack on decisions taken in proceedings on an earlier materially identical EAW, the second proceedings must amount to an abuse of process and must be dismissed. We do not agree that the matter can be put in such absolute terms. Where there are successive warrants or successive extradition requests, if proceedings on the subsequent warrants can properly be characterised as a collateral attack on a decision in proceedings on the first warrant, the latter proceedings are capable of amounting to an abuse of process. It may be possible to go further and say that ordinarily this will be the case. But the outcome in any given situation must depend on the overall merits- based assessment of public interests and careful evaluation of the facts, referred to at paragraph 32 in judgment of Giese."*

---

275 see e.g. Hamburg Public Prosecutor's Office, Germany v Altun [2011] EWHC 397 (Admin), Auzins v Prosecutor General's Office of the Republic of Latvia [2016] EWHC 802 (Admin), [2016] 4 WLR 75, Giese v Government of the United States of America [2018] EWHC 1480 (Admin), [2018] 4 WLR 103)

Accordingly, proceedings on a second or later warrant will not necessarily amount to an abuse of process resulting in those proceedings being dismissed.[276] However, when an issuing judicial authority invokes the assistance of the courts in the United Kingdom to secure extradition, it is under a corresponding duty to bring forward the entirety of its case as soon as possible and to cooperate and supply information where this is sought.[277] If it fails to do so, and the Requested Person is discharged, then there is a risk the second warrant that may be found to be an abuse of process on a broad, merits-based review.[278]

The special objective in extradition proceedings requires the court to have regard to the importance of conducting extradition proceedings in accordance with its obligation to deal swiftly with extradition requests.[279] As such, the need for efficiency, economy and finality in legal proceedings, which underpins the application of the abuse of process jurisdiction to re-litigation, may apply as much in the context of extradition proceedings as it does to other areas of litigation.[280] Whether the subsequent proceedings are an abuse of process will require an analysis of all of the facts of the case[281]:

> *"The key, in our judgment, to cases where it is said that the requesting state failed in the first set of proceedings such that the second set are an abuse of process is to make a broad, merits-based judgment which takes account of the public and private interest involved and also takes account of all the facts of the case, see Johnson v Gore Wood ..."*

---

276 Jasvins v General Prosecutor's Office, Latvia [2020] EWHC 602 (Admin) at [17].

277 *Warwryzczek v Poland* [2021] EWHC 64 (Admin) at [106].

278 *Warwryzczek v Poland* [2021] EWHC 64 (Admin) at [106]; *Bacau District Court, Romania v Iancu* [2023] EWHC 1274 (Admin) at [39].

279 Criminal Procedure Rules, 50.2.

280 Rymarski v Regional Court of Szczecin, Poland [2023] EWHC 3389 (Admin) at [31]

281 Giese v Government of the United States of America [2018] EWHC 1480 (Admin) at [32].

A broad, merits-based approach includes considering the gravity of the offending, the nature and cause of the failure of the judicial authority to ascertain and/or provide an assurance or information in earlier proceedings (if relevant), the effect of that on the extent of the public interest in extradition, together with the effect on the Requested Person, whether through change of circumstance or passage of time.[282]

In *Rymarski v Regional Court of Szczecin, Poland*, the court explained that it may be an abuse of process to issue a new arrest warrant as a device for avoiding a litigation disadvantage that might otherwise have applied in earlier proceedings:[283]

> *"It may also be an abuse if a new arrest warrant is issued as a device for avoiding a litigation disadvantage that might otherwise apply on appeal. To take one example, the appellate court does not usually make its own decision as to where the Article 8 balance lies. Rather, it reviews the decision of the district judge in order to determine whether that decision was wrong. It follows that there will be marginal cases where the factors are finely balanced and where different district judges might reach different conclusions. In such cases, an appellate court may dismiss an appeal even if the court would, itself, have reached a different decision as to where the Article 8 balance lies. It would be quite wrong and abusive if, in such a case, a judicial authority simply kept issuing new arrest warrants until it found a first instance judge who reached a conclusion in its favour on the Article 8 balance."*

Incorrect or misleading particulars

A request that contains statutory particulars which are (or have become) incomplete, is capable of being an abuse of process, but only if the information omitted is material to the operation of the statutory scheme. In *Zakrzewski v Regional Court in Lodz, Poland*, [2013] UKSC 2, [2013] 1 WLR 324, Lord Sumption JSC, in commenting on *The Criminal Court*

282 Bacau District Court, Romania v Iancu [2023] EWHC 1274 (Admin) at [36].

283 Rymarski v Regional Court of Szczecin, Poland [2023] EWHC 3389 (Admin) at [36].

at the National High Court, 1st Division (a Spanish Judicial Authority) v Murua [2010] EWHC 2609 (Admin), made four observations as to the availability of the challenge.

- Firstly, the statements in the warrant must comprise statutory particulars which are wrong or incomplete in a manner which is misleading;
- Secondly, the true position must be "clear and beyond legitimate dispute";
- Thirdly, the error must be material to the operation of the statutory scheme; and
- Fourthly, the sole basis for the enquiry into the accuracy of the particulars is by means of abuse of process. If the error goes to the validity of the warrant, materiality is irrelevant.

It would be abusive for a Requesting State to seek extradition, knowing that it has no sustainable case against the Requested Person i.e. where they could not prosecute them or the prosecution would be doomed to fail.[284] However, as noted by Lord Sumption JSC in *Zakrezewski*, at [13], the abuse of process challenge *"...is not therefore to be used as an indirect way of mounting a contentious challenge to the factual or evidential basis for the conduct alleged in the warrant, this being a matter for the requesting court."*

In summary, the threshold is inevitably a high one. There is a strong presumption that a Requesting State with whom we have extradition arrangements is acting in good faith.[285] However, the jurisprudence demonstrates that, in certain circumstances, the courts are willing to intervene. Decided cases may be of limited assistance in considering whether there has been an abuse of process, save insofar as they serve to explain the principles to be applied: what may be a strong indicator of

284 *Patel v The Government of India* [2013] EWHC 819 (Admin), [2013] ACD 90, at [15]

285 *Patel*, at [13]

abuse in one case may be of less weight in another.[286] In each case it is a question of weight to be attributed to each individual factor, when considered overall.[287] Nevertheless, previous cases may demonstrate the kinds of factors which it will be necessary to consider.

[286] Bacau District Court, Romania v Iancu [2023] EWHC 1274 (Admin) at [42].

[287] Bacau District Court, Romania v Iancu [2023] EWHC 1274 (Admin) at [43].

CHAPTER FOUR

HUMAN RIGHTS

Introduction

Pursuant to section 21/87 a District Judge must decide whether a Requested Person's extradition would be compatible with the European Convention on Human Rights.

There is an assumption that Member States of the Council of Europe are presumed to be able and willing to fulfil their obligations under the ECHR, in the absence of clear, cogent and compelling evidence to the contrary[288]. This presumption is of even greater importance where a European Union Member State is involved[289]. Notwithstanding the UK's exit from the European Union, the assumption that the UK will continue to comply with its Convention obligations will remain intact[290]. It is envisaged that, at least insofar as the majority of the protections conferred by the ECHR, the same process and jurisprudence that applied prior to Brexit will continue to be of relevance. The obtaining of assurances, whilst commonplace in Part 1 cases since *Criminal Proceedings against Aranyosi and Caldararu* [2016] QB 921, has now been enshrined in the TCA. Article 604(c) of the TCA provides: '*if there are substantial grounds for believing that there is a real risk to the protection of the fundamental rights of the requested person, the executing judicial authority may require, as appropriate, additional guarantees as to the treatment of the requested person after the person's surrender before it decides whether to execute the arrest warrant.*'

This chapter will explore some of the more common challenges to extradition where a breach of the ECHR has been alleged.

---

288 See *Krolik v Regional Court in Czestochowa, Poland* [2012] EWHC 2357 (Admin), [2013] 1 WLR 490, at [4]

289 *Krolik*, at [5]

290 *Criminal Proceedings against RO* (Case C-327/18 PPU), at [52].

Article 2 ECHR

Article 2 protects the right to life, and reads:

> *'1. Everyone's right to life shall be protected by law. No one shall be deprived of his life intentionally save in the execution of a sentence of a court following conviction for which this penalty is provided by law.*
>
> *2. Deprivation of life shall not be regarded as inflicted in contravention of this article when it results from the use of force which is no more than absolutely necessary:*
>
>> *(a) in defence of any person from unlawful violence;*
>>
>> *(b) in order to effect a lawful arrest or to prevent the escape of a person lawfully detained;*
>>
>> *(c) in action lawfully taken for the purpose of quelling a riot or insurrection.'*

Article 2 has been raised in the extradition context, not only where the threat to a Requested Person is from the State, for example where the death penalty has been or will be imposed,[291] but also where the threat is from non-state actors. In *Government of South Africa v Dewani*,[292] the Requested Person alleged that the risk of attack and HIV infection by fellow prisoners gave rise to a prospective breach of Article 2, and in *McLean v High Court of Dublin, Ireland* the Requested Person alleged that he faced a real risk of death at the hands of rival gang members.[293] More recently, in *Elmeris v The General Prosecutor's Office, Latvia*[294] and

291 *Launder v United Kingdom* (Application no. 27279/94, decision of 8 December 1997). See also *Government of Republic of Ghana v Gambrah* [2014] EWHC 1569 (Admin), [2014] 1 WLR 4464.

292 [2012] EWHC 842 (Admin), [2013] 1 WLR 82, [29]-[35].

293 [2008] EWHC 547 (Admin), [2008] Extradition LR 182. See also *Georgiev v Sofia Prosecutor's Office* [2012] EWHC 3979 (Admin); *Clingain v High Court Ireland* [2011] EWHC 2768 (Admin).

294 [2022] EWHC 2992 (Admin).

Burghelea v Bucharest Tribunal Romania,[295] the Requested Persons submitted, unsuccessfully, that the risk of death emanated from their status as police informants. The burden is on the Requested Person to demonstrate that, if extradited, s/he faces a real risk of being killed. Where the risk is from a non-state actor, s/he must show that the State cannot provide reasonable protection.[296] Clear and cogent evidence is always required.

The test is very difficult to satisfy, indeed Lord Bingham in *R (on the application of Ullah) v Special Adjudicator* expressed that "... *successful reliance demands presentation of a very strong case*".[297] His Lordship continued that in *Dehari v Netherlands*,[298] the European Commission doubted whether a "*real risk*" was enough to resist removal under Article 2, suggesting that the loss of life must be shown to be a "*near certainty*".[299]

Article 3 ECHR

Article 3 ECHR provides:

> '...*No one shall be subjected to torture or to inhuman or degrading treatment or punishment*'

---

295 [2021] EWHC 2261 (Admin).

296 *McLean*. See also *R (Bagdanavicius) v Secretary of State for the Home Department* [2005] UKHL 38, [2005] 2 AC 668, [24] and *Lord Advocate v Dean* [2017] UKSC 44, [2017] 1 WLR 2721, [26]-[27]. Although the latter cases deal with Article 3, the test is equally applicable to Article 2.

297 [2004] UKHL 26, [2004] 2 AC 323, [24].

298 (2000) 29 EHRR CD 74.

299 However, in *McLean* the Court observed that it would be unsatisfactory to adopt a stricter test in relation to Article 2 than in relation to Article 3, where the risk was of less serious harm. Ultimately, it left the point undecided as it was common ground that on the particular facts of that case, where both Articles 2 and 3 were raised in tandem based on the same circumstances, the "real risk" test fell to be applied.

The Article 3 question to be determined is whether there are "*substantial grounds*" for believing there is a "*real risk*" of being subjected to such treatment.[300]

The test is one of real, and not merely fanciful, risk. It requires more than a mere possibility. However, it does not require proof on the balance of probabilities, and may be established by something less than proof of 51% probability.[301] Once such evidence has been adduced, it is for the Government to dispel any doubts about it.[302]

There is a strong but rebuttable presumption that EU Member States will comply with the ECHR, so Requested Persons must show "*strong grounds*" for believing there is a "*real risk*".[303] This presumption is unaffected by the UK's departure from the EU[304]; the UK remains a signatory to the ECHR, and other signatories to the Convention will be presumed to be able and willing to fulfil their obligations thereunder, in the absence of clear, cogent and compelling evidence to the contrary.[305]

In the majority of extradition cases, arguments under Article 3 relate to overcrowding and material conditions in the Requesting State's prisons, although issues sometime arise concerning threats from non-state actors. The following are examples of Article 3 challenges which have been raised in the extradition context.

---

300 Criminal proceedings against ML (Case C-220/18 PPU), at [62].

301 *Saadi v Italy* (2009) 49 EHRR 30, [140]; *AS and DD v SSHD (Libya)* [2008] EWCA Civ 289, [2008] HRLR 28, [60]; *Bajinya v Government of Rwanda* [2009] EWHC 770 (Admin), [2009] Extradition L.R. 197, [34].

302 *Saadi*, [129].

303 *R (Ullah)*, [24].

304 *Criminal Proceedings against RO* (Case C-327/18 PPU), at [52].

305 See Targosinski v Judicial Authority for Poland [2011] EWHC 312 (Admin) at [5]; Agius v Court of Magistrates Malta [2011] EWHC 759 (Admin) at [12]-[20].

(i) Torture

The term "*torture*" encompasses inhuman treatment, deliberately inflicted for a prohibited purpose, causing very severe suffering, whether physical or mental.[306] As defined in Article 1 of the United Nations Convention Against Torture:[307] "*the term torture means any act by which severe pain or suffering, whether physical or mental, is intentionally inflicted on a person for such purposes as obtaining from him or a third person information or a confession, punishing him for an act he or a third person has committed or is suspected of having committed, or intimidating or coercing him or a third person, or for any reason based on discrimination of any kind*". It is an aggravated form of cruelty, inhuman or degrading treatment or punishment.[308]

Where a Requested Person can demonstrate a future risk of torture, Article 3 will be satisfied.[309] However, it is rarely argued in the extradition context that there is a real risk the Requested Person will be *tortured* if extradited, and still less does a Requested Person succeed on this basis.[310] Merely showing that the Requested Person has been tortured in the past in the requesting country is unlikely, without more, to be enough.

In *Charles v Mugla Public Prosecution Office, Turkey*[311] the Court found that *historic* physical and psychological mistreatment by prison officers and fellow prisoners on account of Mr Charles race and sexuality '*might satisfy the test for torture, and certainly satisfies the test of inhuman and degrading treatment*' (emphasis added)[312] . Irwin LJ and Garnham J relied

306 Ireland v United Kingdom (2018) 67 EHRR SE1.

307 Which came into force on 26 June 1987.

308 Article 1 of Resolution 3452 adopted by the General Assembly of the United Nations on 9 December 1975.

309 *Konuksever v The Government of Turkey* [2012] EWHC 2166 (Admin). [58]-[61].

310 It was argued unsuccessfully in *Patel v Government of India* [2013] EWHC 819 (Admin), [2013] ACD 90, see [57]-[61].

311 [2017] EWHC 952 (Admin),

312 [44]

on new assurances provided by the Turkish authorities that Mr Charles would be accommodated in a separate prison for gay prisoners and therefore the Court found that this element of the risk was unsubstantiated[313]. Despite this, the Court concluded that there was a real risk that Mr Charles would be held in solitary confinement and that this would cross the threshold of inhuman and degrading treatment.[314]

(ii) Physical ill-treatment by non-state actors

ECHR State parties are obliged to secure to everyone within their jurisdiction the rights and freedoms set out in the Convention and to take positive measures to ensure that individuals are not subjected to torture or inhuman or degrading treatment, including ill-treatment administered by non-state actors: Article 1, ECHR.[315] Consequently, acts of violence by non-state actors which are of such a degree of severity as to engage Article 3, do not absolve the State from its obligations and duties under this provision.[316] Although this positive obligation should not impose an excessive burden on the authorities to guarantee that inhuman or degrading treatment is never inflicted by one individual on another, the State remains obliged to provide at least effective protection of persons within its jurisdiction, including by taking reasonable steps to prevent ill-treatment of which State authorities had or ought to have had knowledge.[317]

The applicable test was established by the decision of the House of Lords in *R (Bagdanavicius)*[318] and applied by the Supreme Court in the case of *Lord Advocate v Dean*.[319] In *R (Bagdanavicius)* Lord Brown drew attention to the difference between "*the risk of serious harm on the one hand and the risk of treatment contrary to article 3 on the other*": at [24].

313 [57]

314 ibid

315 See *A. v the United Kingdom* (25599/94) (1999) 27 EHRR 611 at [22].

316 *Premininy v Russia* (App. 44973/04) [2011] ECHR 252, at [71].

317 *O'Keeffe v Ireland* (App. 35810/09) [2014] ECHR 28, at [144].

318 Op cit.

319 Op cit.

Lord Brown established that liability for the actions of non-state actors is incurred by the State where it fails to provide *reasonable protection* (*ibid.*). That test was expressly adopted by the Supreme Court in *Dean*, at [27].

Thus, where the authorities knew or ought to have known that a prisoner was suffering from ill-treatment at the hands of their cellmates, or was at risk of being subjected to such ill-treatment, it must take reasonable steps to eliminate those risks and to protect them from such abuse.[320] In *Bartulis and Others v Lithuania*, a Divisional Court requested "*further evidence, assurances and/or guarantees*" in order to meet a risk of breach of Article 3 ECHR in relation to inter-prisoner violence.[321]

(iii) Prison conditions: overcrowding and material conditions

The Grand Chamber of the ECtHR provided guidance on the type of prison conditions which would amount to a violation of Article 3 ECHR in *Mursic v Croatia*.[322] It is not possible to specify a particular number of square metres that should be allocated to each detainee in order to comply with Article 3; however, there is "*a weighty but not irrebuttable presumption of a violation of article 3*" if individual personal space falls below $3m^2$. At the same time, the overall and cumulative effect of any compensatory factors should be considered.[323]

The strong presumption of a violation of Article 3 could normally be rebutted only if the following factors were <u>cumulatively</u> met:

(i) The periods of confinement in less than $3m^2$ per person were short (measured in days), occasional and minor;

(ii) Such reductions were accompanied by sufficient time out of

320 See for example *Premininy v Russia* (op cit), at [84].

321 See *Bartulis and Others v Lithuania* [2019] EWHC 3504 (Admin), at [9]-[10].

322 (2017) 65 EHRR 1. The principles espoused by the ECtHR were confirmed to apply domestically in *Grecu v Romania* [2017] EWHC 1427 (Admin), [2017] 4 WLR 139.

323 *Mursic*, at [103]-[110], [122]-[126].

cell, together with out of cell activities; and

(iii) The applicant is in an "*appropriate*" detention facility and there are no other aggravating aspects of his detention.[324]

Where a detainee is allocated between 3-4m², a violation is likely to be found if other aspects of the physical conditions are inappropriate: in particular, insufficient access to outdoor exercise, natural light or air; inadequate ventilation or room temperature; insufficient access to private commodes; and non-compliance with basic sanitary and hygiene requirements.[325]

In *Criminal Proceedings against ML* the CJEU found that the executing state is "*required to assess the conditions of detention in the prisons in which, according to the information available to them, it is actually intended that the person concerned will be detained*" and "*must review the conditions of detention of the person concerned in those...prisons*".[326] In practice, one would think that this means that the Court must know in which prison(s) the Requested Person is likely to be held. However, the High Court in *Duarte v Comarca De Lisboa, Portugal*[327] held that it was not necessary for the Requesting State to identify the relevant prison where a general assurance had been provided.

Since the majority of Article 3 challenges in extradition cases concern prison conditions, the courts' approach to such challenges, to the evidence required to establish a "*real risk*" of a breach, and to assurances by the Requesting State, are considered in more detail below.

(iv) Healthcare

The impact of extradition on a Requested Person's health is usually argued under s.25 (in Part 1 cases) or s.91 (in Part 2 cases) of the 2003 Act, which bar extradition (or require it to be postponed) where the

---

324 *Mursic*, at [137].

325 *Mursic*, at [139].

326 Case C-220/PPU, at [87] and [89], respectively.

327 [2018] EWHC 2995 (Admin) at [43]

Requested Person's physical or mental condition would render extradition unjust or oppressive (see chapter 3). However, this type of argument may also be deployed under the auspices of Article 3, provided the threshold is met. A number of cases have considered the application of Article 3 to healthcare cases, most often in the deportation context where there is no statutory bar equivalent to ss.25 and 91 of the 2003 Act.

The Article 3 threshold is not easily met in healthcare cases. Until recently, it was thought that Article 3 would generally only prevent removal where there was an "*imminent risk of death*" in the Requesting State. Thus, non-availability of healthcare would only found an Article 3 argument where "*the applicant's illness has reached such a critical stage (i.e. he is dying) that it would be inhuman treatment to deprive him of the care which he is currently receiving and send him home to an early death unless there is care available there to enable him to meet that fate with dignity*".[328] The more recent ECtHR case of *Paposhvili v Belgium*[329] has widened the range of circumstances in which Article 3 may prevent removal on grounds of ill-health. In that case, the Grand Chamber held that the remit of Article 3 included "*situations involving the removal of a seriously ill person in which substantial grounds have been shown for believing that he or she, although not at imminent risk of dying, would face a real risk, on account of the absence of appropriate treatment in the receiving country or the lack of access to such treatment, of being exposed to a serious, rapid and irreversible decline in his or her state of health resulting in intense suffering or to a significant reduction in life expectancy*".[330] The implications of *Paposhvili* were considered by the Supreme Court in the recent case of *AM (Zimbabwe) v Secretary of State for the Home Department*,[331] a deportation case in which it was claimed that the absence of appropriate medical treatment (namely anti-retrovirals which were suitable to treat the applicant's HIV infection) in the receiving country would result in a

328 *N v Secretary of State for the Home Department* [2005] UKHL 31, [2005] 2 WLR 1124, at [69], applying *D v UK* (1997) 24 EHRR 423.

329 (App. 41738/10), [2017] Imm. AR 867.

330 *Paposhvili*, at [183].

331 [2020] UKSC 17, [2020] 2 WLR 1152.

breach of Article 3. The Supreme Court accepted that *Paposhvili* created a new criterion, extending Article 3 to situations *other than* those in which there was an "*imminent risk of death*" in the returning state.[332] The Court held that a "*significant*" reduction in life expectancy meant "*substantial*", and that anything less than that would not attain the minimum level of severity which Article 3 required.[333]

(v) Life imprisonment without parole

The key case which set out the principles governing Article 3 ECHR and "*irreducible*" life sentences is the ECtHR judgment in *Vinter and Others v UK*.[334] The Court held that for a sentence of life imprisonment to be compatible with Article 3, there had to be a possibility of review and a possibility of release. Were it otherwise, a prisoner could be forcibly deprived of his/her freedom without striving towards his/her rehabilitation and providing him/her with the chance to regain that freedom at a later date. This would be incompatible with the rehabilitative purpose of incarceration and with the fundamental human dignity of the prisoner.[335] The review required by Article 3 had to permit an assessment of any changes in the prisoner's circumstances and any progress made towards rehabilitation.[336]

The ECtHR returned to the issue in *Murray v The Netherlands*.[337] The court held that a failure to provide treatment for a mentally ill life prisoner, and thereby provide him with the possibility of rehabilitation, had resulted in the prisoner continuing to present a high risk of

---

332 *AM (Zimbabwe) v Secretary of State for the Home Department* (op cit), at [22]-[23]. See also the judgment of the Fourth Section of the ECtHR in *Savran v Denmark* [2019] ECHR 651; and of the Grand Chamber (App 57467/15) Judgment of 7 December 2021 finding no violation of article 3 but finding a violation of article 8 ECHR.

333 *Ibid.*, at [27]-[31].

334 (Apps. 66069/09, 130/10 and 3896/10), [2013] ECHR 645.

335 Vinter and Others, [113].

336 Vinter and Others, [119].

337 (App. 10511/10), [2016] ECHR 408.

recidivism so as to make his sentence *de facto* irreducible. Although the Convention did not guarantee a right to rehabilitation *per se*, life prisoners were to be provided with an opportunity to rehabilitate themselves, so as to avail themselves of the review mechanism that was required by Article 3. In the context of mentally ill life prisoners, whose health and wellbeing the state is required to secure under Article 3, this included undertaking an assessment of their needs and providing appropriate treatment with a view to facilitating their rehabilitation.[338]

The following principles on the subject can be derived from these cases:

(i) The imposition of a life sentence is not in itself incompatible with Article 3 ECHR; contracting states are free to impose such sentences.[339]

(ii) No issues arise if a life sentence is both *de jure* and *de facto* reducible. However, the imposition of a life sentence may raise an issue under Article 3 ECHR where it is *de jure* or *de facto* irreducible.[340]

(iii) Where domestic law provides no mechanism or possibility for review of a whole life sentence, the incompatibility with Article 3 arises at the moment of the imposition of that sentence.[341]

(iv) When determining whether a sentence is irreducible, the court has to ascertain whether a life prisoner can be said to have any prospect of release. However, a life sentence does not become irreducible by the mere fact that in practice it may be served in full. If a prisoner is refused release on the grounds that s/he poses a danger to the public, no Article 3 issue would arise since a State has an obligation to protect the public.[342]

---

338 *Murray*, [99]-[108] and [113]..

339 *Kafkaris v Cyprus* (2009) EHRR 35 [99] and *Vinter and Others*, [106].

340 *Kafkaris*, [97] and *Vinter and Others*, [107]-[108].

341 Vinter and Others, [122].

342 Kafkaris, [98]; Vinter and Others, [108]; Murray, [99].

(v) Where national law affords a sufficient possibility of review with a view to the commutation, remission, or termination of the life sentence, or conditional release, this will be sufficient to satisfy Article 3.[343]

(vi) It is not for the court to determine *when* that review ought to take place, but comparative and international law materials show clear support for a dedicated review mechanism to guarantee a review <u>no later than 25 years after the imposition of a life sentence, with further periodic reviews thereafter</u>.[344]

(vii) In *Vinter* at [199], the essence of the required review was described as follows:

> "*... a review which allows the domestic authorities to consider whether any changes in the life prisoner are so significant, and such progress towards rehabilitation has been made in the course of the sentence, as to mean that continued detention can no longer be justified on legitimate penological grounds*".[345]

(viii) "*... [A] whole life prisoner is entitled to know... what he or she must do to be considered for release and under what conditions*".[346] Consequently, the assessment must be based on rules which have a sufficient degree of clarity and certainty.[347] It must also be based on objective and established criteria.[348]

343 Kafkaris, [98]; Vinter and Others, [109]; Murray, [99].

344 *Vinter and Others*, [117]-[118], [120].

345 Endorsed in *Murray*, at [100].

346 Vinter and Others, [122].

347 *Vinter and Others*, [125] and [129]; *Murray*, at [100].

348 *Trabelsi v Belgium* (App. 140/10), (2015) 60 EHRR 21 at [137]; *Murray*, [100].

(ix) The review must have sufficient procedural guarantees and be safeguarded by access to judicial review.[349]

(x) As noted above, the State must also provide sufficient opportunity for the prisoner to rehabilitate him/herself, so that s/he can in practice avail him/herself of the review mechanism. As the court explained in *Murray* at [13]: "*... a life prisoner must be realistically enabled, to the extent possible within the constraints of the prison context, to make such progress towards rehabilitation that it offers him or her the hope of one day being eligible for parole or conditional release. This could be achieved, for example, by setting up and periodically reviewing an individualised programme that will encourage the sentenced prisoner to develop himself or herself to be able to lead a responsible and crime-free life*". In the case of mentally ill prisoners, the state may also be required to assess their needs and provide suitable treatment.

(xi) In determining whether a prisoner has, *de facto*, any prospect of release, it may be relevant to take account of statistical information on prior use of the review mechanism, including the number of persons who have been granted release.[350]

In *Trabelsi v Belgium* (op cit), the ECtHR held that Article 3 imposed a universal standard in relation to life sentences, and ruled that Belgium could not extradite a prisoner to the U.S. to face a life sentence. In the most recent cases on the subject, *Hafeez v United States* and *Sanchez v United States*,[351] which also concerned the U.S. system of 'life without parole', the High Court endorsed the traditional view and refused to apply *Trabelsi*.[352] Further, in both cases the High Court held that the U.S. system was compliant with the Convention, as it offered a sufficient

349 *Kafkaris*, [105]; *Murray*, [100].

350 *Kafkaris*, [103]; *Murray*, [100].

351 [2020] EWHC 155 (Admin) and [2020] EWHC 508 (Admin), respectively.

352 *Hafeez*, at [56]-[57]; *Sanchez*, at [60]-[61].

prospect of release to satisfy the requirements of Article 3.[353] Whilst that scheme only permitted release on compassionate grounds and did not contemplate release based purely on a prisoner's progress in rehabilitating himself, rehabilitation could be relevant combined with other factors. Such factors included legitimate penological grounds such as punishment and deterrence. The other route to release, namely executive clemency, could also be taken into account as the review mechanism required by Article 3 did not have to be judicial. That route had clear criteria set out in guidance documents.

In *Sanchez-Sanchez v UK* (2023) EHRR 16, [at 95-96], the ECtHR overruled *Trabelsi*, emphasising the need to appreciate the different contexts between domestic and extradition cases. The Court held that *Trabelsi* had not addressed, as a preliminary step, the question of whether there had existed a real risk that the applicant would be sentenced to life without parole. The Court held that the life sentence that the Applicant would serve in the U.S. if extradited was not irreducible, noting the two routes by which a prisoner could seek a reduction in sentence: compassionate release and executive clemency. The Court set down the following two stage test for the extradition context:

> (1) Has the applicant adduced evidence capable of proving that there are substantial grounds for believing that if extradited, and in the event of conviction, there is a real risk of a sentence of life imprisonment without parole? It is for the applicant to demonstrate that such a penalty will be imposed. Such a risk will more readily be established if the applicant faces a mandatory sentence of life imprisonment.
>
> (2) If so, it must be ascertained by the relevant authorities of the sending state that there exists in the requesting state a mechanism of sentence review which allows the competent authorities there to consider whether any changes in the life prisoner are so significant, and such progress towards rehabilitation has been made in the course of the sentence, as to mean that continued

[353] *Hafeez*, at [58]; *Sanchez*, at [60]-[61].

detention can no longer be justified on legitimate penological grounds.

It should be noted that Article 3 issues relating to life sentences rarely if ever arise in respect of Part 1 countries. In any event, Article 604(a) of the TCA enables the executing court to make surrender conditional on the Requesting State providing a guarantee that it "*will review the penalty or measure imposed, on request or at the latest after 20 years, or will encourage the application of measures of clemency for which the person is entitled to apply under the law or practice of the issuing State, aiming at the non-execution of such penalty or measure*".[354]

Approach to Article 3 in prison conditions cases

The majority of Article 3 arguments in extradition cases concern prison conditions. Where there is evidence of a real risk of inhuman or degrading treatment of individuals detained in the issuing Member State, the Requested State must adopt a three-stage approach when considering whether to order extradition: *Criminal Proceedings against Aranyosi and Caldararu*.[355] Although *Aranyosi* was a decision of the CJEU, a similar approach had been (and continues to be) adopted by the English courts in relation to both Part 1 and Part 2 cases.[356]

At the first stage, the court must consider whether there is evidence of a real risk of inhuman or degrading treatment by virtue of general conditions of detention in the requesting country. In arriving at this decision, the court must rely on "*information that is objective, reliable, specific and properly updated on the detention conditions prevailing in the [requesting] state*" which "*demonstrates that there are deficiencies*" within

354 Previously enshrined in Article 5(2) of the 2002 Framework Decision.

355 [2016] QB 921.

356 See for example *Government of Ecuador v Larco* [2020] EWHC 1797 (Admin), [2020] ACD 121, at [43]-[44] and *Government of USA v Assange* [2021] EWHC 3313 (Admin) [2022] 4 WLR 11 at [42]-[46].

its prison system.[357] The types of evidence which might establish this include judgments of the ECtHR, domestic decisions, and documents of the Council of Europe, although this list is not exhaustive.[358]

If the stage one threshold is surpassed, the court does not automatically discharge the Requested Person but rather looks to the next stage of the assessment, at which it "*make[s] a further assessment, specific and precise, of whether there are substantial grounds to believe that the individual concerned will be exposed to [the] risk because of the conditions for his detention envisaged in the [requesting] state*".[359] The mere existence of systemic or generalised deficiencies "*does not necessarily imply that, in a specific case, the individual concerned will be subject to inhuman or degrading treatment in the event that he is surrendered*",[360] and the executing court is "*bound to determine, specifically and precisely, whether, in the particular circumstances of the case*" substantial grounds exist in relation to that particular individual.[361] Thus, at the second stage, the executing court should consider only the prisons at which it is actually intended the Requested Person will be held,[362] and it should if appropriate request further information and assurances from the Requesting State.[363]

---

357 Aranyosi, at [89]. Thus, the deficiencies "may be systemic or generalised, or … may affect certain groups of people, or … may affect certain places of detention", provided that the Requested Person's Article 3 rights are engaged: ibid.

358 *Szalai and Zabolotnyi v Hungary* [2019] EWHC 934 (Admin), [37].

359 *Aranyosi* (op cit), at [92].

360 *Aranyosi* (op cit), at [93].

361 *Criminal proceedings against ML* (Case C-220/18 PPU), at [61]-[62].

362 Criminal proceedings against ML (op cit).

363 *Aranyosi* (op cit), at [95]. Previously, the power to request further information of issuing Judicial Authorities in EU member states derived from Art 15(2) of the 2002 Framework Decision; this provision is now replicated in Article 613(2). Also of relevance is Article 604(c) of the TCA, which had no equivalent in the 2002 Framework Decision and provides: "*if there are substantial grounds for believing that there is a real*

At stage three, if, having received and considered the supplementary information from the Requesting State, the court cannot discount the existence of a risk of inhuman or degrading treatment in relation to the Requested Person, it "*must decide whether the surrender procedure should be brought to a close*".[364]

Tips for practitioners

Type of evidence required

The following is a list of the type of evidence which a Requested Person might adduce in order to meet the first stage of *Aranyosi.* The most powerful will generally be a Pilot Judgment of the ECtHR, but the absence of such a judgment is by no means fatal.[365] Common types of evidence include reports by local experts, and reports by the Committee for the Prevention of Torture (CPT).[366]

Most common way to seek to rebut the presumption of compliance with Article 3:

- *Expert reports*
- *CPT reports*

---

risk to the protection of the fundamental rights of the Requested Person, the executing judicial authority may require, as appropriate, additional guarantees as to the treatment of the Requested Person after the person's surrender before it decides whether to execute the arrest warrant". In relation to Part 2 countries, the power to request further information derives from the UK's formal extradition arrangements with the relevant country.

364 *Aranyosi* (op cit), at [104].

365 See for example *Jane v Lithuania* [2018] EWHC 1122 (Admin), in which the required international consensus was established by reference to a CPT inspection in September 2016, followed by a report published in 2018.

366 The latter would "*clearly qualify*" as the type of evidence that could be relied upon: *Mohammed v Portugal* [2017] EWHC 3237 (Admin), at [50] per Beatson LJ.

- *US DOJ reports / NGO reports*
- *Helsinki Committee reports*
- *Ombudsman reports*
- *Judgments of other member states' courts*
- *ECtHR judgments*
- *ECtHR Pilot Judgments*

Experts

It is important to check whether the expert that is intended to be instructed is in fact likely to be regarded as an "*expert*". Their report must meet the requirements of CrimPR 19.4. Authoritative guidance on the issue was provided by Collins J in *Brazuks v Latvia* [2014] EWHC 1021 (Admin):

> *"Approval should not be given to pay such experts who have no direct personal experience of the conditions in a particular country. If they do have such experience and it is relevant, they can of course give evidence of what they have observed. They may also have knowledge of the economic situation or of any views expressed by government officials which may mean that any shortcomings will not be likely to be dealt with. Thus their knowledge of the existing situation and their added knowledge of the prospects of improvements may entitle them to put forward expert opinions. But if they do not have any such expertise, they will be doing no more than giving factual evidence."*[367]

If an expert can arrange a visit to the prison and interview prisoners, this will be the best source of evidence. The expert will also need to review domestic case law relating to Article 3 violations, any Ombudsman and local NGO reports, and news reports containing quotes from government officials regarding the situation in that

367 [2014] EWHC 1021 (Admin), at [42].

country's prisons. The topics which are likely to be useful for the expert to report on include: prison capacity and current population, cell size (exact measurements), material conditions, food, health care, natural light, inter-prisoner violence, staff violence, time out of cell, activities, toilet facilities (access day and night), washing facilities, corruption, complaint and oversight mechanisms.

Approach to assurances

As set out in *Greece v Hysa* [2022] EWHC 2050 (Admin) at [132] the High Court may admit an assurance on appeal by applying the following principles:

> *"(1) The High Court may admit an assurance by the Receiving State, even if it is offered for the first time at the appeal stage;*
>
> *(2) Such an assurance is not fresh evidence. It is not evidence at all. Rather, it is an 'issue' for the purposes of section 29(4) [of the 2003 Act];*
>
> *(3) This means that the assurance should not be admitted unless it would have resulted in the District Judge deciding the relevant question differently, if it had been placed before the District Judge;*
>
> *(4) However, the appellate court is not bound to admit the assurance, even if it would or might have resulted in the District Judge deciding the relevant question differently. There is a prior question. This is whether the appellate court should, in its discretion, be prepared to admit the assurance.*
>
> *(5) In this regard, the Court must examine the reasons why the assurances have been offered at a late stage and consider the practicability or otherwise of the Requesting State having put them forward earlier. It is also necessary to consider whether the Requesting State has delayed the offer of assurances for tactical reasons or has acted in bad faith.*
>
> *(6) If the requested assurance has not been provided within a reasonable time, and was supplied outside the time limit laid down*

for its supply, this may be a reason for refusing to admit the assurance on appeal."

In *Pojega v Romania*[368] , the Divisional Court summarised the "*applicable test... [as] whether it is in the interests of justice to admit the material in question.*"

Where the court determines that the first stage of the *Aranyosi* test has been met, and it seeks further information or "*assurances*" from the Requesting State as to the conditions of detention, it must then assess the reliability and sufficiency of those assurances. The principle of mutual trust also applies to assurances.[369]

In *Romania v Zagrean and Others*,[370] Cranston J set out four factors by reference to which assurances are to be evaluated.[371] These factors are consistent with the approach set out in *Othman v United Kingdom*,[372] and require that:

(i) The terms of assurances must be such that, if they are fulfilled, the person returned will not be subject to treatment contrary to Article 3;

(ii) The assurances must be given in good faith;

(iii) There must be a sound, objective basis for believing the assurances will be fulfilled; and

(iv) Fulfilment of the assurances must be capable of being verified.

---

368 [2023] EWHC 997 (Admin) at [36]

369 Zabolotnyi v The Mateszalka District Court, Hungary [2021] UKSC 14, [2021] 1 WLR 2569, at [44]

370 [2016] EWHC 2786 (Admin), [2016] ACD 140.

371 The factors are those identified by Mitting J in *BB v Secretary of State for the Home Department*, SC/39/205, a decision of the Special Immigration Appeals Commissions, and approved on appeal by the Court of Appeal: [2015] EWCA Civ 9.

372 (2012) 55 EHRR 1.

In *Zabolotnyi v The Mateszalka District Court, Hungary* [2021] UKSC 14, [2021] 1 WLR 2569, Lord Lloyd-Jones commented on how the courts should approach previous breaches of assurances. At [46] he held:

> *"A critical consideration here is whether evidence is relevant to the determination of a fact in issue (see generally Shagang Shipping Co Ltd v HMA Group Co Ltd (Liberty intervening) [2020] UKSC 34; [2020] 1 WLR 3549, para 104 per Lord Hamblen and Lord Leggatt). In deciding whether an assurance can be relied upon, evidence of past compliance or non-compliance with an earlier assurance will obviously be relevant. A state's failure to fulfil assurances in the past may be a powerful reason to disbelieve that they will be fulfilled in the future. (Jane per Hickinbottom LJ at para 55; Georgiev at para 61). The weight to be attached to a previous breach of assurance would be likely to vary from case to case depending on all the circumstances, including how specific the previous assurance was and whether the breach was deliberate or inadvertent (see, for example, Klenovski v Hungarian Judicial Authority [2017] EWHC 2560 (Admin), paras 21-22 per Bean LJ). The breach would, however, clearly be relevant (see GS , per Burnett LJ at para 32). In the same way, the absence of evidence that a state has ever acted in breach or in disregard of an assurance of this nature would be relevant (Duarte v The Comarca De Lisboa (A Portuguese Judicial Authority) [2018] EWHC 2995 (Admin), para 44 per Holroyde LJ)."*

In *Zabolotnyi*, the Supreme Court confirmed that breaches of assurances provided to other Member States are relevant, and that *"[t]here exists no special rule of admissibility or other heightened legal test which prevents an appellant from relying on evidence of breach of assurances given to a third state."*[373]

The Supreme Court also provided guidance that assurances issued from bodies other than the requesting judicial authority would require additional scrutiny[374]. The Supreme Court found that it was required "*to undertake a free evaluation of the assurance, which requires the court to*

---

373 At [50].

374 At [33-34]

examine and assess all relevant evidence"[375] as opposed to simply applying previous case law.

Article 5 ECHR

Article 5 provides:

> '*1. Everyone has the right to liberty and security of person. No one shall be deprived of his liberty save in the following cases and in accordance with a procedure prescribed by law:*
>
> *a. the lawful detention of a person after conviction by a competent court;*
>
> *b. the lawful arrest or detention of a person for non-compliance with the lawful order of a court or in order to secure the fulfilment of any obligation prescribed by law;*
>
> *c. the lawful arrest or detention of a person effected for the purpose of bringing him before the competent legal authority on reasonable suspicion of having committed an offence or when it is reasonably considered necessary to prevent his committing an offence or fleeing after having done so;*
>
> *d. the detention of a minor by lawful order for the purpose of educational supervision or his lawful detention for the purpose of bringing him before the competent legal authority;*
>
> *e. the lawful detention of persons for the prevention of the spreading of infectious diseases, of persons of unsound mind, alcoholics or drug addicts or vagrants;*
>
> *f. the lawful arrest or detention of a person to prevent his effecting an unauthorised entry into the country or of a person against whom action is being taken with a view to deportation or extradition.*

375 At [50]

2. *Everyone who is arrested shall be informed promptly, in a language which he or she understands, of the reasons for his arrest and of any charge against him.*

3. *Everyone arrested or detained in accordance with the provisions of paragraph 1.c of this article shall be brought promptly before a judge or other officer authorised by law to exercise judicial power and shall be entitled to trial within a reasonable time or to release pending trial. Release may be conditioned by guarantees to appear for trial.*

4. *Everyone who is deprived of his liberty by arrest or detention shall be entitled to take proceedings by which the lawfulness of his detention shall be decided speedily by a court and his release ordered if the detention is not lawful.*

5. *Everyone who has been the victim of arrest or detention in contravention of the provisions of this article shall have an enforceable right to compensation.'*

In *Othman v United Kingdom* (2012) 55 EHRR 1 at [233] the ECtHR confirmed that it was possible for Article 5 to apply in an expulsion context, however there must be a "*real risk of a flagrant breach of that article*". In providing examples as to what could constitute a "*flagrant breach*" in this context, the court held, at [233]:

> *"233. The Court therefore considers that, despite the doubts it expressed in Tomic, it is possible for art.5 to apply in an expulsion case. Hence, the Court considers that a Contracting State would be in violation of art.5 if it removed an applicant to a state where he or she was at real risk of a flagrant breach of that article. However, as with art.6, a high threshold must apply. A flagrant breach of art.5 would occur only if, for example, the receiving state arbitrarily detained an applicant for many years without any intention of bringing him or her to trial. A flagrant breach of art.5 might also occur if an applicant would be at risk of being imprisoned for a substantial period in the receiving state, having previously been convicted after a flagrantly unfair trial."*

That the threshold is high was noted by the House of Lords in *R (Ullah) v Special Adjudicator* [2004] 2 AC 323, [2004] UKHL 26 at [24] where Lord Bingham said *"The lack of success of applicants relying on Articles 2, 5 and 6 before the Strasbourg court highlights the difficulty of meeting the stringent test which that court imposes."*

In general, pre-trial detention will fall within the exception in Article 5(1)c). It is theoretically possible that this exception will not apply if a person is held in custody without a present intention to prosecute, but it is not difficult for a Requesting State to establish that there will be an intention to prosecute, and even a very significant period of detention pre-trial may not breach Article 5[376]. See for example, *Neave v Italy* [2012] EWHC 358 (Admin) at [34] to [37] where a delay of some three months before making a final decision to charge would not necessarily constitute a flagrant breach of Article 5, and *Othman v United Kingdom* (2012) 55 EHRR 1 at [235], where the ECtHR agreed with the House of Lords that being held incommunicado for 50 days prior to being brought to trial fell far short of a flagrant breach of Article 5.

Article 5 has been relied upon in a series of cases which arise from federal and state regimes of 'civil commitment' in the United States[377]. The question of whether there is a 'real risk' that an individual might, if convicted, be made the subject of a civil commitment order is, ultimately, a question of fact.

In *Sullivan v United States* [2012] EWHC 1680 (Admin), [2012] 156(25) SJLB 31, the relevant civil commitment regime was that of Minnesota, which had a particularly draconian regime of potentially indefinite civil commitment. Having accepted that there was a real risk of civil commitment, the court concluded at [33] that it would be a flagrant denial of Mr Sullivan's rights under Art. 5.1 because the very broad Minnesotan regime fell outside the provisions of Art. 5.1(e), as it did not require proof that the person was of unsound mind.

---

376 See s.12A of the 2003 Act, which applies to Part 1 EAW cases regarding absence of prosecutorial decisions.

377 'Civil commitment' is a form of *indeterminate confinement* in a secure facility which may be imposed in civil proceedings against a person who has been convicted of, and who has served their sentence for, certain types of sexual offence.

In *United States v Giese* [2015] EWHC 2733 (Admin), [2016] ACD 4 the Requested Person succeeded in establishing that there was a real risk that he would be subjected to civil commitment in California. As in *Sullivan*, civil commitment in California did not fall within the exception in Article 5(1)(e). The correct starting point was the ECtHR's interpretation of 'unsound mind' in Article 5(1)(e). The High Court in *Giese* at [48] drew six principles from the ECtHR jurisprudence:

> *"(1) the term "unsound mind" in Article 5(1)(e) is not fixed or immutable because scientific investigation and knowledge on the mental state of humans is continuously advancing and society's attitudes to "mental illness" are constantly changing. However, a distinction is to be drawn between a person being dangerous and being of "unsound mind". Only in the case of a serious mental disorder would detention under Article 5(1)(e) be justified. 16 (2) The mental state of the person must be established by objective medical expertise and must be based on the actual state of mental health of the person concerned and not solely on past events. (3) The mental state of the person must be of a kind or degree warranting compulsory confinement. This may be necessary either because the person needs therapy, medication or other clinical treatment to cure or alleviate his condition, or because the person needs control and supervision to prevent him from causing harm to himself or other persons. 17 (4) The validity of continued confinement must depend on the continuance of such a mental disorder. (5) Article 5(1)(e) cannot be used to permit the detention of a person simply because his views or behaviour deviate from the norms prevailing in a particular society. To hold otherwise would be contrary to the terms of Article 5(1), and the exceptions to that rule must be given a narrow interpretation. (6) Except in urgent cases, or where it is otherwise not possible to obtain medical advice, the detention should only be made after obtaining the opinion of a medical expert."*

The US Government provided adequate assurances in order to permit extradition to take place in *Giese*[378], whilst in *Castle v United States* [2013] EWHC 1048 (Admin) the High Court was satisfied that was no real risk that the Requested Person would actually be subjected to federal civil

[378] [2018] EWHC 1480 (Admin), [2018] 4 WLR 103

commitment, as the United States government had stated that deportation (a far cheaper option for the State) would be pursued instead[379].

Articles 5 and 6 are strongly linked because if someone has suffered a flagrant denial of justice contrary to Article 6 their detention is unlawful and therefore contrary to Article 5.

Article 6 ECHR

Article 6 provides:

> '*1. In the determination of his civil rights and obligations or of any criminal charge against him, everyone is entitled to a fair and public hearing within a reasonable time by an independent and impartial tribunal established by law. Judgment shall be pronounced publicly but the press and public may be excluded from all or part of the trial in the interest of morals, public order or national security in a democratic society, where the interests of juveniles or the protection of the private life of the parties so require, or the extent strictly necessary in the opinion of the court in special circumstances where publicity would prejudice the interests of justice.*
>
> *2. Everyone charged with a criminal offence shall be presumed innocent until proven guilty according to law.*
>
> *3. Everyone charged with a criminal offence has the following minimum rights:*
>
> *(a) to be informed promptly, in a language which he understands and in detail, of the nature and cause of the accusation against him;*
>
> *(b) to have adequate time and the facilities for the preparation of his defence;*

379 See also, *Mitchell v United States* [2016] EWHC 2649 (Admin)

(c) to defend himself in person or through legal assistance of his own choosing or, if he has not sufficient means to pay for legal assistance, to be given it free when the interests of justice so require;

(d) to examine or have examined witnesses against him and to obtain the attendance and examination of witnesses on his behalf under the same conditions as witnesses against him;

(e) to have the free assistance of an interpreter if he cannot understand or speak the language used in court.'

As with Article 5, there is a high threshold to establish a breach i.e. a 'real risk' that there would be a "flagrant denial of justice". In *Othman*, the ECtHR provided examples as to what might satisfy this threshold. At [259], the court held:

> *"259. In the Court's case law, the term "flagrant denial of justice" has been synonymous with a trial which is manifestly contrary to the provisions of art.6 or the principles embodied therein. Although it has not yet been required to define the term in more precise terms, the Court has nonetheless indicated that certain forms of unfairness could amount to a flagrant denial of justice. These have included:*
>
> - *conviction in absentia with no possibility subsequently to obtain a fresh determination of the merits of the charge;*
> - *a trial which is summary in nature and conducted with a total disregard for the rights of the defence;*
> - *detention without any access to an independent and impartial tribunal to have the legality the detention reviewed;*
> - *deliberate and systematic refusal of access to a lawyer, especially for an individual detained in a foreign country."*

(i) Trials in absentia

Recourse will ordinarily be had to the statutory bar under section 20/85 of the 2003 Act when arguing that a Requested Person was convicted in their absence and is no longer entitled to a retrial. However, where this is unavailable, an argument may still be pursued under Article 5/6 (see

Elashmawy v Court of Brescia, Italy [2015] EWHC 28 (Admin), at [33]). In *Van der Kramer v Federal Magistrate in the Federal Prosecution Office, Belgium* [2013] EWHC 560 (Admin), Mitting J held that, as the trial had already taken place, the challenge should be pursued under Article 5 (as opposed to 6).

Whereas the statutory bar does not require a Requested Person to demonstrate a "flagrant breach", the same challenge under Articles 5/6 does require that this high threshold be met.

(ii) Legal assistance and procedural matters

The case of *Klemis v United States* [2019] EWHC 3403 (Admin), [2020] ACD 16, a decision on permission to appeal, illustrates the difficulty in overcoming the assumption the court must make "*that the courts of another state with which this country has an extradition treaty will exercise its judicial functions properly and fairly*" [40]. Although American law did not provide a right to state funded counsel for a particular application, in the absence of evidence to demonstrate otherwise, the assumption was that judicial discretion would be exercised fairly (and the US government had given an undertaking not to object to state funding).

Other examples which did not meet the threshold are: *Pimenta v Brazil* [2017] EWHC 2588 (Admin), a national chronic shortage of public defenders but prisoners at the particular prison had access to free legal counsel and the state public defender had a strong presence, trial by video-link did not come close to the threshold; *Meadows v Spain* [2019] EWHC 2084 (Admin), no real risk of a flagrantly unfair trial in Spain for an individual who had been born deaf and who would require an interpreter, specifically a lip-speaker with a Liverpool accent; *Devani v Kenya* [2015] EWHC 3535 (Admin) being subject to four separate trials, which were incredibly slow partly due to the Requested Person's absence and where prosecution witnesses had already given evidence in his absence but he was entitled to challenge the continuation of the trials; *Yilmaz v Turkey* [2017] EWHC 1617 (Admin) laws passed following an attempted coup d'etat in Turkey in 2016 allowed detention for up to 30 days before trial, violated the lawyer-client privilege and allowed interception of confidential data, had not been shown to actually apply to the Requested Person and there were specific assurances from the Requesting State.

(iii) Judicial independence

There may (depending on individual circumstances) be a real risk of a flagrant breach of the right to a fair trial when there is sufficient concern about the independence of the judiciary from the executive in the Requesting State. Evidence of widespread corruption in Albania was sufficient for the matter to be remitted in *Kapri v Lord Advocate* [2013] UKSC 48, [2013] 1 WLR 2324. There Lord Hope said at [28] that:

> *"It is, of course, hard to get at the true facts. But there is no smoke without fire, and where allegations of corruption are widespread they must be taken seriously. So too must an appreciation of what corruption may lead to when it affects the whole system. ... Everyone whose case comes before the courts of that country where practices of that kind are widespread is at risk of suffering an injustice. Those who are familiar with the system may know how much they need to pay, or what they have to do, to obtain a favourable decision but be quite unable to come up with what is needed to achieve that. Those who are not familiar with it will be at an even greater disadvantage".*

Remitting the matter, the Supreme Court thought it was possible that the appellant would suffer a flagrant denial of justice if he were to be extradited, and this deserved further exploration: "*It is impossible to say that any individual who is returned to such a system will receive that most fundamental of all the rights provided for by article 6 of the Convention, which is the right to a fair trial.*" Lord Hope at [32].

In *Popoviciu v Curtea De Apel Bucharest* [2023] UKSC 39, [2023] 1 WLR 4256 the Supreme Court considered how Articles 5 and 6 ECHR work together. Mr Popoviciu had been arrested on a European Arrest Warrant issued by a court in Romania which sought his extradition to serve a seven-year sentence for offences of being an accessory to aggravated abuse of power and bribery. The District Judge ordered his extradition but the Divisional Court allowed his appeal. However the Supreme Court allowed the appeal, even though by the time it considered his case the warrant had been withdrawn. It was alleged that the judge in Romania had been biased and a challenge to extradition on the basis of Articles 5 and 6 was brought. The Supreme Court found at [78] that if alleging judicial bias it would be necessary to show not only that there was a real risk that the allegations of bias and corruption were true but that they had to prove, on the balance of probabilities, that the trial had been flagrantly unfair. It was insufficient to demonstrate that there were substantial grounds for believing that there was a real risk that the trial had been flagrantly unfair. The reason for this is that when someone had, in the past, been subject to a flagrant denial of justice it required this historical fact to be proved to the civil standard [67]. It has nothing to do with an assessment of future risk.

Where there is no 'pilot judgment' or evidence of an international consensus about the lack of judicial independence in a particular country, and particularly where that country is a signatory to the ECHR, it will be difficult to establish that there is a sufficiently widespread lack of judicial independence, see in relation to Romania *Adamescu v Romania* [2020] EWHC 2709 (Admin).

Where new evidence on appeal demonstrated that the appellant would be subjected to trial without a jury, and the evidence was that the acquittal rate in judge only trials in Chechnya was less than 1%, the High Court found that there were sufficient grounds to remit the decision to the Magistrates' court in *Zarmaev v Russia* [2017] EWHC 2705 (Admin), [2017] ACD 140.

In *Lis v Poland (No.1)* [2018] EWHC 2848 (Admin), [2018] ACD 141 the High Court found that those sought for ordinary criminal offences, with no political or sensitive content, seemed unlikely to be able to establish a real risk of a flagrantly unfair trial. In *Lis v Poland (No.2)* [2019] EWHC 674 (Admin), neither appellant succeeded given their particular circumstances [22].

There followed similar arguments which were refreshed by the Divisional Court in relation to Poland in the case of *Wozniak v Circuit Court in Gniezno, Poland* [2021] EWHC 2557 (Admin). *Wozniak* addressed the position in Poland up until July 2021. In that case it was argued that legislative changes concerning the judiciary, and promoted by then governing party, the Law and Justice Party, had undermined the principle of judicial independence and also Polish rule of law to such an extent that the UK would have had to halt extradition to that country.

Wozniak considered earlier decisions of the CJEU in such cases as *LM* [2019] 1 WLR 1004 (July 2018) and *L and P* C-354/20 PPU and C-412/20 PPU (December 2020) which both addressed the developments in Poland. In *LM* [52] The Court observed [58] that

> *"the high level of trust between Member States on which the European arrest warrant mechanism is based is thus founded on the premiss that the criminal courts of the other Member States- which following executing of a European arrest warrant, will have to conduct the criminal procedure for the purpose of prosecution, or of enforcement of a custodial sentence or detention order, and the substantive criminal proceedings – meet the requirements of effective judicial protection, which include, in particular, the independence and impartiality of those courts."*

In the following paragraph the Court held that the "*existence of a real risk that the person... will... suffer a breach of his fundamental right to a fair trial... is capable of permitting the executing judicial authority to refrain... by way of exception from giving effect to that European arrest warrant.*"

The Court, in *Wozniak*, concluded [217] that the Appellants' offending consisted of "*ordinary criminal offences (some at a fairly low level) with no political overtones, or indeed <u>any</u> feature of any note. They are unremarkable and unexceptional.... Their cases must be typical of hundreds, if not thousands, of cases in Poland each year.*" The Court remarked that there was no evidence that any of the judges who issued the EAWs were not independent [221]. Whilst it could be said that there were "*structural weaknesses*" [222] in the Polish judicial system it could not lead to a conclusion that the judges lacked independence even if some individuals had been disciplined.

Finally, and importantly, the Divisional Court stressed at [225] that the Appellants would have lawyers to represent them and they would be able to challenge the witnesses, make legal arguments, and the trials would be held in public. All of these are safeguards in relation to fair trial rights.

The Courts then moved on to consider, in a number of decisions, the rule of law in Hungary. In *Bogdan v Judge of Law Enforcement at Veszprem, Hungary* [2022] EWHC 1149 (Admin) (a renewed application for permission to appeal) Julian Knowles J considered the decision in *Wozniak* and was not persuaded that his earlier judgment was wrong [63]. In the same month of 2022 Fordham J also considered the arguments about Hungary in *Nemeth v Hungarian Judicial Authorities* [2022] EWHC 273 (Admin) and, again rejected them, refusing permission to appeal in relation to individuals of Roma ethnic origin.

In *Rwanda v Nteziryayo* [2017] EWHC 1912 (Admin) the five Requested Persons were sought for a second time by the government of Rwanda trial on various charges arising from the genocide in Rwanda in 1994. The evidence justified *"a bleak view of the political context within which the Rwandan judiciary are obliged to operate. Certainly, were these Respondents to be thought of as political opponents of the Rwandan government, a very high level of anxiety would be justified as to their prospects of a fair trial. […] it is an important consideration whether the Respondents fall into such a category, or whether they will be regarded as 'merely' alleged genocidaires, and of less interest to the authorities."* [150]. Various matters, including "*the long and continuing history of the influence of political will over the justice system where the case is perceived to matter*" and evidence of witnesses in other trials pointed to *"a high level of risk of pressure within the system"* [234]. In that context, an effective defence was *"absolutely central"* [377]. As the arrangements for the defence were *"clearly inadequate"* the threshold was met [378].

Evidence that some trials are corrupted is not necessarily sufficient. In *Ioskevic v Russia* [2018] EWHC 696 (Admin), [2018] ACD 55 the features of the case did not match the criteria for a risk of a rigged or corrupt trial. The Requested Person "*was not the sort of rich and powerful businessman who could or would use his influence to rig judicial proceedings*" [61]. See also *Cato v Peru* [2016] EWHC 914 (Admin), [2016] ACD 91 at [57-61].

(iv) Evidence obtained by torture

In *Pham v USA* [2014] EWHC 4167 (Admin), [2015] ACD 62 the court analysed a series of ECtHR cases from [26] to [29]. The Divisional Court stated that the ECtHR had "*distinguished between evidence obtained "directly as a result of torture" and that which was obtained in breach of other Article 3 rights that fell short of torture. In the first case the use of such evidence automatically made the criminal proceedings unfair and in breach of Article 6. In the second case the use of such "material evidence" would not be contrary to Article 6 "unless it is shown that the breach of Article 3 had a bearing on the outcome of the proceedings, that is, had an impact on the conviction or the sentence*"[380]. In *Pham* itself there was no evidence the testimony complained of had been obtained by torture (or other Article 3 breach) and in any event its admissibility could be challenged in the court of the Requesting State.

Article 8 ECHR

Article 8 ECHR provides:

> '***Right to respect for private and family life***
>
> *i. Everyone has the right to respect for his private and family life, his home and his correspondence.*
>
> *ii. There shall be no interference by a public authority with the exercise of this right except such as is in accordance with the law and is necessary in a democratic society in the interests of national security, public safety or the economic well-being of the country, for the prevention of disorder or crime, for the protection of health of morals or for the protection of the rights and freedoms of others."*

In extradition cases, there is often a significant tension between the rights of the Requested Person and their family, and the public interest in extradition taking place. In *Norris v Government of United States of America* [2010] UKSC 9, [2010] 2 AC 487, Lord Mance stated, at [108], that "*the number of potential extraditees who can successfully invoke article 8 to resist extradition will be a very small minority of all those extradited, but that expectation must not be converted into an a priori assumption or into a part of the relevant legal test*". He cautioned against "formulations"

380 At [29]

because some of the *"circumstances which might influence a court to consider that extradition would unduly interfere with private or family life can hardly be described as "exceptional" or "striking and unusual"* [109].

The most recent Supreme Court guidance on Article 8 in an extradition context is *HH v Deputy Prosecutor of the Italian Republic, Genoa* [2012] UKSC 25, [2013] 1 AC 338[381], Baroness Hale held, at [8]:

> *"8. We can, therefore, draw the following conclusions from Norris: (1) There may be a closer analogy between extradition and the domestic criminal process than between extradition and deportation or expulsion, but the court has still to examine carefully the way in which it will interfere with family life. (2) There is no test of exceptionality in either context. (3) The question is always whether the interference with the private and family lives of the extraditee and other members of his family is outweighed by the public interest in extradition. (4) There is a constant and weighty public interest in extradition: that people accused of crimes should be brought to trial; that people convicted of crimes should serve their sentences; that the United Kingdom should honour its treaty obligations to other countries; and that there should be no "safe havens" to which either can flee in the belief that they will not be sent back. (5) That public interest will always carry great weight, but the weight to be attached to it in the particular case does vary according to the nature and seriousness of the crime or crimes involved. (6) The delay since the crimes were committed may both diminish the weight to be attached to the public interest and increase the impact upon private and family life. (7) Hence it is likely that the public interest in extradition will outweigh the article 8 rights of the family unless the consequences of the interference with family life will be exceptionally severe."*

Lord Judge made clear in *HH* at [132], when dealing with the position of children, that:

---

381 The Supreme Court, itself, considered its own previous decision on article 8 ECHR in the extradition context of *Norris v Government of the United States of America (No 2)* [2010] UKSC 9, [2010] 2 AC 487

> *"When resistance to extradition is advanced, as in effect it is in each of these appeals, on the basis of the article 8 entitlements of dependent children and the interests of society in their welfare, it should only be in very rare cases that extradition may properly be avoided if, given the same broadly similar facts, and after making proportionate allowance as we do for the interests of dependent children, the sentencing courts here would nevertheless be likely to impose an immediate custodial sentence: any other approach would be inconsistent with the principles of international comity. At the same time, we must exercise caution not to impose our views about the seriousness of the offence or offences under consideration or the level of sentences or the arrangements for prisoner release which we are informed are likely to operate in the country seeking extradition. It certainly does not follow that extradition should be refused just because the sentencing court in this country would not order an immediate custodial sentence: however it would become relevant to the decision if the interests of a child or children might tip the sentencing scale here so as to reduce what would otherwise be an immediate custodial sentence in favour of a non-custodial sentence (including a suspended sentence)."*

Further guidance was provided by a Divisional Court in *Polish Judicial Authorities v Celinski & Ors* [2015] EWHC 1274 (Admin), [2016] WLR 551, where Lord Thomas CJ sought to clarify the approach to be taken:

(a) *HH* concerned three cases involving the interests of children. The judgments of the Supreme Court must therefore be read in that context [8].

(b) The public interest in ensuring that extradition arrangements are honoured and in discouraging persons seeing the UK as a State willing to accept fugitives from justice are both very high. Accordingly, both factors should be addressed in the District Judge's reasoned judgment [9].

(c) The decisions of the issuing Judicial Authority should be accorded a proper degree of confidence and respect. As the UK was subject to the jurisdiction of the CJEU since 1st December 2014, it is also important to have regard to that court's jurisprudence in respect of the 2002 Framework Decision [10].

(d) Decisions on whether to prosecute an offender in England and Wales are ordinarily matters for the independent decision of the prosecutor. Accordingly, the independence of prosecutorial decisions must be borne in mind when considering issues under Article 8 [11].

(e) Factors mitigating the gravity of the offence or culpability will ordinarily be matters for the court in the Requesting State to take into account. This should be borne in mind by the District Judge when considering an accusation EAW [12].

(f) Similarly, the District Judge must bear in mind that, although personal factors relating to family life will weigh in the Article 8 balancing exercise, they will also be considered by the court in the Requesting State in the event of conviction [12].

(g) In conviction cases:

- The District Judge at the extradition hearing will seldom have the detailed knowledge of the foreign proceedings, the background or the previous offending history of the Requested Person which the sentencing judge had before him [13(i)].

- Each Member State is entitled to set its own sentencing regime and levels of sentence. Provided it is in accordance with the ECHR, it is not for a UK judge to second-guess that policy. The prevalence and significance of certain types of offending are matters for the Requesting State and its judiciary to decide. By way of example, UK courts should respect the importance in foreign courts seeking to enforce non-compliance with the terms of a previously suspended sentence [13(ii)].

- It will only rarely be appropriate for the UK court to consider whether the sentence was very significantly different from what a UK court would have imposed, let alone to approach extradition issues by substituting its own view of what the appropriate sentence should have been [13(iii)].

(h) Because Article 8 cases are invariably fact-specific, it should rarely, if ever, be necessary to cite decisions on Article 8 other than *Norris* and *HH* (and *Celinski* itself) [14(iii)].

At [16] the court proposed that District Judges adopt a "balance sheet" in which they set out each of the factors for and against extradition. The judge should then set out their conclusions with reference to the balance sheet.

Regarding the question that the Court must answer on appeal, Lord Thomas CJ stated, at [24]:

> *"The single question therefore for the appellate court is whether or not the district judge made the wrong decision. It is only if the court concludes that the decision was wrong, applying what Lord Neuberger said, as set out above, that the appeal can be allowed. Findings of fact, especially if evidence has been heard, must ordinarily be respected. In answering the question whether the district judge, in the light of those findings of fact, was wrong to decide that extradition was or was not proportionate, the focus must be on the outcome, that is on the decision itself. Although the district judge's reasons for the proportionality decision must be considered with care, errors and omissions do not of themselves necessarily show that the decision on proportionality itself was wrong."*

More recently, in *Koc v Turkey* [2021] EWHC 1234 (Admin), Fordham J provided some nuance to this argument, stating that it may be helpful [28]: "*acting always with discipline, rigour and focus — to place before the Court 'working illustrations' of principles and legal tests 'in action'. Such examples can assist the Court's appreciation. That does not mean there should be a proliferation of authorities, in a game of 'tit for tat'. The temptation to overload authorities' bundles — a temptation which is the greater when the bundle is electronic — must always be avoided.*" However, in *Deb v Greek Judicial Authority* [2024] EWHC 1131 (Admin) Kerr J stated that the value of this comparative exercise [146] "*is in inverse proportion to the time it takes to carry it out.*"

Notwithstanding the fact that the High Court in *Celinski* cautioned against citation of fact-specific decisions on Article 8, there are nevertheless particular themes which have been highlighted as reducing the public interest in extradition.

Delay

In *H(H),* Baroness Hale stated, at [8] that "*[t]he delay since the crimes were committed may both diminish the weight to be attached to the public interest and increase the impact upon private and family life*". More recently, in *Konecny v District Court in Brno-Venkov, Czech Republic* [2019] UKSC 8, [2019] 1 WLR 1586, Lord Lloyd-Jones, at [57], said: "*Passage of time is clearly capable of being a relevant consideration in weighing the article 8 balance in extradition cases. (See H (H) v Deputy Prosecutor of the Italian Republic, Genoa (Official Solicitor intervening) [2013] 1 AC 338, paras 6 and 8, per Baroness Hale JSC.) It is capable of having an important bearing on the weight to be given to the public interest in extradition. In the article 8 balancing exercise, the relevant period of time will not be subject to the restrictions which appear in section 14.*"

Whilst a finding that one is a fugitive will almost invariably prevent a Requested Person from relying on the passage of time bar under s.14/82[382], the same finding will not preclude reliance upon Article 8; although it will certainly weigh against them. The court will often be reticent to conclude that the Requesting Authority has been "culpable" for the delay, or has failed to adequately explain their actions over the ensuing years.[383] However, there exists a number of decisions where the lack of a sufficient explanation has weighed against the public interest.[384]

382 See Gomes v Government of the Republic of Trinidad and Tobago [2009] UKHL 21, [2009] 1 WLR 1038.

383 See e.g. *T v Circuit Court in Tarnobrzeg, Poland* [2017] EWHC 1978 (Admin), [2017] 4 WLR 137, at [61]

384 See e.g. Stryjecki v District Court in Lublin, Poland [2016] EWHC 3309 (Admin)

Seriousness of the offence

Whilst the public interest will always carry great weight, the weight to be attached to it in the particular case "*does vary according to the nature and seriousness of the crime or crimes involved*"[385]. In *Lipski v Regional Court in Torin, Poland* [2020] EWHC 1257 (Admin), [2020] 4 WLR 87, Mr Justice Fordham sought to explain the manner in which our courts should approach the serious of the offence, whilst showing respect and deference for other sentencing regimes. At paragraph 43, he held:

> "*The appropriate comparison to be conducted is not between (a) the way in which the Polish authorities have characterised and responded to criminal conduct and (b) the way in which the UK authorities would do so. The appropriate comparison, rather, is between: (i) the conduct in the present case, including the way in which it has been characterised by the Polish authorities; and (ii) other conduct on the spectrum of criminal behaviour. That is an entirely appropriate, indeed necessary, exercise for the UK court to conduct.*"

In *Koc v Turkey* [2021] EWHC 1234 (Admin) – Fordham J held [25]:

> "*The seriousness of the offending, and the length of a custodial term to be served in a conviction case, are highly significant features in the evaluative exercise of considering oppression by reason of the passage of time. There is a spectrum of seriousness, just as there is a spectrum as to other features of a case which inform the outcome*".[386]

Impact on children

Whilst Requested Persons have been able to successfully rely on Article 8 based solely on their private life[387], a significant number of successful cases have been due to the impact that extradition will have on young children, either because of an underlying health condition which will render the provision of their care more difficult for the remaining

385 Per *H(H)*, at [8].

386 See also *Toleikis v Lithuania* [2015] EWHC 904 (Admin)

387 Chmura v District Court of Lublin, Poland [2013] EWHC 3896 (Admin), at [20].

parent[388], or where the child faces a risk of being taken into care[389]. As is stressed throughout the authorities, these decisions are highly fact specific.

However it is important always to record the decision of the House of Lords in the immigration case of *Beoku-Betts v Secretary of State for the Home Department* [2009] AC 115 [43], where it was said that "the family unit had to be considered as a whole, and each family member had to be regarded as a victim. This position was given approval in an extradition context by Lord Philips in *Norris* [64].

Time remaining to be served

In cases where the amount of time left to serve is equal to or near equal to the total sentence imposed it may no longer be proportionate for extradition to take place. In *Kasprzak v Warsaw Regional Court* [2010] EWHC 2966 (Admin) McCombe J at [21] accepted that, in certain circumstances the fact that a very short period of time remains to be served may be taken into account, although it will depend on the individual case. Mr Justice Fordham summarised the relevant principles, at [11] in *Molik v Judical Authority of Poland* [2020] EWHC 2836 (Admin):

> *"11. The fact that the Appellant has the period left to be served of 6 weeks does not in my judgment fall within the category described in the authorities, deliberately, as "a very short period of time": see Kasprzak at paragraph 21 and the subsequent cases quoting and endorsing that approach. The Court considering Article 8 proportionality must, in principle, respect the time left to be served and which is required, by the requesting state authorities, to be served there: see Kasprzak again at paragraph 21 ("If a sentence has been passed this court should take the view that the sentence is, all things being equal, to be served") and Ostrzycki at paragraph 34 ("There is a high public interest in*

[388] See e.g. Ode v High Court, Criminal Courts of Justice, Dublin, Ireland [2013] EWHC 3718 (Admin).

[389] See e.g. Moczko v the Circuit Court in Katowice (Poland) [2017] EWHC 2812 (Admin).

honouring extradition arrangements and that public interest is not diminished by reason of the length of time left to be served in custody"). The court does not evaluate whether sufficient time has been served: see Kloska paragraph 27 ("except in most unusual circumstances, it cannot be for the courts in England to form a view on whether the person to be extradited has or has not served enough of his sentence that was imposed by the requesting judicial authority") and Zakrzewski at paragraph 48. This is not a case like Jesionowski where, although there was still a month of an eight-month sentence to be served, the Court was satisfied that early release provisions applicable in the requesting state would irresistibly have been applied to entitle the appellant to immediate release upon return: see paragraph 19. I accept that all cases are fact sensitive and that the threshold is only reasonable arguability. But, in my judgment, a reliable illustrative working example is the case of Malar : see paragraph 13. In that case Supperstone J explained that "there is nothing inherently disproportionate in the surrender of the appellant to serve a sentence that amounts to weeks rather than months". On the facts of that case the appellant had served 4 months 1 week and 2 days of a 5 month term. His extradition was held to be proportionate and article 8 compatible. That conclusion does not drive the conclusion in the present case, but it serves to illustrate and reinforce the points made about mutual respect and "a very short period" being capable of being a factor (Kasprzak paragraph 21).see also Newman v District Court of Krakow, Poland [2012] EWHC 2931 (Admin).

A curfew can be taken into account in the Article 8 balancing exercise even when no specific period of time falls to be deducted from the amount of time served: *Hojden v. District Court, Gorzow, Wielkopolski, Poland* [2022] EWHC 2725, [49-50] but this depends entirely on the facts of any case.[390]

[390] See also *Brindusa v Romania* [2023] EWHC 3372 (Admin) and *Bakai v Slovakia* [2024] EWHC 1768 (Admin)

Uncertainty over the legal landscape after Brexit

In *Antochi v Richterin Am Amstegericht of the Amstgericht Munchen (Munich), Germany* [2020] EWHC 3092 (Admin), [2021] ACD 15 Fordham J held that the uncertainty concerning Brexit was a relevant factor in the Article 8 balancing exercise, both in terms of the subjective "anguish" that might be occasioned by uncertainty, and in terms of the objective prospect that the appellant might not be able to return to the UK.

However after Brexit and the transition period Swift J had the opportunity to consider the issue of Brexit uncertainty in the case of *Gurskis v Latvia* [2022] EHC 1305 (Admin), [2022] 4 WLR 82. At paragraphs 30 and 31 the Court considered the Immigration (European Economic Area) Regulations 2016 which were in force until 31 December 2020 under the transition arrangements. The Court addressed Appendix FM of the Immigration Rules [§26] which deal with individuals convicted of offences. The rules refer to "exceptional circumstances" at GEN.3.2.(2) where an individual applies to enter the UK and refusal of entry clearance would result in a breach of Article 8 ECHR "because such a refusal would result in unjustifiably harsh consequences for the applicant, their partner, a relevant child or another family member whose article 8 rights it is evidence from that information would be affected by a decision to refuse the application."

Swift J held at [33] that:

> *"Fordham J's notion of Brexit uncertainty has now been overtaken by events." Requested Persons with settled status are subject to the immigration rules". It is for that reason that any arguments in relation to an individual's immigration position must be made in a way which is "fully formulated, takes account of all relevant statutes, regulations and immigration rules, and that relevant authority is provided to the court". As Sir Peter Lane explained in Hojden v District Court, Gorzow, Wielkopolski, Poland [2022] EWHC 2725 (Admin) [§59] "if they ever existed, the days when it was sufficient merely to refer to "Brexit uncertainty" in order to have it added to the Article 8 mix are over."*

Early release provisions

In *Andrysiewicz v. Circuit Court in Lodz, Poland* [2024] EWHC 1399 (Admin) [2024] 4 WLR 74, Swift J stated at [30]: "*The important issue is the weight that ought properly attach [sic] to a submission based on article 77 of the Polish Penal Code for the purposes of the article 8 proportionality balance.*" The Court was considering the provision of Polish law which permitted an offender to be released early on licence after at least half of a custodial sentence has been served.

Swift J set out the three possible options as follows:

i. "*One is the option that is the logical consequence of the judgment of the Divisional Court in Sobczyk. This is that any application of article 77 of the Polish Penal Code is solely a matter for the Polish court. It would follow that no weight would attach to the possibility of release on licence pursuant to article 77*" [30].

ii. "*The second option rests on the premise that it is unrealistic not to recognise the existence of article 77 of the Polish Penal Code*" ... "*However, accepting the simple existence of the article 77 power only permits a requested person to point to the bare possibility that that power to release on licence might be exercised in her favour. This will add little weight to the submission that extradition would be a disproportionate interference with article 8 rights*" [31] and [32].

iii. "*The third option requires the court to form a view on the likely merits of the requested person's application under article 77 of the Polish Penal Code. It is only this option that allows the possibility that reliance on article 77 might add significant weight in support of the conclusion that extradition would be a disproportionate interference with article 8 rights*" [33].

Swift J concluded at [34]:

> *"34 Notwithstanding the approach taken in Chmura, Borkowski and Dobrowolski, I do not consider the court should go further than the second option I have described above. There is practical sense that favours recognising the existence of the power of the Polish court under article 77 of the Polish Penal Code to release prisoners on licence. But I can see no good reason for going further. In principle it ought to be a rare case in which it will be appropriate for this court to take an approach that anticipates the Polish court's application of article 77. In practice, even if a court decided it was appropriate to embark on such a task, it ought to do so only on provision of appropriate evidence."*

On 19 July 2024, Swift J certified the following as raising points of law of general public importance:

> *"When the court is considering whether extradition pursuant to a conviction warrant would be a disproportionate interference with Article 8 rights,*
>
> *(a) what weight can attach to the possibility that, following surrender, pursuant to the warrant, the requesting judicial authority might in exercise of its power under articles 77, 78, 80 and 82 of the Polish Penal Code, permit the requested person's release on licence ("the early release provisions"); and*
>
> *(b) to what extent (if at all) should the court assess the likely merits of an application under the early release provisions, either that the requested person has made, or that he may make".*

The Supreme Court listed this case for hearing on 13 March 2025.

CHAPTER FIVE

THE SECRETARY OF STATE'S ROLE

Certification

The role of the Secretary of State for the Home Department in extradition proceedings remains unchanged following the UK's exit from the European Union. Whilst it had been thought that the UK would have recourse to the European Convention on Extradition to govern our extradition arrangements (which would have significantly increased the Secretary of State's workload), as a result of signing the Trade and Co-operation Agreement this eventuality did not occur. This Chapter considers the Secretary of State's role under Part 2 of the 2003 Act.

Before the Extradition Hearing:

The Secretary of State's initial involvement in extradition proceedings under Part 2 of the Act includes issuing a certificate and sending the relevant papers in support of the extradition request to the District Judge at Westminster Magistrates' Court.[391] Where a valid request for extradition has been received the Secretary of State *'must'* issue a certificate under Part 2 of the Act,[392] save in the limited circumstances set out in section 70(2). Section 70(2) provides that the Secretary of State *'may'* refuse to issue a certificate if: (a) she has a power under section 126 to order that the proceedings on the request be deferred (see further below), (b) the Requested Person has been recorded by the Secretary of State as a refugee within the meaning of the Refugee Convention, or (c) the Requested Person has been granted leave to enter or remain in the

---

391 Where under section 70 of the Act, the Secretary of State receives a valid request for extradition from a Category 2 territory they must, subject to section 70(2), issue a certificate under section 70(1), which must be sent to the appropriate judge together with the supporting documents.

392 Section 70(3) – (7) set out the criteria of a "valid request".

United Kingdom on the ground that it would be a breach of Articles 2 or 3 of the Human Rights Convention to remove him to the territory to which extradition is requested.

After the Extradition Hearing:

Pursuant to section 87(3) if, at the conclusion of extradition proceedings, the appropriate judge determines that there are neither any bars, nor human rights reasons why extradition cannot be ordered, they must send the case to the Secretary of State to decide whether the Requested Person is to be extradited. Section 93 then applies, which governs the exercise of the Secretary of State's discretion to order extradition. Section 93(2) requires the Secretary of State to decide whether she is prohibited from ordering extradition in light of any the following matters:

- The death penalty
- Speciality
- Earlier extradition to United Kingdom from another territory, or the International Criminal Court

The Secretary of State *must* consider each of these matters whether or not representations are received. Section 208 of the Act makes provision for the Secretary of State to refuse a request, or potential request for extradition because of reasons of national security.

The Secretary of State will consider any representations made to her during a four-week period, beginning from the appropriate day, following the case being sent to her by the appropriate Judge (section (93(6)). The Secretary of State will not make an order for extradition during this period in which representations can be made. The Secretary of State is not required to consider any representations made after this period (section 93(5)).

If no issues are found by the Secretary of State, then she will make an order for extradition[393] which can be appealed to the High Court.

[393] Unless one of the situations in section 93(4) applies.

Where there have been simultaneous asylum and immigration applications or proceedings and the Requested Person has been recorded by the Secretary of State as a refugee under the Refugee Convention, or has been granted leave to remain in the United Kingdom on the grounds that it would be a breach of Articles 2 or 3 of the Human Rights Convention to remove the person to the territory to which extradition is requested, then the Secretary of State *may* order the Requested Person's discharge (section 93(6A). Any *bona fide* claim for asylum should be resolved before the Secretary of State makes an extradition order. In *R v (on the application of Troitino) v National Crime Agency)* [2017] EWHC 931 (Admin), [2017] ACD 78, the Divisional Court recalled that pursuant to section 39 of the Act, where an order for extradition has been made and the person has made an asylum claim (whether before or after the issue of the warrant) the person must not be extradited until the asylum claim is finally determined. Burnett LJ, delivering the judgment of the Divisional Court, made the following observations at [55–57]:

> *"55…if an asylum claim has been made, it is not finally determined for the purposes of s39 unless it has run its course within the procedures specified in s39 itself. But that in turn emphasises the importance, where there is any extradition background, and even more so in an EU case, for a clear claim for asylum to have been made so that the SSHD knows that she has a claim to investigate and decide…"*
>
> *56. Any contention by a claimant that a document or action rejected by the SSHD as constituting an asylum claim must be tested and resolved swiftly, if there is an extradition background and not left to languish in uncertainty in the appeal process, whether for tactical purposes or not. The Magistrates' Court and Divisional Court must be kept fully informed as to the precise position with any actual or purported asylum claim. The human rights bars in ss21 and 21A , and the extraneous consideration bar in s13 of the 2003 Act should be fully presented and resolved in the extradition proceedings. They should not be reserved for any asylum claim nor should the extradition proceedings be adjourned to await the outcome of the asylum proceedings, unless very good reason to the contrary is shown.*

Where a Requested person consents to their extradition under section 127 of the Act and the appropriate Judge has sent the case to the Secretary of State under section 128, then section 93(7) provides that the Secretary of State need not wait before ordering the Requested Person's extradition and need not consider any representations after the order is made.

Death penalty

Section 94(1) provides that the Secretary of State must not order a person's extradition to a Category 2 territory if the Requested Person could be, will be, or has been sentenced to death for the extradition offence. Section 94(2) provides that section 94(1) does not apply if the Secretary of State receives a written assurance, which she considers adequate, that any death sentence that could be imposed, will not be imposed, or if it is imposed, will not be carried out. These provisions were considered in the case of *Government of Republic of Ghana v Gambrah* [2014] EWHC 1569 (Admin), [2014] 1 WLR 4464. An assurance had been provided that if convicted, whilst a death sentence would be imposed (it being mandatory), it would not be implemented. The Divisional Court held that it was not open to our courts to reject the assurance.[394] It also rejected the submission that the imposition of the sentence barred extradition.[395] Instead, the Court had to assess whether the sentence would actually be implemented. The UK would not be in breach of Article 2 ECHR if there was no risk of Mr Gambrah actually being executed although the imposition of the death penalty and being held on death row amounted to a breach of Article 3 ECHR in the circumstances of the case.[396]

Specialty

Speciality protection ensures that a Requested Person is only dealt with by the Requesting State for the offence, or offences for which they were extradited. Under Part 2 of the Act, the Secretary of State must determine whether the Requested Person has adequate specialty protection. Section 95 of the Act sets out the applicable law regarding specialty and category

394 *Government of Republic of Ghana v Gambrah* [2014] EWHC 1569 (Admin), [2014] 1 WLR 4464 [9].

395 *Ibid.*, [15].

396 *Ibid.*, [15] & [47].

2 territories. It is important that the Secretary of State's Order makes it clear in respect of which offences extradition has been ordered.

Section 95(1) provides that the Secretary of State must not order a person's extradition if there are no specialty arrangements with the category 2 territory. However, section 95(1) does not apply if the Requested Person has consented to their extradition under section 127 before their case was sent to the Secretary of State (section 95(2)).[397]

It is possible for a Requesting State to make a request to prosecute a Requested Person for further offences which did not form part of the original extradition request, following their extradition to the Requesting State. Section 129 of the Act makes provision for this situation and provides as follows:

> *'129. Consent to other offences being dealt with*
>
> *(1) This section applies if—*
>
> > *(a) a person is extradited to a category 2 territory in accordance with this Part;*
> >
> > *(b) the Secretary of State receives a valid request for his consent to the person being dealt with in the territory for an offence other than the offence in respect of which he was extradited.*
>
> *(2) A request for consent is valid if it is made by an authority which is an authority of the territory and which the Secretary of State believes has the function of making requests for the consent referred to in subsection (1)(b) in that territory.*
>
> *(3) The Secretary of State must serve notice on the person that he has received the request for consent, unless he is satisfied that it would not be practicable to do so.*

397 See sections 127 (Consent to extradition: general) and 128 (consent to extradition before case sent to the Secretary of State) of the Act.

(4) The Secretary of State must decide whether the offence is an extradition offence.

(5) If the Secretary of State decides the question in subsection (4) in the negative he must refuse his consent.

(6) If the Secretary of State decides that question in the affirmative he must decide whether the appropriate judge would send the case to him (for his decision whether the person was to be extradited) under sections 79 to 91 if—

(a) the person were in the United Kingdom, and

(b) the judge were required to proceed under section 79 in respect of the offence for which the Secretary of State's consent is requested.

(7) If the Secretary of State decides the question in subsection (6) in the negative he must refuse his consent.

(8) If the Secretary of State decides that question in the affirmative he must decide whether, if the person were in the United Kingdom, his extradition in respect of the offence would be prohibited under section 94, 95 or 96.

(9) If the Secretary of State decides the question in subsection (8) in the affirmative he must refuse his consent.

(10) If the Secretary of State decides that question in the negative he may give his consent.'

Section 129 is therefore intended to protect the Requested Person's specialty rights. Section 129(3) requires the Secretary of State to serve notice on the person that she has received the request for consent. This will involve locating the Requested Person, who may, for example, be in a prison in the Requesting State. The Requested Person may then respond, consenting, or not, to the request. The Secretary of State must serve such notice, unless it would not be practical to do so. In practice, section 129 involves the Secretary of State considering the same provisions under the Act as the appropriate Judge would have done, should the offence have been subject to an extradition hearing. The disadvantage for the Requested Person is the manner in which the

Secretary of State considers these representations i.e. without an oral hearing, by contrast the position under part 1 of the 2003 Act where a consent hearing is held in open Court and can be contested.

Section 95(3) sets out when there are specialty arrangements with a category 2 territory. It states that:

> *'(3) There are specialty arrangements with a category 2 territory if (and only if) under the law of that territory or arrangements made between it and the United Kingdom a person who is extradited to the territory from the United Kingdom may be dealt with in the territory for an offence committed before his extradition, only if–*
>
> *(a) the offence is one falling within subsection (4), or*
>
> *(b) he is first given an opportunity to leave the territory.'*

The offences under section 95(4) are:

> *'(a) the offence in respect of which the person is extradited;*
>
> *(b) an extradition offence disclosed by the same facts as that offence, other than one in respect of which a sentence of death could be imposed;*
>
> *(c) an extradition offence in respect of which the Secretary of State consents to the person being dealt with;*
>
> *(d) an offence in respect of which the person waives the right that he would have (but for this paragraph) not to be dealt with for the offence.'*

Section 95(5) specifically provides that arrangements made with a category 2 territory which is a Commonwealth country, or a British overseas territory may be made for a particular case, or more generally. A certificate issued by or under the authority of the Secretary of State confirming the existence of arrangements with a category 2 territory which is a Commonwealth country, or a British overseas territory and stating the terms of those arrangements is conclusive evidence of those matters (section 95(6)).

There are a number of cases providing guidance on section 95 of the Act. In *Cokaj v Albania* [2007] EWHC 238 (Admin), [2007] Extradition LR 51 the Requested Person, who had been convicted of murder and sentenced to 15 years' imprisonment, had escaped from prison and had fled to the United Kingdom. He had additionally been convicted in his absence in respect of an offence of robbery and sentenced to 10 years' imprisonment. This sentence was then merged with the sentence imposed for murder, creating an aggregate sentence of 20 years' imprisonment. The Requested Person was discharged in relation to the robbery conviction as the court could not be satisfied that he would be entitled to a retrial. However, the request pertaining to the murder conviction was sent to the Secretary of State. The Requested Person made representations to the Secretary of State that his extradition was barred under section 95 because there was no provision under Albanian law to dis-aggregate the sentence. Albania stated that it was bound by the rule of specialty contained in the European Convention on Extradition and gave an undertaking that the Requested Person would only serve the sentence imposed following the conviction for murder. The Requesting State did not, however, identify the provision under which the cumulative sentence could be dis-aggregated. The Requested Person's extradition was ordered and a Divisional Court dismissed the subsequent appeal. Clarke J, giving the judgment of the Divisional Court at [31] held:

> *"I am satisfied that by virtue of the European Convention being part of the law of Albania, taking precedence over any domestic provision with which it is inconsistent, and by virtue of Article 504(2) of the Albanian Code of Criminal Procedure (set out at paragraph 21 (iv) above), the law of Albania contains the speciality provision required by section 95(3). Albania's Minister of Justice has guaranteed both that this is the law and that he expressly accepts that it applies in the appellant's case. These guarantees have been given in absolute and unequivocal terms, and I am not persuaded that the absence of an identified specific procedural provision for "de-merging" the sentences undermines the assurance that the appellant will not be required to serve more than his sentence in respect of the murder conviction".*

Another example is *Barnes v USA* [2011] EWHC 2218 (Admin). In that case, the Requested Person's extradition had been ordered in respect of an indictment alleging 29 counts of wire fraud. The allegation was that the Requested Person was the leader of a criminal group which defrauded three companies of about 1.7 million US dollars. The information in support of the request for extradition also referred to further offending, namely the attempted fraud of various other companies. On behalf of the Requested Person, it was argued that there would be a breach of specialty and his extradition would be unlawful, if it were proposed to deal with him in relation not only to the extradition offence in the indictment but also the attempted thefts referred to in the supporting papers. In dismissing the appeal and finding that there would be no breach of specialty, Laws LJ ruled at [14] that:

> *"I am quite clear in this case that if the appellant is convicted of the extradition offence the attempt offences may properly be deployed for the purposes of sentencing him in the United States courts subject of course to all relevant rules and conditions there prevailing. Such a procedure would not violate the specialty rule given by section 95 of the 2003 Act".*

In so concluding, Laws LJ referred to the *ratio decidendi* in the earlier case of *Welsh and Thrasher v SSHD* [2006] EWHC 156 (Admin), [2007] 1 WLR 1281, adopted in the subsequent cases of *R (Berming-ham and Others) v Director of the Serious Fraud Office* [2006] EWHC 200 (Admin), [2007] 1 QB 727 and *Norris v Government of the United States of America* [2009] EWHC (Admin) 995, [2009] Lloyd's Rep FC 475, at [138] of the judgment of Mr Justice Ouseley:

> *"For my part I do not consider therefore that the absence of an arrangement which would prevent the extradited person being punished for the extradition offence in the way in which he could be under the now discretionary United States sentencing guidelines shows that the requisite arrangement for section 95 is not in place. Such a person is not being "dealt with" within the scope of that phrase in the Act for an offence for which he is not been or could not have been extradited. He is being dealt with for that very offence by reference to the conduct which is relevant to the gravity of the way in which he committed the offence of to the offending behaviour".*

At [11] of *Barnes*, Laws LJ explained:

> *"Mr Justice Ouseley's reference to conduct which is relevant to the gravity of the means of committing the extradition crime or to the offending behaviour shows I think that there must be some reasonable nexus between the extradition crime and the extraneous behaviour sought to be relied upon for the purposes of sentencing. Where that extraneous behaviour consists of offending in which the extraditee has in effect deployed the same modus operandi as in the extradition offence, such a reasonable nexus is likely to be established. It shows system, which is no doubt why it may if all else is equal be admitted in proof of the extradition offence and it may exacerbate the gravity of that offence depending of course on the particular facts, because it may demonstrate propensity, planning, professionalism or sheer determination".*

The decision in *Welsh and Thrasher* was recently endorsed by the Divisional Court in *Wienzierl v Government of the USA* [2025] EWHC 391 (Admin) at [165]-[184].

Earlier extradition to the United Kingdom

Sections 96 and 96A concern the potential onward extradition of a Requested Person to another Requesting State, in circumstances where the Requested Person has already been extradited to the United Kingdom from another category 2 territory, either to face a trial, or serve a sentence of imprisonment (section 96), or from the International Criminal Court (ICC) to serve a sentence of imprisonment imposed by that court (section 96A). The Secretary of State is prohibited from ordering extradition without the consent of the extraditing category 2 territory (if required under arrangements with that jurisdiction), or the Presidency of the ICC, respectively. However, Section 96A (2) specifically states that the consent of the President of the ICC is not required where the Requested Person has remained voluntarily in the United Kingdom for 30 days after serving their ICC sentence, or has left the United Kingdom and returned to it.

Deferral of extradition

Pursuant to section 97, if a person is charged with an offence in the United Kingdom while the case is pending before the Secretary of State, then the Secretary of State must not make a decision about the Requested Person's extradition until: either the charge is disposed of or withdrawn; proceedings are discontinued; or an order is made for the charge(s) to lie on the file. If a sentence of imprisonment is imposed in respect of the charged offence(s), the Secretary of State *may* defer making a decision on the Requested Person's extradition until the person is released from detention, whether on licence or otherwise (section 97(3)).

Pursuant to section 98, if the case is sent to the Secretary of State by the appropriate Judge and the Requested Person is serving a sentence of imprisonment, the Secretary of State *may* defer making a decision with regard to the person's extradition until the Requested Person is released from detention, whether on licence or otherwise.

Alternatively, the Secretary of State may seek assurances from the authorities in the Requesting State that, if extradited to face a trial, the Requested Person will then be returned to complete the remainder of their sentence in the UK before completing any sentence of imprisonment for the extradition offence in the Requesting State (in other words "temporary surrender"). For an example of such a scenario see the cases of *Klemis v Government of USA* [2013] EWHC 4454 (Admin) and *Klemis v Government of USA* [2019] EWHC 3403 (Admin), [2020] ACD 16. The Government of the USA sought Mr Klemis' extradition in relation to the supply of heroin. At the time of the extradition proceedings, he was serving a domestic sentence in relation to the supply of class A drugs. His extradition was ordered to the United States on the condition that an undertaking was provided by the Requesting State to return him following trial to serve the balance of his sentence. He was convicted and sentenced to 20 years' imprisonment in the USA, after which he was surrendered back to the UK to serve the remainder of his sentence. He subsequently, unsuccessfully appealed his re-extradition to the United States, which had been ordered by the Senior District Judge.

Competing claims

On occasions where two different category 2 territories have made requests for an individual's extradition, the Secretary of State must decide between the competing requests and determine which one will be deferred.

Section 126 applies where three conditions are met: (a) the Secretary of State receives a valid request for a person's extradition to a category 2 territory; (b) the person is in the United Kingdom and (c) before the person is extradited in pursuance of the request or discharged, the Secretary of State receives another valid request for the person's extradition. Where the Secretary of State is in receipt of two competing extradition requests, she may take one of two steps:

(1) She may order proceedings (or further proceedings) on one of the requests to be deferred until the other one has been disposed of, if neither of the requests has been disposed of; or

(2) She may order the person's extradition in pursuance of the request under consideration to be deferred until the other request has been disposed of, if an order for their extradition in pursuance of the request under consideration has been made.

In deciding which of these steps to take, the Secretary of State must take account of the following matters:

(a) the relative seriousness of the offences concerned;

(b) the place where each offence was committed (or was alleged to have been committed);

(c) the date when each request was received; and

(d) whether, in the case of each offence, the person is accused of its commission (but not alleged to have been convicted) or is alleged to be unlawfully at large after conviction.

Section 179 makes similar provision where there is a competing Part 2 Extradition Request and a Part 1 Warrant. It is for the Secretary of State to determine which request should take priority and which should be deferred. Sections 180 and 181 govern the resumption of proceedings. Section 180 of the Act governs the procedure where proceedings have been deferred because of a competing extradition claim. Section 181 governs the procedure where the Requested Person's extradition, rather than their extradition proceedings have been deferred. Time limits for the resumption of proceedings have been imposed (s.180(6) and s.181(6)). Where those time limits have not been complied with it is open to the Requested Person to apply for their discharge from the extradition proceedings.

Time limits

Once the appropriate Judge has sent the case to the Secretary of State under Part 2 of the Act, the Secretary of State has two months to make an order for extradition (section 99(3)). The two months period starts on the day on which the case is sent to the Secretary of State.[398] If the Secretary of State does not order extradition within the required period, then the Requested Person must be discharged (section 99(2)). However, the time period to make the decision can be extended on application to Westminster Magistrates' Court (section 99(4)). Such decisions can only be challenged by way of an Application for Judicial Review[399].

Information (section 100)

If the Secretary of State orders the Requested Person's extradition she must (a) inform the Requested Person of the order, (b) inform the Requested Person that they have a right to appeal to the High Court and

398 *R. on the application of Zaporozhchenko v Westminster Magistrates' Court* [2011] EWHC 34 (Admin), [2011] 1 WLR 994. Following an application for judicial review, a Divisional Court held that the claimants in that case were entitled to be discharged pursuant to the 2003 Act s.99(2) as the Secretary of State had not ordered their extradition within the required period of two months. The time limit under s.99(3) expired not on the corresponding date of the later month, but on the previous day.

399 R. on the application of Lynch v Westminster Magistrates' Court, Secretary of State for the Home Department and Government of the USA [2022] EWHC 142 (Admin).

(c) inform a person acting on behalf of the category 2 territory of the order (section 100(1)). Where the Requested Person has consented to their extradition (b) does not apply as they will have forfeited their appeal rights by consenting to their extradition (section 100(2)). In circumstances where the Secretary of State has received an assurance, such as regarding the death penalty (see section 94(2)) above), the Secretary of State must provide the Requested Person with a copy of this assurance alongside the order for their extradition (section 100(3)). In circumstances where the Secretary of State decides to discharge the Requested Person, she must inform both the Requested Person and the person acting on behalf of the category 2 territory.

Making of order for extradition or discharge (section 101)

Pursuant to section 101 of the Act, an order for extradition must be made under the hand of one of the following: (a) the Secretary of State; (b) a Minister of State; (c) a Parliamentary Under-Secretary of State; (d) or a senior official (which is defined as a member of the Senior Civil Service, or a member of the Senior Management Structure of Her Majesty's Diplomatic Service). In practice, orders for extradition are usually made by a Home Office Minister in person.

The appropriate day (section 102)

Section 102 of the Act sets out in detail when the "appropriate day" begins for the purpose of the time limits in relation to the various scenarios discussed in this Chapter. The important dates to remember include:

- If the appropriate judge sends the case to the Secretary of State under section 92, then the Secretary of State has a period of 2 months to order extradition pursuant to section 99, which starts from the day on which the case is sent to her.

- If a person is charged with an offence in the United Kingdom whilst the case is pending before the Secretary of State pursuant to section 97, the Secretary of State must not make a decision about the Requested Person's extradition until: either the charge is disposed of; it is withdrawn; proceedings are discontinued; or an order is made for the charge(s) to lie on the file. The two month period begins on the day on which one of those events occurs (section 102(2).

- If under section 97(3) or 98 the Secretary of State defers making a decision because the Requested Person is serving a sentence or imprisonment, then the two month period begins on the day on which the Requested Person is released from detention (whether on licence or otherwise) (section 102(3).

Time for removal where no appeal (section 117)

If there is no appeal against the Secretary of State's order, the Requested Person will be extradited to the category 2 territory within 28 days of the decision. Unlike in part 1 cases, that period cannot be extended upon an application to Westminster Magistrates' Court. A person who Is not removed within the statutory timescale can apply to the Court to be discharged and the judge must order their discharge unless reasonable cause Is shown for the delay.

Where a person is charged with an offence in the UK or is a serving prisoner after an extradition order has been made, sections 118C and 118D of the 2003 Act require (in the case of a person charged with an offence) and permit (in the case of a serving prisoner) the appropriate Judge to make an order deferring the extradition order from being carried out until the charge is disposed of or withdrawn or discontinued or until the person is released from detention where they are a serving prisoner.

CHAPTER SIX

APPEALS

Appeals by Requested Persons

In Part 1 cases, the Requested Person may appeal against a decision of the appropriate Judge to order extradition (s.26(1) of the 2003 Act). In Part 2 matters, the Requested Person may either appeal the appropriate Judge's decision to send a case to the Secretary of State ('SSHD') (s.103(1) of the 2003 Act), or they may appeal the SSHD's decision to order extradition (s.108(1) of the 2003 Act).[400]

In either case, the appeal lies to the High Court and permission to appeal is required.

Basis of appeal

An appeal may be brought on a question of law or fact (ss.26(3)(a), 103(4)(a), 108(3)(a)).

In order for their appeal to be allowed, the Requested Person must show that the decision-maker (be it the appropriate judge or the SSHD) '*ought to have decided a question before him differently*' and that '*if he had decided the question in the way he ought to have done, he would not have ordered the person's extradition*' (ss.27(3), 104(3), 109(3)). In layman's terms, the appellate court must determine whether any of the challenged decisions taken by the appropriate judge was "*wrong*".[401]

Further or alternatively, in an appeal under s.26 or s.103, the Requested Person must show that '*an issue is raised that was not raised at the*

---

400 Though if a Requested Person appeals under s.103 of the 2003 Act before the SSHD has decided whether to order extradition, the appeal cannot be heard until after that decision is made: s.103(5).

401 *Love v Government of the United States of America* [2018] EWHC 172 (Admin), [2018] 1 WLR 2889 at [26]

extradition hearing or evidence is available that was not available at the extradition hearing'; that '*the issue or evidence would have resulted in the judge deciding a question before him at the extradition hearing differently*'; and that '*if he had decided the question in that way, he would have been required to order the person's discharge*' (ss.27(4), 104(4)). The equivalent provision in relation to appeals under s.108 is that '*an issue is raised that was not raised when the case was being considered by the SSHD or information is available that was not available at that time*'; that '*the issue or information would have resulted in the SSHD deciding a question before him differently*'; and that '*if he had decided the question in that way, he would not have ordered the person's extradition*' (s.109(4)). The right to raise a new issue, evidence or information is not unfettered; this is considered further below.

In a Part 2 appeal under s.103, the High Court does not just have the power to allow or dismiss an appeal; it also has the power to remit the case to the appropriate Judge to decide again a question which they decided at the extradition hearing (s.104(1)(b)). This power is considered further below.

Filing the application for permission to appeal

In a Part 1 case, the Requested Person must apply for permission to appeal within seven days of the extradition order being made (s.26(4) of the 2003 Act). It is very important to note that this period includes the day on which the order was made.

In a Part 2 case, permission to appeal must sought within 14 days starting with the day on which the SSHD informs the Requested Person (under s.100(1) of the 2003 Act) that an order for their extradition has been made (ss.103(9) and 108(4) of the 2003 Act).

It should be noted that, notwithstanding the deeming provisions in Crim PR 4.11, the Requested Person has until midnight on the last day to lodge the application.[402] Further, if the deadline falls on a day when the Administrative Court Office ('ACO') is closed, for example a Sunday or

---

402 *Mucelli v Government of Albania* [2009] UKHL 2, [2009] 1 WLR 276, at [82]. Of course, in practice this only applies where a method of filing is used which does not rely on the physical court office being open, see [85].

a Bank Holiday, the application must be lodged by the end of the next working day.[403]

The application for permission to appeal must be in writing, and it must:[404]

- Specify the date of the Requested Person's arrest under Part 1 or Part 2 of the 2003 Act (as the case may be);
- Specify the decision which the Requested Person wishes to appeal and the date of that decision;
- Identify and explain each ground of appeal relied upon;[405]
- Summarise the relevant facts;
- Identify any document or other material that the appellant thinks the court will need to decide the appeal; and
- Identify those on whom the appeal notice has been served.

In practice, what this means is that Form EXN161 (the appellant's notice) must be lodged, along with the Requested Person's grounds of appeal, the TCA arrest warrant or extradition request (as the case may be), the judgment of the appropriate Judge and if applicable the decision

---

403 *Mucelli*, at [84].

404 (Crim PR 50.20(3)):

405 This includes setting out which question(s) the appropriate judge or SSHD (as the case may be) should have decided differently, explaining how the question(s) should have been decided, and explaining why the Requested Person would have been discharged if they had been decided differently (Crim PR 50.20(6)(a) and 50.20(7)(a)). If the Requested Person seeks to raise a new issue or introduce fresh evidence which they say would have led to their discharge, they must identify the new issue or fresh evidence, explain why it was not raised or available at the extradition hearing or when the case was being considered by the SSHD, and explain why it would have led to the appropriate judge or SSHD deciding a question differently and thus ordering their discharge (Crim PR 50.20(6)(b) and 50.20(7)(b)).

of the SSHD, and any other documents relied upon (typically, further information and evidence adduced at first instance).

The relevant court fee must be paid at the same time as the application is lodged (or the conditions for any remission of the fee must be satisfied at that time).[406]

Service of the application for permission to appeal

Sections 26(4), 103(9) and 108(4) of the 2003 Act require "*notice of application for leave to appeal*" to be given within the specified time limits. This has been held to entail not just filing the application for permission to appeal, but also notifying the respondent of the appeal. In *Mucelli v Government of Albania* it was held that such notice could only be given by serving the application on the respondent in the manner contemplated by rules of court; failure to do so before the deadline would result in the appeal being out of time, even if it was filed with the ACO in time.[407] In *Pomiechowski v Poland*, however, it was clarified that the Act itself does not specify the form of notice to be given, so something less than formal service might suffice provided that the respondent has adequate notice of the appeal.[408]

However, any failure to comply with the rules regarding service will amount to an irregularity, which the Requested Person will need to apply to the court to cure.[409] Lord Mance in *Pomiechowski v Poland* cautioned that, ordinarily, the Requested Person will be expected to have served "*a complete copy of the sealed [appeal notice]*", so good reasons will be required to persuade the court to exercise its discretion in their favour.

Crim PR 50.19 sets out what is required. The Requested Person must serve a copy of the appeal notice not only on the CPS as the Requesting State's representative, but also on the NCA (in Part 1 cases) or the SSHD (in Part 2 cases), within the time limits stipulated in the 2003 Act. The

---

406 See Crim PR 50.31 for the consequences of failure to pay the fee on time.

407 Mucelli.

408 *Pomiechowski v Poland* [2012] UKSC 20, [2012] 1 WLR 1604, at [18].

409 Though the Court has no power to dispense with service altogether in extradition appeals: *Mucelli*

form and content of the appeal notice is spelled out at Crim PR 50.20 (discussed above). Once the appeal notice has been lodged and sealed and issued by the ACO, a sealed copy should also be served on the CPS, the NCA, and the SSHD (as applicable), as Lord Mance observed.

Approach to out of time applications:

The Court has no general power to extend the time limits for filing or service of the application for permission to appeal, nor does it have any power to dispense with service. Although it has such powers in the other types of appeal, its powers in extradition appeals are circumscribed by the provisions of the 2003 Act.[410]

When enacted the 2003 Act did not make any provision for extending the time limits specified by ss.26(4), 103(9) and 108(4) of the 2003 Act. Consequently, these time limits were treated as strict and unqualified, tempered only by the fact that a Requested Person could file or serve their application up to midnight (as opposed to by close of business) on the day of the deadline, or the next working day if the deadline fell on a Sunday or Bank Holiday.[411]

Three developments ameliorated the position somewhat. First, in *Pomiechowski v Poland*,[412] the Supreme Court held that, where a British citizen sought leave to appeal against an extradition decision, Art 6 of the ECHR was engaged, since such persons had a common law right to enter and remain in the UK, which was affected by such a decision. Consequently, the time limits laid down in the 2003 Act must not be such as to impair "*the very essence*" of the right to appeal, must pursue a legitimate aim, and must involve a "*reasonable relationship of proportionality between the means employed and the aim sought to be achieved*". Since the statutory provisions were strict and unqualified, they did not meet this standard, with the result that the Court had to read in the qualification that there was a discretion to extend time for a British citizen to file and serve a notice of appeal. The discretion only

410 See *Zuckerman on Civil Procedure* (4th Edn., Sweet & Maxwell: 2021), paras 25.79-25.80.

411 *Mucelli,* [73] ff.

412 Pomiechowski

empowered the court to extend time "*where [the] statutory provisions would otherwise operate to prevent an appeal in a manner conflicting with the right of access to an appeal process ... under [Art 6 ECHR]*", and thus would be exercised only in exceptional circumstances.[413]

Next, in 2013 s.108 was amended to enable a Requested Person in a Part 2 case to introduce human rights grounds out of time, after their extradition has been ordered by the SSHD.[414] This was a corollary of the removal of the SSHD's obligation to consider human rights issues when making an extradition decision; instead, the Requested Person had to take such issues up with the courts, but could do so up until the time of surrender. The Court may only give leave to appeal on such grounds out of time where '*(a) the appeal is necessary to avoid real injustice, and (b) the circumstances are exceptional and make it appropriate for the appeal to be heard*'.[415]

Finally, and most significantly, all three sections were amended by the Anti-Social Behaviour, Crime and Policing Act 2014 ('the 2014 Act'), so as to require the High Court to not '*refuse to entertain*' an application for leave to appeal on account of it being out of time, '*if the [requested] person did everything reasonably possible to ensure that the notice was given as soon as it could be given*'.[416] It should be noted that the amendments do not afford the court a general discretion to extend time; rather, the Requested Person must overcome the statutory test and show that they did everything reasonably possible to give the required notice as soon as possible. The prejudice to the Requested Person if time is not extended, the absence of any prejudice to the respondent, and the merits of the appeal, are all irrelevant to this test.[417]

---

413 Pomiechowski, at [39].

414 Sections 108(5)-(6) of the 2003 Act, inserted by the Crime and Courts Act 2013, s.61(2), Sch. 20 para 12.

415 Section 108(7) of the 2003 Act.

416 Sections 26(5), 103(10) and 108(7A) of the 2003 Act, inserted by s.160 of the 2014 Act.

417 *Szegfu v Hungary* [2015] EWHC 1764 (Admin), [2016] 1 WLR 322, at [13]-[14].

In *Szegfu v Hungary*, the High Court In London held that it is not just the Requested Person's own conduct that matters; anything their legal representatives did (or failed to do) is relevant.[418] Thus, even if a Requested Person ensured that their representatives had all the necessary instructions, information and paperwork to file the appeal on time, but they negligently forgot to do so, the Requested Person may be regarded as falling foul of the statutory test. This approach was disapproved by the Divisional Court in Northern Ireland in *O'Connor v Greece* [2017] NIQB 77, which held that a distinction should be drawn between the actions of a Requested Person and those of their solicitor. In *O'Connor v Greece* [2022] UKSC 4, [2022] 1 WLR 903 the Supreme Court clarified that, properly interpreted, references to 'the person' in section 26 of the 2003 should be read as the Individual whose extradition is sought, not their legal representatives. To that extent the Supreme Court disapproved of the approach taken in *Szegfu*, which it described as the surrogacy principle, attributing the fault of a legal representative to a prospective appellant (judgment at [48-52]).

If a Requested Person files and serves the application for permission to appeal after the expiry of the time limit, the appeal notice must explain what they did to ensure that the notice was filed/served as soon as it could be, and must include or attach the evidence they rely upon to support that explanation.[419] Where the appeal is on human rights grounds against an order for extradition made by the SSHD, the appeal notice must explain why the appeal is necessary to avoid real injustice, and must identify the circumstances that are said to be exceptional and make it appropriate to consider the appeal.[420]

Amending the application for leave to appeal:

An application for leave to appeal can be amended without the court's permission, if the amended application is filed and served no later than 10 working days after service of the original application.[421] This enables

418 *Szegfu*, at [15]-[16].

419 Crim PR 50.20(4)(a)(i).

420 Crim PR 50.20(4)(b)(i) and (ii).

421 Crim PR 50.20(5)(a).

Requested Persons to lodge abbreviated or 'holding' grounds within the statutory time limit, and to serve 'perfected' grounds later if need be. If a Requested Person wishes to amend their appeal notice after the 10-day time limit, they must seek the High Court's permission. Crim PD 50B.18(iii) underlines that any such application should be made as soon as practicable and well in advance of any hearing, especially if there is a risk that the respondent may need to seek time to answer the proposed amendment.

Respondent's notice:

A person on whom the application for permission to appeal has been served must file and serve a respondent's notice if they wish to make representations to the High Court, or if the High Court directs them to do so.[422] The deadlines for the respondent's notice are: (i) 10 working days after service of the amended appeal notice, or the expiry of the time limit for service of such amended appeal notice; (ii) five working days after service of a notice renewing an application for permission to appeal; or (iii) five working days after a direction to serve a respondent's notice.[423]

The respondent's notice must state the date on which they were served with the appellant's notice/renewal notice (as applicable) summarise any relevant facts not already summarised in the appeal notice. It must also identify each ground of opposition on which the respondent relies, and the ground of appeal to which such ground of opposition relates; and it must identify any document or other material that the Court will need to decide the appeal.[424]

A respondent has no window of opportunity to perfect their notice without the Court's permission[425]. Again, such applications should be made as soon as the need arises, and well in advance of any hearing (Crim PD 50B.19(iii)).

[422] Crim PR 50.21(1).

[423] Crim PR 50.21(3).

[424] Crim PR 50.21(4).

[425] CrimPR 50.17(6)(b)

Grant and refusal of permission to appeal:

Permission to appeal will be granted in respect of grounds of appeal which are "*reasonably arguable*".[426] The High Court will consider the application for permission on the papers in the first instance. If it grants permission, then unless otherwise stated permission is taken to have been granted on every ground identified in the appeal notice, and the court will give directions to progress the matter to a full appeal hearing.[427]

If permission is refused, or is refused on some of the grounds identified in the appeal notice, the Requested Person may renew their application for leave to appeal or may apply to restore the excluded grounds (as the case may be).[428] If so, they must serve a notice to that effect on the High Court officer, respondent, and any other person on whom the appeal notice was served, not more than five working days after service of the High Court's decision refusing permission on some or all of their grounds.[429] The application for leave to appeal, or to restore excluded grounds, will then be reconsidered at an oral permission hearing[430] by a judge other than the one who determined the application on the papers.[431] In *Opalfvens v Belgium* [2015] EWHC 2808 (Admin) Irwin J held that renewal grounds "*must grapple with the reasons given by the single judge and set out, briefly and concisely, why it is said the judge's decision was wrong. If that is not done, the appellant may be held to have failed to lodge grounds for renewal, to have failed to have applied for renewal, and the matter may be dismissed without a renewal hearing.*" [14] Where an application for an extension of time to file a notice of renewal is refused on the papers there is no right to seek an oral hearing of that application,

426 Cf. Crim PR 50.17(4)(b).

427 Crim PR 50.17(4)(a) and (c).

428 Crim PR 50.22(2).

429 Crim PR 50.21(5).

430 Crim PR 50.17(1)(b)(ii).

431 Crim PR 50.30(3)(a). Or, the renewed application may be heard by a Divisional Court: Crim PR 50.30(3)(b).

the only route then open is to seek to re-open the appeal under Crim PR 50.27 (Crim PD 12.3).

High Court's powers on appeal by a Requested Person:

On a full appeal, the High Court may dismiss the appeal,[432] allow it,[433] or in the case of an appeal under s.103, it may direct the appropriate judge to decide again a question which they decided at the extradition hearing.[434]

As noted above, the appeal may only be allowed if the relevant conditions are satisfied.[435] If it is allowed, the court must quash the order for extradition and order the person's discharge (ss.27(5), 104(5) and 109(5)).

The purpose of the High Court's power to remit a case under s.104(1)(b) is generally to correct an error of law on the appropriate judge's part (for example, as to whether the conduct alleged was an extradition offence) and require them to apply the correct legal principles to the facts.[436] Although the 2003 Act does not expressly provide that the conditions in s.104(4) must be satisfied in order for this power to be exercised, the High Court has held that this does not mean that a Requested Person can circumvent the restrictions on fresh evidence contained in s.104(4), by simply inviting the Court to remit the case to the appropriate Judge.[437] Thus, the power under s.104(1)(b) will be exercised where the District Judge erred and the appropriate course is to remit the case, but if the Requested Person wishes to rely on fresh evidence to demonstrate the

---

432 Sections 27(1)(b), 104(1)(c), and 109(1)(b) of the 2003 Act.

433 Sections 27(1)(a), 104(1)(a), and 109(1)(a) of the 2003 Act.

434 Section 104(1)(b) of the 2003 Act.

435 That is, the conditions under ss.27(3), 27(4), 104(3), 104(4), 109(3) or 109(4), as the case may be.

436 See *Hafeez v United States* [2020] EWHC 155 (Admin), [2020] 1 WLR 1296, at [38]. See also *Dempsey v United States* [2020] EWHC 603 (Admin), [2020] 1 WLR 3103.

437 See *Hafeez*, at [40].

error, they must satisfy the court that the evidence was "*not available*" below (this test is discussed later on in the chapter).

If the appropriate Judge comes to a different decision on any question which they have been directed to answer by virtue of s.104(1)(b), they must order the Requested Person's discharge (s.104(6)). However, if they come to the same decision as they did at the original extradition hearing, the appeal must be taken to have been dismissed by decision of the High Court (s.104(7)).

Appeals by Requesting States

Just as a Requested Person may appeal a decision to extradite them, so may a Requesting State appeal against a decision ordering their discharge. Thus, in Part 1 cases, the authority which issued the arrest warrant may appeal against a decision of the appropriate Judge to order the Requested Person's discharge (s.28(1) of the 2003 Act). In Part 2 matters, the category 2 territory may appeal the appropriate Judge's decision to order the Requested Person's discharge (s.105(1) of the 2003 Act); or, if the case was sent to the SSHD but the SSHD discharged the Requested Person, the category 2 territory may appeal that decision (s.110(1) of the 2003 Act).

The rules and principles governing appeals by Requesting States are similar to those governing appeals by Requested Persons, albeit with some important differences. Thus, an appeal against discharge lies to the High Court,[438] may be brought on a question of fact or law,[439] and permission to appeal is required.

Announcing intention to appeal

Where a Requested Person is discharged, they are obviously entitled to be released from custody or from the conditions of their bail, but the Requesting State may wish to avoid this if it is going to appeal the decision. The Requesting State may therefore inform the appropriate Judge of its intention to appeal "*immediately*" after discharge is ordered

438 Sections 28(4)(a), 105(4)(a), 110(4)(a) of the 2003 Act.

439 Sections 28(4)(b), 105(4)(b), 110(4)(b) of the 2003 Act.

(or, in the case of an appeal under s.110, it may inform the SSHD of its intention to appeal within three days starting with the day on which discharge is ordered), in which case the judge must remand the Requested Person in custody or on bail whilst the appeal is pending.[440]

Basis of appeal

A Requesting State may appeal on the basis that the appropriate Judge '*ought to have decided a question before him differently*' and that '*if he had decided the question in the way he ought to have done, he would not have been required to order the person's discharge*' (ss.29(3), 106(4));[441] or on the basis that '*an issue is raised that was not raised at the extradition hearing or evidence is available that was not available at the extradition hearing*', that '*the issue or evidence would have resulted in the judge deciding a question before him at the extradition hearing differently*', and that '*if he had decided the question in that way, he would not have been required to order the person's discharge*' (ss.29(4), 104(5)).[442] As with appeals by Requested Persons, the Requesting State does not have an unrestricted ability to raise a new issue, evidence or information on appeal; this is considered further below.

Filing and service of the application for permission to appeal

As with appeals by Requested Persons, the Requesting State's application for permission to appeal must be filed and served by the time limit specified in the statutory provisions. In the case of appeals under s.28 of the 2003 Act, this is seven days starting with the day on which discharge

440 Sections 30, 107 and 112 of the 2003 Act, respectively.

441 In the case of appeals under s.110, the equivalent provision is that if the SSHD "had decided the question in the way he ought to have done, he would have ordered the person's extradition": s.111(3)(b).

442 The equivalent provision in relation to appeals under s.110 is s.111(4), which provides that the appeal may be allowed if "an issue is raised that was not raised when the case was being considered by the SSHD or information is available that was not available at that time", "the issue or information would have resulted in the SSHD deciding a question before him differently", and "if he had decided the question in that way, he would have ordered the person's extradition".

is ordered. In Part 2 cases, the permitted period is 14 days starting with the day on which discharge is ordered (in the case of appeals under s.105) or the day on which the SSHD informs the CPS of the discharge order under s.100(4) (in the case of appeals under s.110).

Unlike appeals by Requested Persons, however, the time limits remain rigid where the appeal is against discharge. Unless the Requesting State gives notice within the requisite time limit, the court has no jurisdiction to entertain the appeal.[443]

The form and content of the appeal notice is spelled out at Crim PR 50.20 (discussed above), and Crim PR 50.19 (also discussed above) sets out the service requirements. The Requesting State must serve a copy of the appeal notice on the Requested Person, and the NCA (in Part 1 cases) or the SSHD (in Part 2 cases).

Amending the application for leave to appeal, respondent's notice, permission to appeal

The provisions governing amendments to the appeal notice, the requirement for a respondent's notice, the test on applications for permission to appeal, and the consequences of a grant or refusal of permission, are the same as for appeals by Requested Persons (discussed above).

High Court's powers on appeal by a Requesting State:

On a full appeal, the High Court may dismiss the appeal,[444] allow it,[445] or in the case of an appeal under s.105, it may direct the appropriate judge to decide again a question which they decided at the extradition hearing.[446]

---

443 See The Public Prosecutor's Office of the Appeal Court of Eastern Crete, Greece v Andrew [2018] EWHC 441 (Admin).

444 Sections 29(1)(b), 106(1)(c), and 111(1)(b) of the 2003 Act.

445 Sections 29(1)(a), 106(1)(a), and 111(1)(a) of the 2003 Act.

446 Section 106(1)(b) of the 2003 Act.

If the appeal is dismissed, the order discharging the Requested Person will take effect, unless the High Court is immediately informed that the Requesting State intends to apply for leave to appeal to the Supreme Court. If so, the appeal is treated as still pending and the order remanding the Requested Person in custody or on bail will continue in force.[447]

In an appeal under ss.28 or 105, if the relevant conditions are satisfied[448] and the appeal is allowed, the Court must quash the order discharging the Requested Person, remit the case to the appropriate Judge, and direct them to proceed as they would have been required to do if they had decided the issue which resulted in the Requested Person's discharge differently (ss.29(5), 106(6)).

If, rather than allowing an appeal outright, the High Court exercises its power under s.106(1)(b) to direct the appropriate Judge to decide again a question which they decided at the extradition hearing, the appeal is treated as dismissed by order of the High Court if they come to the same decision as before (s.106(8)). If the appropriate Judge decides the question differently, then as where the appeal is allowed, they must proceed as they would have been required to do if they had decided it differently at the extradition hearing (s.106(7)).

It should be noted that where a case is remitted and the appropriate judge is required to proceed as they would have had to do if they had decided the relevant issue differently (i.e. under s.29(5), s.106(6), or s.106(1)(b) together with s.106(7)), it is not open to the Requested Person to raise new issues which were not raised at the original extradition hearing, at the further hearing before the appropriate Judge.[449]

New issues and fresh evidence on appeal

There is conflicting authority as to what, if any, conditions must be satisfied in order for a new issue (as opposed to fresh evidence) to be raised in an appeal to the High Court. In *Hoholm v The Government of*

---

447 Sections 30(4)(b), 107(4)(b) and 112(4)(b) of the 2003 Act.

448 That is, the conditions under ss.29(3), 29(4), 106(4) or 106(5) of the 2003 Act, as the case may be.

449 *Dempsey, Gurau v Romania* [2024] EWHC 1924 (Admin)

Norway [2009] EWHC 1153 (Admin), a Divisional Court held that the appellant did *not* have to show that the issue could not have been raised at first instance. Whilst parties were generally expected to bring forward their entire case at first instance, issues which do not require the introduction of fresh evidence are less problematic than those which do, and "*the court is concerned to ensure that those who are the subject of conforming requests for extradition are lawfully extradited*", whilst at the same time ensuring that the legal requirements for extradition are observed.[450] Consequently, "*where an issue was available to be raised by an appellant on the evidence adduced at the extradition hearing, she is in general, if not always, entitled to raise that issue on appeal to this Court, even though the issue was not raised at that hearing*".[451]

In *Khan v Government of the United States of America* [2010] EWHC 1127 (Admin), however, a Divisional Court held that where a new issue was raised on appeal, the appellant would have to show that there was a good reason for not raising it below. Since the High Court was concerned with the correctness of the appropriate Judge's decision on the material before them, "*it should be only in special circumstances that the Court is invited to overrule a decision on the grounds of… an issue which could have been raised in the Magistrates' Court but was not*".[452]

It appears that the weight of authority is now clearly in favour of the approach in *Hoholm*: see for example *Adedeji v The Public Prosecutor's Office, Germany* [2012] EWHC 3237 (Admin); *Gruchala v Poland* [2013] EWHC 1177 (Admin); and more recently, *Troka v Government of the Republic of Albania* [2020] EWHC 408 (Admin), [2020] ACD 35. In *Troka*, the court held that the proper approach is to consider the new point *de bene esse*, and to permit it to be raised afresh if it has merit.[453] In *Romania v Gurau* [2023] EWHC 439 (Admin) the Divisional Court held (at [32-38] & [51-60]) that there was no means under the statutory

---

450 *Hoholm v The Government of Norway* [2009] EWHC 1513 (Admin), Times, October 13, 2009, at [19].

451 *Hoholm,* at [19].

452 *Khan v United States* [2010] EWHC 1127 (Admin), at [42].

453 *Troka v Government of the Republic of Albania* [2020] EWHC 408 (Admin), [2020] ACD 35, at [24].

scheme of the 2003 Act for a successful respondent to cross-appeal on issues on which they had not succeeded at first instance.

The position is different where the appellant seeks to rely on fresh evidence, whether in support of a point raised at first instance or in order to advance a new point.[454] In *Szombathely City Court, Hungary v Fenyvesi*, a Divisional Court defined evidence that was "*not available at the extradition hearing*" for the purposes of the relevant provisions of the 2003 Act[455] as:

> "*... evidence which either did not exist at the time of the extradition hearing, or which was not at the disposal of the party wishing to adduce it and which he could not with reasonable diligence have obtained. If it was at the party's disposal or could have been so obtained, it was available. It may on occasions be material to consider whether or when the party knew the case he had to meet. But a party taken by surprise is able to ask for an adjournment. In addition, the court needs to decide that, if the evidence had been adduced, the result would have been different resulting in the person's discharge. This is a strict test, consonant with the parliamentary intent and that of the Framework Decision, that extradition cases should be dealt with speedily and should not generally be held up by an attempt to introduce equivocal fresh evidence which was available to a diligent party at the extradition hearing. A party seeking to persuade the court that proposed evidence was not available should normally serve a witness statement explaining why it was not available.*"[456]

The Court in *Fenyvesi* recognised, however, that where the appellant is a Requested Person, and it is alleged that their Convention rights may be

---

454 Where an appellant wishes to advance a new point by reference to fresh evidence, it is the restrictions on the introduction of fresh evidence that will be the limiting factor: see *Satkunas v Prosecutor General's Office of Republic of Lithuania* [2015] EWHC 3962 (Admin).

455 That is, ss.27(4), 29(4), 104(4), 106(5), 109(4), and 111(4) of the 2003 Act.

456 *Szombathely City Court, Hungary v Fenyvesi* [2009] EWHC 231 (Admin), [2009] 4 All ER 324 at [32].

breached if the fresh evidence is not considered, the strict approach set out above must be modified:

> "*Section 29(4) of the 2003 Act is not expressed in terms which appear to give the court a discretion; although a degree of latitude may need to be introduced from elsewhere. As Latham LJ said in Miklis, there may occasionally be cases where what might otherwise be a breach of the European Convention on Human Rights may be avoided by admitting fresh evidence, tendered on behalf of a defendant, which a strict application of the section would not permit. The justification for this would be a modulation of s 29(4) with reference to s.3 of the 1998 Act* ..."[457]

Even in these circumstances, however, the threshold "*remains high ... [i]n short, the fresh evidence must be decisive*".[458]

It should be noted that ss.27(4), 29(4), 104(4), 106(5), 109(4), and 111(4) of the 2003 Act do not set up rules of *admissibility*, but rather establish the conditions for allowing an appeal.[459] If fresh evidence is admitted, strictly speaking that is done pursuant to the inherent jurisdiction of the High Court to control its own procedure, although the court's inherent jurisdiction may be influenced or circumscribed by statute.[460] Thus, when considering whether to admit fresh evidence, the court will have regard to the statutory provisions. If it is clear that the evidence will inevitably fall foul of them (for example, because it is "*plain that it was available at the extradition hearing*"), then the court is unlikely to spend much more time and expense considering it.[461] In practice, the court will often consider fresh evidence *de bene esse*, and with some care, in order to decide whether it is admissible under the normal rules of

457 *Fenyvesi* at [34]. Section 3 of the Human Rights Act 1998 requires that primary legislation be read and given effect in a way which is compatible with Convention rights.

458 *Fenyvesi,* at [35].

459 Zabolotnyi v The Mateszalka District Court, Hungary [2021] UKSC 14, [2021] 1 WLR 2569 at [57].

460 *FK v Germany* [2017] EWHC 2160 (Admin), at [31].

461 *Fenyvesi,* at [33].

criminal evidence, what would be involved if it were to be formally admitted (for example, whether there would need to be a full rehearing), and whether it appears likely to pass or fail the statutory test.

Where a respondent seeks to rely on fresh evidence, or where the High Court is considering whether to seek further information from one of the parties by way of clarification, the position is rather different. In such circumstances, ss.27(4), 29(4), 104(4), 106(5), 109(4), and 111(4) of the 2003 Act do not apply,[462] and the court will reach its decision based on what would be in the interests of justice.[463] This does not mean a respondent has *carte blanche* to apply to admit fresh evidence, but a relevant factor will be whether the evidence was available to the respondent at first instance, but only as one of several material considerations.[464]

Practical matters

Funding on appeal

All Requested Persons are entitled to legal aid on appeal, since the means test does not apply.[465] To apply, a completed CRM14 must be sent to the ACO, and a nominated legal officer will make a representation order under delegated powers with effect from the day the completed form was submitted.[466] Since the earliest the completed CRM14 can be submitted is along with the appeal notice, work done to prepare the appeal notice will be covered by the Magistrates' Court representation order (if there

---

462 *FK*, at [34]-[35].

463 *FK*, at [39].

464 *FK*, at [40].

465 See s.21 of the Legal Aid, Sentencing and Punishment of Offenders Act 2012, reg.17 of the Criminal Legal Aid (Financial Resources) Regulations 2013. Extradition cases are automatically taken to pass the interests of justice test.

466 Although representation orders may also be granted by a Lord Justice of Appeal, a Single Judge of the High Court, a Master of the Administrative Court (see Crim PD 50C.1), in practice they are most often dealt with by the nominated legal officers.

was one). Further work done to prepare the appeal notice after the CRM14 is submitted (for example, the preparation of perfected grounds of appeal) will be covered by the High Court representation order.

The High Court representation order automatically covers the work of a litigator and junior counsel.[467] Requested Persons may wish to apply to extend the representation order to cover the instruction of Queen's Counsel (to appear alone or with junior counsel), for prior authority to cover the cost of obtaining expert evidence, or to extend the representation order to cover the translation of documents.

Applications to extend the representation order may be determined by a Lord/Lady Justice of Appeal, a Single Judge of the High Court, a Master of the Administrative Court, or a nominated legal officer (see Crim PD 12.4.1). No specific form is required, and no fee is payable (Crim PD 12.4.2).

Applications to extend the representation order to cover the instruction of Queen's Counsel to appear alone or with junior counsel are governed by regulation 18 of the Criminal Legal Aid (Determinations by a Court and Choice of Representative) Regulations 2013. In essence, if the application is to instruct Queen's Counsel alone, the applicant must satisfy the Court that the case involves '*substantial novel or complex issues of law or fact which could not be adequately presented except by a Queen's Counsel*', and either that the case is '*exceptional compared with the generality of cases involving similar offences*', or that Queen's Counsel has been instructed on behalf of the Requesting State (reg.18(2)). If the application is to instruct Queen's Counsel to appear with junior counsel, the case must involve "*substantial novel or complex issues of law or fact which could not be adequately presented except by a Queen's Counsel assisted by a junior advocate*". Additionally, the exceptionality condition must be met, or two advocates must have been instructed on behalf of the Requesting State *and* the 'prosecution condition' in reg.18(7) must be met (reg.18(4)).

467 See reg.18 of the Criminal Legal Aid (Determinations by a Court and Choice of Representative) Regulations 2013.

Accordingly, Crim PD 12.4.4 specifies that the application must:

> "(i) *identify the substantial novel or complex issues of law or fact in the case;*
>
> (ii) *explain why these may only be adequately presented by a Queen's Counsel;*
>
> (iii) *state whether a Queen's Counsel has been instructed on behalf of the respondent;*
>
> (iv) *explain any delay in making the request;*
>
> (v) *be supported by advice from junior advocate or Queen's Counsel."*

Crim PD 12.4.6 spells out what is required of an application for prior authority to cover the cost of obtaining expert evidence. It must (as appropriate):

> (i) *confirm that the evidence sought has not been considered in any previous appeals determined by the appellate courts;*
>
> (ii) *explain why the evidence was not called at the extradition hearing in Westminster Magistrates' Court and what evidence can be produced to support that;*
>
> (iii) *explain why the new evidence would have resulted in the District Judge deciding a question at the extradition hearing differently and whether, if so, the District Judge would have been required to make a different order as to discharge of the Requested Person;*
>
> (iv) *explain why the evidence was not raised when the case was being considered by the Secretary of State for the Home Department or information was available that was not available at that time;*
>
> (v) *explain why the new evidence would have resulted in the Secretary of State deciding a question differently, and if the question had been decided differently, the Secretary of State would not have ordered the person's extradition;*
>
> (vi) *state when the need for the new evidence first became known;*

(vii) *explain any delay in making the request;*

(viii) *explain what relevant factual, as opposed to expert evidence, is being given by whom to create the factual basis for the expert's opinion;*

(ix) *explain why this particular area of expertise is relevant: for example why a child psychologist should be appointed as opposed to a social worker;*

(x) *state whether the Requested Person has capacity;*

(xi) *set out a full breakdown of all costs involved including any VAT or other tax payable, including alternative quotes or explaining why none are available;*

(xii) *provide a list of all previous extensions of the representation order and the approval of expenditure to date;*

(xiii) *provide a timetable for the production of the evidence and its anticipated effect on the time estimate and hearing date;*

(xiv) *set out the level of compliance to date with any directions order.*

The criteria for applications to extend the representation order to cover the translation of documents are set out in Crim PD 12.4.10.

Case management in the High Court:

The High Court has the same case management powers as under Crim PR, Part 3, subject to Crim PR 50.2 which requires it to have regard to the importance of (a) mutual trust and confidence and (b) expedition in extradition matters when exercising these powers.

Crim PD 12.6 and 12.7 gives a robust reminder that the High Court takes its case management role seriously. Thus, the parties are expected to cooperate with each other and the Court to ensure that the directions set are appropriate and realistic, for example by making sure that the issues are clearly identified, and that any requests for further information are promptly and clearly drawn up.[468]

Interim applications (save for applications to extend the representation order) must be made on the proper form and the applicable fee must be paid (Crim PD 12.5.1.a). Applications should be made as soon as the need to do so becomes apparent, especially where the application is to vary directions or to extend or shorten a time limit (Crim PD 12.5.1). Indeed, where an application to vary directions is made after the expiry of the relevant deadline, this "*will generally result in the refusal of the application unless good reasons are shown*" (Crim PD 12.5.8). Applications to extend or shorten time limits, or to otherwise vary directions, should provide a full and proper explanation for why directions have not been complied with, contain the views of the other parties to the appeal and include a draft order setting out in full the timetable and directions as varied (Crim PD 12.5.7-12.5.8).

An application to vacate an appeal hearing which has been fixed by the High Court attracts a fee if it is made within 14 days of the hearing date (Crim PD 12.5.4). The application must explain the reasons why it is being made; detail the views of the other parties to the appeal; and include a draft order with the application notice. Such applications will not be granted lightly; exceptional circumstances are required, especially where the adjournment "*will result in material delay to the determination of the appeal*" (Crim PD 12.5.5).

Failure to comply with rules, practice directions and orders is likely to meet with stern disapproval by the court (see Crim PD 12.5.8), and may lead to it refusing to consider material not filed on time or points not raised in a skeleton argument which was filed on time and even the possibility of referral to the President of the Kings Bench Division to consider whether Counsel or solicitors should be reported to their professional bodies (see Crim PD 12.7).[469] Practitioners' attention is

---

468 See Crim PD 12.1.4.

469 See also, for example, *McIntyre v Government of the United States of America* [2014] EWHC 1886 (Admin), [2015] 1 W.L.R. 507, [65]-[66] and *Michael Turner v High Court of Dublin, Ireland* [2024] EWHC 3294 (Admin).

drawn to the requirements for bundles, authorities and skeleton arguments at Crim PD 12.6.

Time limit for start of appeal hearing:

In relation to Part 1 cases, s.31 of the 2003 Act requires rules of court to prescribe the period within which the High Court must begin to hear an appeal under ss.26 or 28. Under Crim PR 50.23(1), the relevant period is 40 days after the Requested Person's arrest. If the appeal hearing is not begun within this timeframe, the appeal is deemed to have been determined in the Requested Person's favour and they must be discharged, unless the period is extended (s.31(6)-(7)). However, much of the sting is taken out of these provisions by the fact that the period may be extended multiple times, and such extensions may be retrospective (ss.31(4)-(5).

The equivalent provisions in relation to Part 2 cases are to be found in s.113 of the 2003 Act and Crim PR 50.23(2).

Appeal to the Supreme Court

Both the Requested Person and the Requesting State may appeal a decision of the High Court made under ss.26, 28, 103, 105, 108 or 110 to the Supreme Court (ss.32(1) and (2), and ss.114(1) and (2)). Such an appeal only lies with permission of either the High Court or the Supreme Court (ss.32(3) and 114(3)), and permission will only be granted if (a) the High Court has certified that there is a point of law of general public importance involved in the decision, and (b) it appears to the court granting leave that the point is one which ought to be considered by the Supreme Court (ss.32(4) and 114(4)).

An application for leave to appeal to the Supreme Court, when made to the High Court, must be made within 14 days starting with the day on which the High Court makes the decision appealed (ss.32(5) and 114(5)). If leave is refused (but a point of law certified), an application may be made directly to the Supreme Court, and that application must be made within 14 days starting with the day on which the High Court refuses leave (s.32(6) and 114(6)). If permission is granted, the appeal must be brought within 28 days starting with the day leave was granted, otherwise it is taken to have been brought and dismissed (ss.32(7) and (8), and ss.114(7) and (8)).

The Supreme Court may allow or dismiss the appeal (ss.33(1) and 115(1)). Where it allows an appeal by a Requested Person, it must order their discharge and also quash any extant extradition order (ss.33(2)-(3) and 115(2)-(3)).

If the High Court had allowed a Requested Person's appeal but the Supreme Court allows the Requesting State's appeal from that decision, it must quash the order for the Requested Person's discharge and order their extradition (ss.33(4)-(5) and 115(4)-(5)). It must do the same where the Requesting State appealed unsuccessfully under s.110, but the Supreme Court allows its appeal from that decision (ss.115(4)-(5)).

If the Requesting State appealed unsuccessfully to the High Court under s.28, and the Supreme Court allows its further appeal, it must quash the order discharging the Requested Person and order their extradition, if the appropriate Judge would have been required to order extradition if they decided the issue which resulted in discharge differently (ss.33(6) and (7)). If they would not have been required to so order, the Supreme Court must remit the case to them with a direction to proceed as they would have had to do if they had decided the issue as they should have done (ss.33(6) and (8)).

If the Requesting State appealed to the High Court under s.105 but that appeal was dismissed, and the Supreme Court allows its further appeal, it must remit the case to the appropriate judge with a direction to proceed as they would have had to do if they had decided the issue which resulted in discharge differently (ss.115(6)-(7)).

Where the Supreme Court orders extradition or remits the case to the appropriate Judge, it must remand the Requested Person in custody or on bail (ss.33(10), 115(9)), but if they are remanded in custody the High Court may later grant bail (ss.33(11), 115(10)).

Practitioners bringing appeals to the Supreme Court should take note of the Supreme Court Practice Directions, which are available on the Supreme Court website and are also contained, with commentary, in the *White Book* (2024 edn.), Volume 2, Section 4A.

Appeal to the ECtHR

A Requested Person may apply to the *ECtHR* under Article 34 of the ECHR where they have exhausted all domestic remedies (Article 35 ECHR).

They may also (whether along with or ahead of their substantive application under Article 34) make a request for *interim measures* under Rule 39 of the ECtHR's rules of court. In an extradition case, this will generally be to stay their removal unless and until the ECtHR decides it can take place. Interim measures will only be granted in exceptional circumstances, where the applicant would otherwise face a real risk of serious and irreversible harm. It is clear from the statistics that such requests are rarely successful. In 2019, 95 requests for interim measures were made from the UK, and none were granted.[470]

Tips for practitioners

- Practitioners should familiarise themselves with the ECtHR's rules of court and practice direction on interim measures.
- The application must be made in writing and must identify the Convention right(s) likely to be violated if the applicant is extradited, give a detailed explanation of the nature of the alleged risks and the grounds for their fears, and, if interim measures are sought, spell out the potential irreversible harm to the applicant if they are not granted.
- The supporting documentation relied on should substantiate the risk alleged, and must include: a witness statement from the applicant (if feasible to obtain), and/or a statement from their legal representatives or other relevant witnesses, and copies of all of the relevant domestic decisions. If the final judgment is expected imminently, then the date of when it is expected must be set out.
- Requests for interim measures should bear the words "*Rule 39 – Urgent*" in bold on the first page, together with details of a point of contact, the date and time of expected removal, and the destination. Requests must be submitted online at https://r39.echr.coe.int by

[470] https://www.echr.coe.int/Documents/Stats_art_39_01_ENG.pdf

post or fax (+33 (0)388 41 3900). The ECtHR will not accept a request by email. Requests will be accepted between 8am to 4pm (local time; GMT/BST +1). If sent after 4pm, applications will not normally be dealt with until the following day. Faxes of more than 10 pages should be sent in sections.

Challenges outside the statutory appeals scheme

Applications to re-open an appeal

Crim PR 50.27 sets out the procedure for reopening a decision which finally determined an appeal or an application for permission to appeal:

> *"(1) This rule applies where a party wants the High Court to reopen a decision of that court which determines an appeal or an application for permission to appeal.*
>
> *(2) Such a party must—*
>
> *(a) apply in writing for permission to reopen that decision, as soon as practicable after becoming aware of the grounds for doing so; and*
>
> *(b) serve the application on the High Court officer and every other party.*
>
> *(3) The application must—*
>
> *(a) specify the decision which the applicant wants the court to reopen; and*
>
> *(b) give reasons why—*
>
> *(i) it is necessary for the court to reopen that decision in order to avoid real injustice,*
>
> *(ii) the circumstances are exceptional and make it appropriate to reopen the decision, and*
>
> *(iii) there is no alternative effective remedy.*
>
> *(4) The court must not give permission to reopen a decision unless each other party has had an opportunity to make representations'.*

The predecessor to this rule in the Civil Procedure Rules, CPR 52.17, was considered in the context of extradition in *Ignaoua v Italy*.[471] Keane LJ suggested that in order to reopen an extradition appeal, the applicant had to demonstrate that there had been a fundamental change in circumstance or evidence, which demonstrated that the factual basis for the decision was wholly undermined. In *Rexha v Serious Organised Crime Agency*, a Divisional Court approved this and Ouseley J remarked that the threshold is "*high … it is a jurisdiction to be exercised very sparingly and only in cases which truly warrant it*".[472]

In *United States v Bowen*, the Court emphasised that Crim PR 17.27 (now Crim PR 50.27) had a narrow scope, and could not normally be exercised "*unless something has developed after the determination of the appeal*".[473] The Court went on to state that the "*jurisdiction is not designed to allow a disappointed party to the appeal to reconsider his arguments, material and evidence and come back to the court to have another go. Furthermore, we would emphasise the importance of finality in extradition cases by noting the observations of Lord Thomas in Abu Hamza v Government of the United States [2012] EWHC 2736 (Admin) at [21] and [22], namely that there is an overwhelming public interest in both the proper functioning of extradition arrangements and in honouring extradition treaties, as well as there being an equally high importance in the finality of litigation. Finality of litigation is particularly important in extradition cases: 'because of the public interest in an efficient process, the need to adhere to international obligations and to avoid a recurrence of the delays which have so disfigured the extradition process in the past and to which successive appeals over time can subject it*".[474]

471 *Ignaoua v Italy* [2008] EWHC 2619 (Admin), [2009] Extradition L.R. 19.

472 *Rexha v Serious Organised Crime Agency* [2012] EWHC 3397 (Admin), at [8].

473 *United States v Bowen* [2015] EWHC 1873 (Admin), at [9].

474 *Bowen*, at [9].

There is no right to have an application to reopen decided at an oral hearing, unless exceptionally the court directs it (Crim PR 50.17(1)(b)(iv) Crim PD 12.5.15).

Judicial review

Since the Magistrates' court is an inferior tribunal, the High Court exercises supervisory jurisdiction over the acts and omissions of District Judges in extradition proceedings. Two factors operate to limit the scope of judicial review in extradition proceedings. First, judicial review is a remedy of last resort, so if the impugned decision is one which can be challenged under the statutory appeal scheme, judicial review is unavailable. Second, ss.34(1) and 116(1) of the 2003 Act state that a '*decision of the judge under this Part may be questioned in legal proceedings only by means of an appeal under this Part*'. These provisions are not capable of ousting judicial review in respect of extradition proceedings altogether, however they do underline that judges' decisions under the scheme of the Act can only be appealed.

Judicial review is therefore available as a safety valve in three broad types of situation:

- First, where the judge makes a decision within the scheme of the 2003 Act, but the decision is not amenable to appeal under the appeal provisions. For example, where they extend the deadline for removal under ss.35(4), 36(3) or 47(3),[475] or refuse to discharge a Requested Person under ss.35(5), 36(8) or 47(4) where the deadline has been exceeded.[476] Similarly, where they refuse to discharge a Requested Person who has not received the arrest warrant or the s.71 arrest warrant as soon as practicable after arrest (under ss.4(4) and 72(5),

[475] Cf. *Cosar v Governor of HMP Wandsworth* [2020] EWHC 1142 (Admin), [2020] 1 WLR 3846; *Verde v Governor of HMP Wandsworth* [2020] EWHC 1219 (Admin).

[476] See for example R (Caldarelli) v City of Westminster Magistrates' Court [2009] EWHC 107 (Admin).

respectively).[477] Or, where consent to extradition was taken in an erroneous manner.[478]

- Second, where the judge makes a case management or other interlocutory decision, which does not strictly fall within the scope of the 2003 Act at all. This may include decisions to grant or refuse an adjournment,[479] to proceed in the Requested Person's absence,[480] or to refuse to issue a witness summons[481].
- Third, where the judge orders extradition, but the Requested Person cannot succeed under the statutory appeal provisions even though the decision is clearly flawed. Such might be the case where the judge's conduct of the proceedings gave rise to serious procedural unfairness,[482] or where they heard the action even though they were disqualified from doing so. If a serious flaw of this kind is established,

---

477 See *Nikonovs v Governor of Brixton Prison* [2005] EWHC 2405 (Admin), [2006] 1 WLR 1518; *Huczko v Governor of HMP Wandsworth* [2012] EWHC 4134 (Admin); followed in almost identical circumstances in *R (Jochemczk) v Poland* [2012] EWHC 3990 (Admin); and *Komendant v Poland* [2013] EWHC 2712 (Admin).

478 Celczynski v Poland [2019] EWHC 3450 (Admin), R (on the application of Marc Salomon) v Westminster Magistrates' Court [2022] EWHC 83 (Admin).

479 See for instance *Olah v Regional Court in Plzen, Czech Republic* [2008] EWHC 2701 (Admin), [2008] Extradition LR 278; *R (Slavik) v District Court of Nitra, Slovak Republic* [2011] EWHC 265 (Admin); *R (Zmijewski) v Westminster Magistrates' Court* [2013] EWHC 368 (Admin); *Bartys v District Court of Legnica III Criminal Department* [2013] EWHC 1740 (Admin); and *Zubkovs v Court in Riga, Latvia* [2012] EWHC 3331 (Admin).

480 *R (Pasquetti) v Westminster Magistrates' Court* [2010] EWHC 3139 (Admin); *R (Lagocki and Anor) v Westminster Magistrates' Court* [2015] EWHC 3641 (Admin).

481 R (Kaupaitis) v Prosecutor General's Office (Lithuania) [2006] EWHC 2185 (Admin).

482 R (Berners) v Westminster MC & Council of the Criminal Matters Court Regional Court of Riga Latvia [2010] EWHC 1010 (Admin), [2010] ACD 58.

but the appeal cannot be allowed because it cannot be established that the judge "*would have been required to order … discharge*", the only appropriate course is to quash the decision and remit the case the Magistrates' Court. Since there is no power to remit in Part 1 cases, this can only be achieved by way of judicial review. An extreme example of this scenario was found in *Lazarov v Bulgaria*,[483] where the judgment was replete with factual errors and could not stand. The case needed to be remitted so that a proper decision could be taken at first instance, but the High Court had no such power under s.27. The only option was therefore for the Requested Person to bring judicial review proceedings, so that the judge's decision could be quashed as a nullity and the case remitted to the magistrates' court.

Tips for practitioners

- Detailed notes of interim and case management decisions should be kept in case it is necessary to seek judicial review.
- Practitioners should familiarise themselves with the requirements of CPR 54 and of the Pre-Action Protocol for Judicial Review.
- In particular, practitioners should note the short time limit for bringing judicial review claims: *promptly*, and in any event *within three months* (CPR 54.5).
- Whilst it may sometimes be possible to bring a judicial review claim in conjunction with a statutory appeal (for example, whether a late application to adjourn the final extradition hearing is refused, and the appropriate Judge proceeds to order extradition), in other situations it may be necessary to launch judicial review proceedings whilst the first instance proceedings are ongoing.
- If public funding is required, the civil rather than criminal legal aid provisions apply.

483 *Lazarov v Bulgaria* [2018] EWHC 3050 (Admin).

After extradition is ordered

Deadline for removal following appeal

Where the effect of the decision on appeal is that the Requested Person is to be extradited, removal must take place "*before the end of the required period*". In the case of an unsuccessful appeal by the Requested Person under s.26, the "*required period*" is 10 days starting with the day on which the decision of the relevant court on the appeal becomes final, or proceedings on the appeal are discontinued, unless the relevant court agrees to extend the period (s.36). In the case of an unsuccessful appeal by the Requested Person under ss.103 or 108, or a successful appeal by the Requesting State under s.110, the "*required period*" is 28 days starting with the day on which the appeal decision becomes final or the appeal proceedings are discontinued (s.118).

If a Requested Person is not removed within the statutory period, and they apply to the appropriate judge to be discharged, the judge must order discharge unless "*reasonable cause is shown for the delay*" (ss.36(8), 118(7)).

It is apparent that a great deal of latitude is afforded to the Requesting State and NCA when determining what is a "*reasonable cause*" for the delay. In *Mechlinski v Westminster Magistrates' Court*, a Divisional Court outlined the following factors to be taken into account:[484]

> *"a) Administrative error may amount to a reasonable cause for the delay;*
>
> *b) This may encompass cases where there has been negligence but 'not of course, any negligence';*
>
> *c) A rigorous approach will generally be required;*

[484] Mechlinski v Westminster Magistrates' Court [2015] EWHC 2043 (Admin) at [9], following Desai v City of Westminster Magistrates' Court [2014] EWHC 4631 (Admin) [2015] ACD 60.

> *d) The length of the delay should not be disregarded; it may be relevant to the question of whether the delay has or has not a reasonable cause;*
>
> *e) The gravity of the offending or alleged offending is not material".*

"*Administrative error*" has been held to include individual human error, but systemic errors should not be regarded as reasonable.[485] Moreover, whether negligent conduct is reasonable depends on the circumstances. If negligence is "*gross ... such that it [does] not appear to have any sensible explanation in terms of the surrounding circumstances*" or if it is "*repeated*", that is unlikely to be sufficient.[486]

Intervening factors before extradition

The 2003 Act makes provision for certain events which may arise after extradition is ordered but before removal actually takes place. For example, ss.36B and 118C provide for deferral of extradition where the Requested Person is charged with an offence in the UK prior to removal taking place, and ss.36C and 118D address the situation where they are sentenced to a term of imprisonment here before being removed. Equally, if a further arrest warrant or Part 2 extradition request is made or comes to light after extradition has been ordered, the appropriate judge may order that extradition be deferred until such time as proceedings in respect of the competing request have been disposed of (ss.44(4)(b), 179(2)).

Request for consent to other offence being dealt with

In Part 1 cases, one of the exceptions to specialty protection under s.17 applies where the appropriate Judge consents to the Requested Person being dealt with for an offence committed prior to extradition, which did not form part of the arrest warrant (s.17(3)(c)). In Part 2 cases, the equivalent provision allows the SSHD to consent to the Requested

485 Desai.

486 *R (Lezon)* [2018] EWHC 1920 (Admin), [15].

Person being dealt with for offences committed before extradition which were outside the scope of the extradition request (s.95(4)(c)).

The principles governing consent are set out in ss.54-55 (for Part 1 cases) and s.129 (for Part 2 cases)[487]. In Part 1 cases, a Judicial Authority of the category 1 territory must send a request for consent to the NCA, which may certify it under s.54(2) if it believes that the authority is a "*judicial authority*" which "*has the function of making requests for ... consent*". The appropriate Judge must then open the "*consent hearing*" within 21 days starting with the day on which the request for consent was received by the NCA (s.54(5)), unless they extend this period (s.54(6)). The judge must serve notice on the Requested Person that they have received the request for consent, unless they are satisfied that it would not be practicable to do so (s.54(4)). Indeed, in such circumstances Crim PR 50.3(3)(d)(iii) makes clear that the appropriate judge may proceed in the absence of the Requested Person.

At the consent hearing, the appropriate judge effectively conducts a mini-extradition hearing. First, they must decide whether consent is required (s.55(1)). If they decided their consent is not required, they must inform the requesting Judicial Authority of that fact (s.55(2)), and if consent is required, they must proceed to consider whether the offence for which consent is requested is an extradition offence (s.55(3)). If it is not, consent must be withheld (s.55(4)).

If they are satisfied that the offence is an extradition offence, they must proceed to consider whether any of the bars in ss.11-25 would apply if the Requested Person were in the UK and the offence were the subject of an extradition request (s.55(5)). If, applying those provisions, they would hypothetically order extradition, then they must give their consent (s.55(6)), but if they would not then they must refuse consent (s.55(7)).

487 See the chapter on the Secretary of State's role for further information.

APPENDIX A

EXCERPTS FROM THE EXTRADITION ACT 2003[488]

1 **Extradition to category 1 territories**

(1) This Part deals with extradition from the United Kingdom to the territories designated for the purposes of this Part by order made by the Secretary of State.

(2) In this Act references to category 1 territories are to the territories designated for the purposes of this Part.

(3) A territory may not be designated for the purposes of this Part if a person found guilty in the territory of a criminal offence may be sentenced to death for the offence under the general criminal law of the territory.

2 **Part 1 warrant and certificate**

(1) This section applies if the designated authority receives a Part 1 warrant in respect of a person.

(2) A Part 1 warrant is an arrest warrant which is issued by a judicial authority of a category 1 territory and which contains—

[488] In order to avoid overburdening this book with appendices, a decision was taken to re-print the sections of Part 1 of the Act that are frequently referred to at Westminster Magistrates' Court. Legislation has been reproduced, as amended, from the legislation.gov.uk website as at 25th February 2025, the last amendment having been made on 17 September 2021 when the Forum bar in section 11(j) was brought into force in Scotland. Crown copyright applies.

(a) the statement referred to in subsection (3) and the information referred to in subsection (4), or

(b) the statement referred to in subsection (5) and the information referred to in subsection (6).

(3) The statement is one that—

(a) the person in respect of whom the Part 1 warrant is issued is accused in the category 1 territory of the commission of an offence specified in the warrant, and

(b) the Part 1 warrant is issued with a view to his arrest and extradition to the category 1 territory for the purpose of being prosecuted for the offence.

(4) The information is—

(a) particulars of the person's identity;

(b) particulars of any other warrant issued in the category 1 territory for the person's arrest in respect of the offence;

(c) particulars of the circumstances in which the person is alleged to have committed the offence, including the conduct alleged to constitute the offence, the time and place at which he is alleged to have committed the offence and any provision of the law of the category 1 territory under which the conduct is alleged to constitute an offence;

(d) particulars of the sentence which may be imposed under the law of the category 1 territory in respect of the offence if the person is convicted of it.

(5) The statement is one that—

(a) the person in respect of whom the Part 1 warrant is issued has been convicted of an offence specified in the warrant by a court in the category 1 territory, and

(b) the Part 1 warrant is issued with a view to his arrest and extradition to the category 1 territory for the purpose of being sentenced for the offence or of serving a sentence of imprisonment or another form of detention imposed in respect of the offence.

(6) The information is—

(a) particulars of the person's identity;

(b) particulars of the conviction;

(c) particulars of any other warrant issued in the category 1 territory for the person's arrest in respect of the offence;

(d) particulars of the sentence which may be imposed under the law of the category 1 territory in respect of the offence, if the person has not been sentenced for the offence;

(e) particulars of the sentence which has been imposed under the law of the category 1 territory in respect of the offence, if the person has been sentenced for the offence.

(7) The designated authority may issue a certificate under this section if it believes that the authority which issued the Part 1 warrant has the function of issuing arrest warrants in the category 1 territory.

(7A) But in the case of a Part 1 warrant containing the statement referred to in subsection (3), the designated authority must not issue a certificate under this section if it is clear to the designated authority that a judge proceeding under section 21A would be required to order the person's discharge on the basis that extradition would be disproportionate.

In deciding that question, the designated authority must apply any general guidance issued for the purposes of this subsection.

(7B) Any guidance under subsection (7A) may be revised, withdrawn or replaced.

(7C) The function of issuing guidance under subsection (7A), or of revising, withdrawing or replacing any such guidance, is exercisable by the Lord Chief Justice of England and Wales with the concurrence of—

(a) the Lord Justice General of Scotland, and

(b) the Lord Chief Justice of Northern Ireland.

(8) A certificate under this section must certify that the authority which issued the Part 1 warrant has the function of issuing arrest warrants in the category 1 territory.

(9) The designated authority is the authority designated for the purposes of this Part by order made by the Secretary of State.

(10) An order made under subsection (9) may—

(a) designate more than one authority;

(b) designate different authorities for different parts of the United Kingdom.

3 Arrest under certified Part 1 warrant

(1) This section applies if a certificate is issued under section 2 in respect of a Part 1 warrant issued in respect of a person.

(2) The warrant may be executed by a constable or a customs officer in any part of the United Kingdom.

(3) The warrant may be executed by a service policeman anywhere, but only if the person is subject to service law or is a civilian subject to service discipline.

(5) The warrant may be executed even if neither the warrant nor a copy of it is in the possession of the person executing it at the time of the arrest.

(6) …

4 Person arrested under Part 1 warrant

(1) This section applies if a person is arrested under a Part 1 warrant.

(2) A copy of the warrant must be given to the person as soon as practicable after his arrest.

(3) The person must be brought as soon as practicable before the appropriate judge.

(4) If subsection (2) is not complied with and the person applies to the judge to be discharged, the judge may order his discharge.

(5) If subsection (3) is not complied with and the person applies to the judge to be discharged, the judge must order his discharge.

(6) A person arrested under the warrant must be treated as continuing in legal custody until he is brought before the

appropriate judge under subsection (3) or he is discharged under subsection (4) or (5).

5 Provisional arrest

(1) A constable, a customs officer or a service policeman may arrest a person without a warrant if he has reasonable grounds for believing—

(a) that a Part 1 warrant has been or will be issued in respect of the person by an authority of a category 1 territory, and

(b) that the authority has the function of issuing arrest warrants in the category 1 territory.

(2) A constable or a customs officer may arrest a person under subsection (1) in any part of the United Kingdom.

(3) A service policeman may arrest a person under subsection (1) only if the person is subject to service law or is a civilian subject to service discipline.

(4) If a service policeman has power to arrest a person under subsection (1) he may exercise the power anywhere.

6 Person arrested under section 5

(1) This section applies if a person is arrested under section 5.

(2) The person must be brought before the appropriate judge within 48 hours starting with the time when the person is arrested.

(2A) The documents specified in subsection (4) must be produced to the judge within 48 hours starting with the time when the person is arrested but this is subject to any extension under subsection (3B).

(2B) Subsection (3) applies if—

(a) the person has been brought before the judge in compliance with subsection (2); but

(b) documents have not been produced to the judge in compliance with subsection (2A).

(3) The person must be brought before the judge when the documents are produced to the judge.

(3A) While the person is before the judge in pursuance of subsection (2), the authority of the category 1 territory may apply to the judge for an extension of the 48 hour period mentioned in subsection (2A) by a further 48 hours.

(3B) The judge may grant an extension if the judge decides that subsection (2A) could not reasonably be complied with within the initial 48 hour period.

(3C) The judge must decide whether that subsection could reasonably be so complied with on a balance of probabilities.

(3D) Notice of an application under subsection (3A) must be given in accordance with rules of court.

(4) The documents are—

(a) a Part 1 warrant in respect of the person;

(b) a certificate under section 2 in respect of the warrant.

(5) A copy of the warrant must be given to the person as soon as practicable after his arrest.

(5A) Subsection (5B) applies if—

(a) the person is before the judge in pursuance of subsection (2); and

(b) the documents specified in subsection (4) have not been produced to the judge.

(5B) The judge must remand the person in custody or on bail (subject to subsection (6)).

(6) If subsection (2), (2A) or (3) is not complied with and the person applies to the judge to be discharged, the judge must order his discharge.

(7) If subsection (5) is not complied with and the person applies to the judge to be discharged, the judge may order his discharge.

(8) The person must be treated as continuing in legal custody until he is brought before the appropriate judge under subsection (2) or he is discharged under subsection (6) or (7).

(8A) In calculating a period of 48 hours for the purposes of this section no account is to be taken of—

(a) any Saturday or Sunday;

(b) Christmas Day;

(c) Good Friday; or

(d) any day falling within subsection (8B).

(8B) The following days fall within this subsection—

(a) in Scotland, any day prescribed under section 8(2) of the Criminal Procedure (Scotland) Act 1995 as a court holiday in the court of the appropriate judge;

(b) in any part of the United Kingdom, any day that is a bank holiday under the Banking and Financial Dealings Act 1971 in that part of the United Kingdom.

(9) Subsection (10) applies if—

(a) a person is arrested under section 5 on the basis of a belief that a Part 1 warrant has been or will be issued in respect of him;

(b) the person is discharged under subsection (6) or (7).

(10) The person must not be arrested again under section 5 on the basis of a belief relating to the same Part 1 warrant.

7 Identity of person arrested

(1) This section applies if—

(a) a person arrested under a Part 1 warrant is brought before the appropriate judge under section 4(3), or

(b) a person arrested under section 5 is brought before the appropriate judge under section 6 and section 6(2A) is complied with in relation to him.

(2) The judge must decide whether the person brought before him is the person in respect of whom—

(a) the warrant referred to in subsection (1)(a) was issued, or

(b) the warrant referred to in section 6(4) was issued.

(3) The judge must decide the question in subsection (2) on a balance of probabilities.

(4) If the judge decides the question in subsection (2) in the negative he must order the person's discharge.

(5) If the judge decides that question in the affirmative he must proceed under section 8.

(6) In England and Wales, the judge has the same powers (as nearly as may be) as a magistrates' court would have if the proceedings were the summary trial of an information against the person.

(7) In Scotland—

(a) the judge has the same powers (as nearly as may be) as if the proceedings were summary proceedings in respect of an offence alleged to have been committed by the person; but

(b) in his making any decision under subsection (2) evidence from a single source shall be sufficient.

(8) In Northern Ireland, the judge has the same powers (as nearly as may be) as a magistrates' court would have if the proceedings were the hearing and determination of a complaint against the person.

(9) If the judge exercises his power to adjourn the proceedings he must remand the person in custody or on bail.

(10) If the person is remanded in custody, the appropriate judge may later grant bail.

8 Remand etc.

(1) If the judge is required to proceed under this section he must—

(a) fix a date on which the extradition hearing is to begin;

(b) inform the person of the contents of the Part 1 warrant;

(c) give the person the required information about consent;

(d) remand the person in custody or on bail.

(2) If the person is remanded in custody, the appropriate judge may later grant bail.

(3) The required information about consent is—

(a) that the person may consent to his extradition to the category 1 territory in which the Part 1 warrant was issued;

(b) an explanation of the effect of consent and the procedure that will apply if he gives consent;

(c) that consent must be given before the judge and is irrevocable.

(4) The date fixed under subsection (1) must not be later than the end of the permitted period, which is 21 days starting with the date of the arrest referred to in section 7(1)(a) or (b).

(4A) But if proceedings in respect of the extradition are adjourned under section 8A or 8B, the permitted period is extended by the number of days for which the proceedings are so adjourned.

(5) If before the date fixed under subsection (1) (or this subsection) a party to the proceedings applies to the judge for a later date to be fixed and the judge believes it to be in the interests of justice to do so, he may fix a later date; and this subsection may apply more than once.

(6) Subsections (7) and (8) apply if the extradition hearing does not begin on or before the date fixed under this section.

(7) If the person applies to the judge to be discharged the judge must order his discharge, unless reasonable cause is shown for the delay.

(8) If no application is made under subsection (7) the judge must order the person's discharge on the first occasion after the date fixed under this section when the person appears or is brought before the judge, unless reasonable cause is shown for the delay.

8A Person charged with offence in United Kingdom before extradition hearing

(1) This section applies if—

(a) a person has been brought before the appropriate judge under section 4(3) or 6(2) but the extradition hearing has not begun; and

(b) the judge is informed that the person is charged with an offence in the United Kingdom.

(2) The judge must order further proceedings in respect of the extradition to be adjourned until one of these occurs—

(a) the charge is disposed of;

(b) the charge is withdrawn;

(c) proceedings in respect of the charge are discontinued;

(d) an order is made for the charge to lie on the file, or in relation to Scotland, the diet is deserted pro loco et tempore.

(3) If a sentence of imprisonment or another form of detention is imposed in respect of the offence charged, the judge may order further proceedings in respect of the extradition to be adjourned until the person is released from detention pursuant to the sentence (whether on licence or otherwise).

8B Person serving sentence in United Kingdom before extradition hearing

(1) This section applies if—

(a) a person has been brought before the appropriate judge under section 4(3) or 6(2) but the extradition hearing has not begun; and

(b) the judge is informed that the person is in custody serving a sentence of imprisonment or another form of detention in the United Kingdom.

(2) The judge may order further proceedings in respect of the extradition to be adjourned until the person is released from detention pursuant to the sentence (whether on licence or otherwise).

(3) In a case where further proceedings in respect of the extradition are adjourned under subsection (2)—

(a) section 131 of the Magistrates' Courts Act 1980 (remand of accused already in custody) has effect as if a reference to 28 clear days in subsection (1) or (2) of that section were a reference to six months;

(b) Article 47(2) of the Magistrates' Courts (Northern Ireland) Order 1981 (period of remand in custody) has effect as if a reference to 28 days in—

(i) sub-paragraph (a)(iii), or

(ii) the words after sub-paragraph (b),

were a reference to six months.

9 Judge's powers at extradition hearing

(1) In England and Wales, at the extradition hearing the appropriate judge has the same powers (as nearly as may be) as a magistrates' court would have if the proceedings were the summary trial of an information against the person in respect of whom the Part 1 warrant was issued.

(2) In Scotland, at the extradition hearing the appropriate judge has the same powers (as nearly as may be) as if the proceedings were summary proceedings in respect of an offence alleged to have been committed by the person in respect of whom the Part 1 warrant was issued.

(3) In Northern Ireland, at the extradition hearing the appropriate judge has the same powers (as nearly as may be) as a magistrates' court would have if the proceedings were the hearing and determination of a complaint against the person in respect of whom the Part 1 warrant was issued.

(4) If the judge adjourns the extradition hearing he must remand the person in custody or on bail.

(5) If the person is remanded in custody, the appropriate judge may later grant bail.

10 Initial stage of extradition hearing

(1) This section applies if a person in respect of whom a Part 1 warrant is issued appears or is brought before the appropriate judge for the extradition hearing.

(2) The judge must decide whether the offence specified in the Part 1 warrant is an extradition offence.

(3) If the judge decides the question in subsection (2) in the negative he must order the person's discharge.

(4) If the judge decides that question in the affirmative he must proceed under section 11.

11 Bars to extradition

(1) If the judge is required to proceed under this section he must decide whether the person's extradition to the category 1 territory is barred by reason of—

(a) the rule against double jeopardy;

(aa) absence of prosecution decision;

(b) extraneous considerations;

(c) the passage of time;

(d) the person's age;

(e). . . . .

(f) speciality;

(g) the person's earlier extradition to the United Kingdom from another category 1 territory;

(h) the person's earlier extradition to the United Kingdom from a non-category 1 territory.

(i) the person's earlier transfer to the United Kingdom by the International Criminal Court.

(j) forum.

(1A) But the judge is to decide whether the person's extradition is barred by reason of —

(a) absence of prosecution decision, or

(b) forum,

only in a case where the Part 1 warrant contains the statement referred to in section 2(3) (warrant issued for purposes of prosecution for offence in category 1 territory).

(2) Sections 12 to 19F apply for the interpretation of subsection (1).

(3) If the judge decides any of the questions in subsection (1) in the affirmative he must order the person's discharge.

(4) If the judge decides those questions in the negative and the person is alleged to be unlawfully at large after conviction of the extradition offence, the judge must proceed under section 20.

(5) If the judge decides those questions in the negative and the person is accused of the commission of the extradition offence but is not alleged to be unlawfully at large after conviction of it, the judge must proceed under section 21A.

12 Rule against double jeopardy

A person's extradition to a category 1 territory is barred by reason of the rule against double jeopardy if (and only if) it appears that he would be entitled to be discharged under any rule of law relating to previous acquittal or conviction on the assumption—

(a) that the conduct constituting the extradition offence constituted an offence in the part of the

United Kingdom where the judge exercises jurisdiction;

(b) that the person were charged with the extradition offence in that part of the United Kingdom.

12A Absence of prosecution decision

(1) A person's extradition to a category 1 territory is barred by reason of absence of prosecution decision if (and only if)—

(a) it appears to the appropriate judge that there are reasonable grounds for believing that—

(i) the competent authorities in the category 1 territory have not made a decision to charge or have not made a decision to try (or have made neither of those decisions), and

(ii) the person's absence from the category 1 territory is not the sole reason for that failure, and

(b) those representing the category 1 territory do not prove that—

(i) the competent authorities in the category 1 territory have made a decision to charge and a decision to try, or

(ii) in a case where one of those decisions has not been made (or neither of them has been made), the person's absence from the category 1 territory is the sole reason for that failure.

(2) In this section "to charge" and "to try", in relation to a person and an extradition offence, mean—

(a) to charge the person with the offence in the category 1 territory, and

(b) to try the person for the offence in the category 1 territory.

13 Extraneous considerations

A person's extradition to a category 1 territory is barred by reason of extraneous considerations if (and only if) it appears that—

(a) the Part 1 warrant issued in respect of him (though purporting to be issued on account of the extradition offence) is in fact issued for the purpose of prosecuting or punishing him on account of his race, religion, nationality, gender, sexual orientation or political opinions, or

(b) if extradited he might be prejudiced at his trial or punished, detained or restricted in his personal liberty by reason of his race, religion, nationality, gender, sexual orientation or political opinions.

14 Passage of time

A person's extradition to a category 1 territory is barred by reason of the passage of time if (and only if) it appears that it would be unjust or oppressive to extradite him by reason of the passage of time since he is alleged to have—

(a) committed the extradition offence (where he is accused of its commission), or

(b) become unlawfully at large (where he is alleged to have been convicted of it).

Commonwealth country or a British overseas territory and stating the terms of the arrangements is conclusive evidence of those matters.

18 Earlier extradition to United Kingdom from category 1 territory

A person's extradition to a category 1 territory is barred by reason of his earlier extradition to the United Kingdom from another category 1 territory if (and only if)—

(a) the person was extradited to the United Kingdom from another category 1 territory (the extraditing territory);

(b) under arrangements between the United Kingdom and the extraditing territory, that territory's consent is required to the person's extradition from the United Kingdom to the category 1 territory in respect of the extradition offence under consideration;

(c) that consent has not been given on behalf of the extraditing territory.

19 Earlier extradition to United Kingdom from non-category 1 territory

A person's extradition to a category 1 territory is barred by reason of his earlier extradition to the United Kingdom from a non-category 1 territory if (and only if)—

(a) the person was extradited to the United Kingdom from a territory that is not a category 1 territory (the extraditing territory);

(b) under arrangements between the United Kingdom and the extraditing territory, that territory's consent is required to the person's being dealt with in the United Kingdom in respect of the extradition offence under consideration;

(c) consent has not been given on behalf of the extraditing territory to the person's extradition from the United Kingdom to the category 1 territory in respect of the extradition offence under consideration.

19A Earlier transfer to United Kingdom by International Criminal Court

(1) A person's extradition to a category 1 territory is barred by reason of his earlier transfer by the International Criminal Court if (and only if)—

(a) the person was transferred to the United Kingdom to serve a sentence imposed by the Court;

(b) under arrangements between the United Kingdom and the Court, the consent of the Presidency of the Court is required to the person's extradition from the United Kingdom to the category 1 territory in respect of the extradition offence under consideration;

(c) that consent has not been given.

(2) Subsection (1) does not apply if the person has served the sentence imposed by the Court and has subsequently—

(a) remained voluntarily in the United Kingdom for more than 30 days, or

(b) left the United Kingdom and returned to it.

19B Forum

(1) The extradition of a person ("D") to a category 1 territory is barred by reason of forum if the extradition would not be in the interests of justice.

(2) For the purposes of this section, the extradition would not be in the interests of justice if the judge—

(a) decides that a substantial measure of D's relevant activity was performed in the United Kingdom; and

(b) decides, having regard to the specified matters relating to the interests of justice (and only those matters), that the extradition should not take place.

(3) These are the specified matters relating to the interests of justice—

(a) the place where most of the loss or harm resulting from the extradition offence occurred or was intended to occur;

(b) the interests of any victims of the extradition offence;

(c) any belief of a prosecutor that the United Kingdom, or a particular part of the United Kingdom, is not the most appropriate jurisdiction in which to prosecute D in respect of the conduct constituting the extradition offence;

(d) were D to be prosecuted in a part of the United Kingdom for an offence that corresponds to the extradition offence, whether evidence necessary to prove the offence is or could be made available in the United Kingdom;

(e) any delay that might result from proceeding in one jurisdiction rather than another;

(f) the desirability and practicability of all prosecutions relating to the extradition offence taking place in one jurisdiction, having regard (in particular) to—

(i) the jurisdictions in which witnesses, co-defendants and other suspects are located, and

(ii) the practicability of the evidence of such persons being given in the United Kingdom or in jurisdictions outside the United Kingdom;

(g) D's connections with the United Kingdom.

(4) In deciding whether the extradition would not be in the interests of justice, the judge must have regard to the desirability of not requiring the disclosure of material which is subject to restrictions on disclosure in the category 1 territory concerned.

(5) If, on an application by a prosecutor, it appears to the judge that the prosecutor has considered the offences for which D could be prosecuted in the United Kingdom, or a part of the United Kingdom, in respect of the conduct constituting the extradition offence, the judge must make that prosecutor a party to the proceedings on the question of whether D's extradition is barred by reason of forum.

(6) In this section "D's relevant activity " means activity which is material to the commission of the extradition offence and which is alleged to have been performed by D.

19C Effect of prosecutor's certificates on forum proceedings

(1) The judge hearing proceedings under section 19B (the "forum proceedings") must decide that the extradition is not barred by reason of forum if (at a time when the judge has not yet decided the proceedings) the judge receives a prosecutor's certificate relating to the extradition.

(2) That duty to decide the forum proceedings in that way is subject to the determination of any question relating to the prosecutor's certificate raised in accordance with section 19E.

(3) A designated prosecutor may apply for the forum proceedings to be adjourned for the purpose of assisting that or any other designated prosecutor—

(a) in considering whether to give a prosecutor's certificate relating to the extradition,

(b) in giving such a certificate, or

(c) in sending such a certificate to the judge.

(4) If such an application is made, the judge must—

(a) adjourn the forum proceedings until the application is decided; and

(b) continue the adjournment, for such period as appears to the judge to be reasonable, if the application is granted.

(5) But the judge must end the adjournment if the application is not granted.

19D Prosecutor's certificates

(1) A "prosecutor's certificate" is a certificate given by a designated prosecutor which—

(a) certifies both matter A and matter B, and

(b) certifies either matter C or matter D.

(2) Matter A is that a responsible prosecutor has considered the offences for which D could be prosecuted in the United Kingdom, or a part of the United Kingdom, in respect of the conduct constituting the extradition offence.

(3) Matter B is that the responsible prosecutor has decided that there are one or more such offences that correspond to the extradition offence (the "corresponding offences").

(4) Matter C is that—

(a) the responsible prosecutor has made a formal decision as to the prosecution of D for the corresponding offences,

(b) that decision is that D should not be prosecuted for the corresponding offences, and

(c) the reason for that decision is a belief that—

(i) there would be insufficient admissible evidence for the prosecution; or

(ii) the prosecution would not be in the public interest.

(5) Matter D is that the responsible prosecutor believes that D should not be prosecuted for the corresponding offences because there are concerns about the disclosure of sensitive material in—

(a) the prosecution of D for the corresponding offences, or

(b) any other proceedings.

(6) In relation to the extradition of any person to a category 1 territory, neither this section nor any other rule of law (whether or not contained in an enactment) may require a designated prosecutor—

(a) to consider any matter relevant to giving a prosecutor's certificate; or

(b) to consider whether to give a prosecutor's certificate.

(7) In this section "sensitive material" means material which appears to the responsible prosecutor to be sensitive, including material appearing to be sensitive on grounds relating to—

(a) national security,

(b) international relations, or

(c) the prevention or detection of crime (including grounds relating to the identification or activities of witnesses, informants or any other persons supplying information to the police or any other law enforcement agency who may be in danger if their identities are revealed).

19E Questioning of prosecutor's certificate

(1) No decision of a designated prosecutor relating to a prosecutor's certificate in respect of D's extradition (a "relevant certification decision") may be questioned except on an appeal under section 26 against an order for that extradition.

(2) In England and Wales, and Northern Ireland, for the purpose of—

(a) determining whether to give permission for a relevant certification decision to be questioned, and

(b) determining any such question (if that permission is given),the High Court must apply the procedures and principles which would be applied by it on an application for judicial review.

(3) In Scotland, for the purpose of determining any questioning of a relevant certification decision, the High Court must apply the procedures and principles that would be applied by it on an application for judicial review.

(4) In a case where the High Court quashes a prosecutor's certificate, the High Court is to decide the question of whether or not the extradition is barred by reason of forum.

(5) Where the High Court is required to decide that question by virtue of subsection (4)—

(a) sections 19B to 19D and this section apply in relation to that decision (with the appropriate modifications) as they apply to a decision by a judge; and

(b) in particular—

(i) a reference in this section to an appeal under section 26 has effect as a reference to an appeal under section 32 to the Supreme Court;

(ii) a reference in this section to the High Court has effect as a reference to the Supreme Court.

19F Interpretation of sections 19B to 19E

(1) This section applies for the purposes of sections 19B to 19E (and this section).

(2) These expressions have the meanings given—

"D" has the meaning given in section 19B(1);

"designated prosecutor " means—

(a) a member of the Crown Prosecution Service, or

(b) any other person who—

(i) is a prosecutor designated for the purposes of this section by order made by the Secretary of State, or

(ii) is within a description of prosecutors so designated;

"extradition offence " means the offence specified in the Part 1 warrant (including the conduct that constitutes the extradition offence);

"forum proceedings " has the meaning given in section 19C(1);

"part of the United Kingdom " means—

(a) England and Wales;

(b) Scotland;

(c) Northern Ireland;

"prosecutor " means a person who has responsibility for prosecuting offences in any part of the United Kingdom (whether or not the person also has other responsibilities);

"prosecutor's certificate " has the meaning given in section 19D(1);

"responsible prosecutor ", in relation to a prosecutor's certificate, means—

(a) the designated prosecutor giving the certificate, or

(b) another designated prosecutor.

(3) In determining for any purpose whether an offence corresponds to the extradition offence, regard must be had, in particular, to the nature and seriousness of the two offences.

(4) A reference to a formal decision as to the prosecution of D for an offence is a reference to a decision (made after complying with, in particular, any applicable requirement concerning a code of practice) that D should, or should not, be prosecuted for the offence.

20 Case where person has been convicted

(1) If the judge is required to proceed under this section (by virtue of section 11) he must decide whether the person was convicted in his presence.

(2) If the judge decides the question in subsection (1) in the affirmative he must proceed under section 21.

(3) If the judge decides that question in the negative he must decide whether the person deliberately absented himself from his trial.

(4) If the judge decides the question in subsection (3) in the affirmative he must proceed under section 21.

(5) If the judge decides that question in the negative he must decide whether the person would be entitled to a retrial or (on appeal) to a review amounting to a retrial.

(6) If the judge decides the question in subsection (5) in the affirmative he must proceed under section 21.

(7) If the judge decides that question in the negative he must order the person's discharge.

(8) The judge must not decide the question in subsection (5) in the affirmative unless, in any proceedings that it is alleged would constitute a retrial or a review amounting to a retrial, the person would have these rights—

(a) the right to defend himself in person or through legal assistance of his own choosing or, if he had not sufficient means to pay for legal assistance, to be given it free when the interests of justice so required;

(b) the right to examine or have examined witnesses against him and to obtain the attendance and examination of witnesses on his behalf under the same conditions as witnesses against him.

21 Person unlawfully at large: human rights

(1) If the judge is required to proceed under this section (by virtue of section 20) he must decide whether the person's extradition would be compatible with the Convention rights within the meaning of the Human Rights Act 1998 (c. 42).

(2) If the judge decides the question in subsection (1) in the negative he must order the person's discharge.

(3) If the judge decides that question in the affirmative he must order the person to be extradited to the category 1 territory in which the warrant was issued.

(4) If the judge makes an order under subsection (3) he must remand the person in custody or on bail to wait for his extradition to the category 1 territory.

(5) If the person is remanded in custody, the appropriate judge may later grant bail.

21A Person not convicted: human rights and proportionality

(1) If the judge is required to proceed under this section (by virtue of section 11), the judge must decide both of the following questions in respect of the extradition of the person ("D")—

(a) whether the extradition would be compatible with the Convention rights within the meaning of the Human Rights Act 1998;

(b) whether the extradition would be disproportionate.

(2) In deciding whether the extradition would be disproportionate, the judge must take into account the specified matters relating to proportionality (so far as the judge thinks it appropriate to do so); but the judge must not take any other matters into account.

(3) These are the specified matters relating to proportionality—

(a) the seriousness of the conduct alleged to constitute the extradition offence;

(b) the likely penalty that would be imposed if D was found guilty of the extradition offence;

(c) the possibility of the relevant foreign authorities taking measures that would be less coercive than the extradition of D.

(4) The judge must order D's discharge if the judge makes one or both of these decisions—

(a) that the extradition would not be compatible with the Convention rights;

(b) that the extradition would be disproportionate.

(5) The judge must order D to be extradited to the category 1 territory in which the warrant was issued if the judge makes both of these decisions—

(a) that the extradition would be compatible with the Convention rights;

(b) that the extradition would not be disproportionate.

(6) If the judge makes an order under subsection (5) he must remand the person in custody or on bail to wait for extradition to the category 1 territory.

(7) If the person is remanded in custody, the appropriate judge may later grant bail.

(8) In this section "relevant foreign authorities " means the authorities in the territory to which D would be extradited if the extradition went ahead.

21B Request for temporary transfer etc

(1) This section applies if—

(a) a Part 1 warrant is issued which contains the statement referred to in section 2(3) (warrant issued for purposes of prosecution for offence in category 1 territory), and

(b) at any time before or in the extradition hearing, the appropriate judge is informed that a request under subsection (2) or (3) has been made.

(2) A request under this subsection is a request by a judicial authority of the category 1 territory in which the warrant is issued ("the requesting territory")—

(a) that the person in respect of whom the warrant is issued be temporarily transferred to the requesting territory, or

(b) that arrangements be made to enable the person to speak with representatives of an authority in the requesting territory responsible for investigating, prosecuting or trying the offence specified in the warrant.

(3) A request under this subsection is a request by the person in respect of whom the warrant is issued—

(a) to be temporarily transferred to the requesting territory, or

(b) that arrangements be made to enable the person to speak with representatives of an authority in the requesting territory responsible for investigating, prosecuting or trying the offence specified in the warrant.

(4) The judge must order further proceedings in respect of the extradition to be adjourned if the judge thinks it necessary to do so to enable the person (in the case of a request under subsection (2)) or the authority by which the warrant is issued (in the case of a request under subsection (3)) to consider whether to consent to the

request. An adjournment under this subsection must not be for more than 7 days.

(5) If the person or authority consents to the request, the judge must—

(a) make whatever orders and directions seem appropriate for giving effect to the request;

(b) order further proceedings in respect of the extradition to be adjourned for however long seems necessary to enable the orders and directions to be carried out.

(6) If the request, or consent to the request, is withdrawn before effect (or full effect) has been given to it—

(a) no steps (or further steps) may be taken to give effect to the request;

(b) the judge may make whatever further orders and directions seem appropriate (including an order superseding one made under subsection (5)(b)).

(7) A person may not make a request under paragraph (a) or (b) of subsection (3) in respect of a warrant if the person has already given consent to a request under the corresponding paragraph of subsection (2) in respect of that warrant (even if that consent has been withdrawn).

(8) A person may not make a further request under paragraph (a) or (b) of subsection (3) in respect of a warrant if the person has already made a request under that paragraph in respect of that warrant (even if that request has been withdrawn).

(9) If—

(a) a request under subsection (2) or (3) is made before a date has been fixed on which the extradition hearing is to begin, and

(b) the proceedings are adjourned under this section,

the permitted period for the purposes of fixing that date (see section 8(4)) is extended by the number of days for which the proceedings are so adjourned.

22 Person charged with offence in United Kingdom

(1) This section applies if at any time in the extradition hearing the judge is informed that the person in respect of whom the Part 1 warrant is issued is charged with an offence in the United Kingdom.

(2) The judge must adjourn the extradition hearing until one of these occurs—

(a) the charge is disposed of;

(b) the charge is withdrawn;

(c) proceedings in respect of the charge are discontinued;

(d) an order is made for the charge to lie on the file, or in relation to Scotland, the diet is deserted pro loco et tempore.

(3) If a sentence of imprisonment or another form of detention is imposed in respect of the offence charged, the judge may adjourn the extradition hearing until the person is released from detention pursuant to the sentence (whether on licence or otherwise).

(4) If before he adjourns the extradition hearing under subsection (2) the judge has decided under section 11

whether the person's extradition is barred by reason of the rule against double jeopardy, the judge must decide that question again after the resumption of the hearing.

23 Person serving sentence in United Kingdom

(1) This section applies if at any time in the extradition hearing the judge is informed that the person in respect of whom the Part 1 warrant is issued is in custody serving a sentence of imprisonment or another form of detention in the United Kingdom.

(2) The judge may adjourn the extradition hearing until the person is released from detention pursuant to the sentence (whether on licence or otherwise).

(3) In a case where an extradition hearing is adjourned under subsection (2)—

(a) section 131 of the Magistrates' Courts Act 1980 (remand of accused already in custody) has effect as if a reference to 28 clear days in subsection (1) or (2) of that section were a reference to six months;

(b) Article 47(2) of the Magistrates' Courts (Northern Ireland) Order 1981 (S.I. 1981/1675 (N.I. 26)) (period of remand in custody) has effect as if a reference to 28 days in—

(i) paragraph (a)(iii), or

(ii) the words after paragraph (b),

were a reference to six months.

24 Extradition request

(1) This section applies if at any time in the extradition hearing the judge is informed that—

(a) a certificate has been issued under section 70 in respect of a request for the person's extradition;

(b) the request has not been disposed of;

(c) an order has been made under section 179(2) for further proceedings on the warrant to be deferred until the request has been disposed of.

(2) The judge must remand the person in custody or on bail.

(3) If the person is remanded in custody, the appropriate judge may later grant bail.

25 Physical or mental condition

(1) This section applies if at any time in the extradition hearing it appears to the judge that the condition in subsection (2) is satisfied.

(2) The condition is that the physical or mental condition of the person in respect of whom the Part 1 warrant is issued is such that it would be unjust or oppressive to extradite him.

(3) The judge must—

(a) order the person's discharge, or

(b) adjourn the extradition hearing until it appears to him that the condition in subsection (2) is no longer satisfied.

....

64 Extradition offences: person not sentenced for offence

(1) This section sets out whether a person's conduct constitutes an "extradition offence" for the purposes of this Part in a case where the person—

(a) is accused in a category 1 territory of an offence constituted by the conduct, or

(b) has been convicted in that territory of an offence constituted by the conduct but not sentenced for it.

(2) The conduct constitutes an extradition offence in relation to the category 1 territory if the conditions in subsection (3) or (4) are satisfied.

(3) The conditions in this subsection are that—

(a) the conduct occurs in the category 1 territory;

(b) the conduct would constitute an offence under the law of the relevant part of the United Kingdom if it occurred in that part of the United Kingdom;

(c) the conduct is punishable under the law of the category 1 territory with imprisonment or another form of detention for a term of 12 months or a greater punishment.

(4) The conditions in this subsection are that—

(a) the conduct occurs outside the category 1 territory;

(b) in corresponding circumstances equivalent conduct would constitute an extra-territorial offence under the law of the relevant part of the United Kingdom;

(c) the conduct is punishable under the law of the category 1 territory with imprisonment or another form of detention for a term of 12 months or a greater punishment.

(5) *Repealed*

(6) For the purposes of subsections (3)(b) and (4)(b)—

(a) if the conduct relates to a tax or duty, it does not matter whether the law of the relevant part of the United Kingdom imposes the same kind of tax or duty or contains rules of the same kind as those of the law of the category 1 territory;

(b) if the conduct relates to customs or exchange, it does not matter whether the law of the relevant part of the United Kingdom contains rules of the same kind as those of the law of the category 1 territory.

65 Extradition offences: person sentenced for offence

(1) This section sets out whether a person's conduct constitutes an "extradition offence" for the purposes of this Part in a case where the person—

(a) has been convicted in a category 1 territory of an offence constituted by the conduct, and

(b) has been sentenced for the offence.

(2) The conduct constitutes an extradition offence in relation to the category 1 territory if the conditions in subsection (3) or (4) are satisfied.

(3) The conditions in this subsection are that—

(a) the conduct occurs in the category 1 territory;

(b) the conduct would constitute an offence under the law of the relevant part of the United Kingdom if it occurred in that part of the United Kingdom;

(c) a sentence of imprisonment or another form of detention for a term of 4 months or a greater punishment has been imposed in the category 1 territory in respect of the conduct.

(4) The conditions in this subsection are that—

(a) the conduct occurs outside the category 1 territory;

(b) in corresponding circumstances equivalent conduct would constitute an extra-territorial offence under the law of the relevant part of the United Kingdom;

(c) a sentence of imprisonment or another form of detention for a term of 4 months or a greater punishment has been imposed in the category 1 territory in respect of the conduct.

(6) For the purposes of subsections (3)(b) and (4)(b)—

(a) if the conduct relates to a tax or duty, it does not matter whether the law of the relevant part of the United Kingdom imposes the same kind of tax or duty or contains rules of the same kind as those of the law of the category 1 territory;

(b) if the conduct relates to customs or exchange, it does not matter whether the law of the relevant part of the United Kingdom contains rules of the same kind as those of the law of the category 1 territory.

APPENDIX B

EXTRACT FROM THE EU TRADE AND CO-OPERATION AGREEMENT[489]

TITLE VII

SURRENDER

ARTICLE 596

Objective

The objective of this Title is to ensure that the extradition system between the Member States, on the one side, and the United Kingdom, on the other side, is based on a mechanism of surrender pursuant to an arrest warrant in accordance with the terms of this Title.

ARTICLE 597

Principle of proportionality

Cooperation through the arrest warrant shall be necessary and proportionate, taking into account the rights of the requested person and the interests of the victims, and having regard to the seriousness of the act, the likely penalty that would be imposed and the possibility of a State taking measures less coercive than the surrender of the requested person

[489] https://assets.publishing.service.gov.uk/government/uploads/system/uploads/attachment_data/file/982648/TS_8.2021_UK_EU_EAEC_Trade_and_Cooperation_Agreement.pdf

particularly with a view to avoiding unnecessarily long periods of pre-trial detention.

ARTICLE 598

Definitions

For the purposes of this Title, the following definitions apply:

(a) "arrest warrant" means a judicial decision issued by a State with a view to the arrest and surrender by another State of a requested person, for the purposes of conducting a criminal prosecution or executing a custodial sentence or detention order;

(b) "judicial authority" means an authority that is, under domestic law, a judge, a court or a public prosecutor. A public prosecutor is considered a judicial authority only to the extent that domestic law so provides;

(c) "executing judicial authority" means the judicial authority of the executing State which is competent to execute the arrest warrant by virtue of the domestic law of that State;

(d) "issuing judicial authority" means the judicial authority of the issuing State which is competent to issue an arrest warrant by virtue of the domestic law of that State.

ARTICLE 599

Scope

1. An arrest warrant may be issued for acts punishable by the law of the issuing State by a custodial sentence or a detention order for a maximum period of at least 12 months or, where a sentence has been passed or a detention order has been made, for sentences or detention orders of at least four months.

2. Without prejudice to paragraphs 3 and 4, surrender is subject to the condition that the acts for which the arrest warrant has been issued constitute an offence under the law of the executing State, whatever the constituent elements or however it is described.

3. Subject to Article 600, points (b) to (h) of Article 601(1), and Articles 602, 603 and 604, a State shall not refuse to execute an arrest warrant issued in relation to the following behaviour where such behaviour is punishable by deprivation of liberty or a detention order of a maximum period of at least 12 months:

(a) the behaviour of any person who contributes to the commission by a group of persons acting with a common purpose of one or more offences in the field of terrorism referred to in Articles 1 and 2 of the European Convention on the Suppression of Terrorism, done at Strasbourg on 27 January 1977, or in relation to illicit trafficking in narcotic drugs and psychotropic substances, or murder, grievous bodily injury, kidnapping, illegal restraint, hostage-taking or rape, even where that person does not take part in the actual execution of the offence or offences concerned; such contribution must be intentional and made with the knowledge that the participation will contribute to the achievement of the group's criminal activities; or

(b) terrorism as defined in Annex 45.

4. The United Kingdom and the Union, acting on behalf of any of its Member States, may each notify the Specialised Committee on Law Enforcement and Judicial Cooperation that, on the basis of reciprocity, the condition of double criminality referred to in paragraph 2 will not be applied, provided that the offence on which the warrant is based is:

(a) one of the offences listed in paragraph 5, as defined by the law of the issuing State; and

(b) punishable in the issuing State by a custodial sentence or a detention order for a maximum period of at least three years.

5. The offences referred to in paragraph 4 are:

– participation in a criminal organisation;

– terrorism as defined in Annex 45;

– trafficking in human beings;

– sexual exploitation of children and child pornography;

– illicit trafficking in narcotic drugs and psychotropic substances;

– illicit trafficking in weapons, munitions and explosives;

– corruption, including bribery;

– fraud, including that affecting the financial interests of the United Kingdom, a Member State or the Union;

– laundering of the proceeds of crime;

– counterfeiting currency;

– computer-related crime;

– environmental crime, including illicit trafficking in endangered animal species and endangered plant species and varieties;

– facilitation of unauthorised entry and residence;

– murder;

– grievous bodily injury;

– illicit trade in human organs and tissue;

– kidnapping, illegal restraint and hostage-taking;

– racism and xenophobia;

– organised or armed robbery;

– illicit trafficking in cultural goods, including antiques and works of art;

– swindling;

– racketeering and extortion;

– counterfeiting and piracy of products;

– forgery of administrative documents and trafficking therein;

– forgery of means of payment;

– illicit trafficking in hormonal substances and other growth promoters;

– illicit trafficking in nuclear or radioactive materials;

– trafficking in stolen vehicles;

– rape;

– arson;

– crimes within the jurisdiction of the International Criminal Court;

– unlawful seizure of aircraft, ships or spacecraft; and

– sabotage.

ARTICLE 600

Grounds for mandatory non-execution of the arrest warrant

The execution of the arrest warrant shall be refused:

(a) if the offence on which the arrest warrant is based is covered by an amnesty in the executing State, where that State had jurisdiction to prosecute the offence under its own criminal law;

(b) if the executing judicial authority is informed that the requested person has been finally judged by a State in respect of the same acts, provided that, if a penalty has been imposed, it has been enforced, is in the process of being enforced or can no longer be enforced under the law of the sentencing State; or

(c) if the person who is the subject of the arrest warrant may not, owing to the person's age, be held criminally responsible for the acts on which the arrest warrant is based under the law of the executing State.

ARTICLE 601

Other grounds for non-execution of the arrest warrant

1. The execution of the arrest warrant may be refused:

(a) if, in one of the cases referred to in Article 599(2), the act on which the arrest warrant is based does not constitute an offence under the law of the executing State; however, in relation to taxes or duties, customs and exchange, the execution of the arrest warrant shall not be refused on the grounds that the law of the executing State does not impose the same kind of tax or duty or does not contain the same type of rules as regards taxes or duties, customs and exchange regulations as the law of the issuing State;

(b) if the person who is the subject of the arrest warrant is being prosecuted in the executing State for the same act as that on which the arrest warrant is based;

(c) if the judicial authorities of the executing State have decided either not to prosecute for the offence on which the arrest warrant is based or to halt proceedings, or if a final judgment which prevents further proceedings has been passed upon the requested person in a State in respect of the same acts;

(d) if the criminal prosecution or punishment of the requested person is statute-barred under the law of the executing State and the acts fall within the jurisdiction of that State under its own criminal law;

(e) if the executing judicial authority is informed that the requested person has been finally judged by a third country in respect of the same acts provided that, if a penalty has been imposed, it has been enforced, is in the process of being enforced or can no longer be enforced under the law of the sentencing country;

(f) if the arrest warrant has been issued for the purposes of execution of a custodial sentence or detention order and the requested person is staying in, or is a national or a resident of the executing State and that State undertakes to execute the sentence or detention order in accordance with its domestic law; if consent of the requested person to the transfer of the sentence or detention order to the executing State is required, the executing State may refuse to execute the arrest warrant only after the requested person consents to the transfer of the sentence or detention order;

(g) if the arrest warrant relates to offences which:

(i) are regarded by the law of the executing State as having been committed in whole or in part in the territory of the executing State or in a place treated as such; or

(ii) have been committed outside the territory of the issuing State, and the law of the executing State does not allow prosecution for the same offences if committed outside its territory;

(h) if there are reasons to believe on the basis of objective elements that the arrest warrant has been issued for the purpose of prosecuting or punishing a person on the grounds of the person's sex, race, religion, ethnic origin, nationality, language, political opinions or sexual orientation, or that that person's position may be prejudiced for any of those reasons;

(i) if the arrest warrant has been issued for the purpose of executing a custodial sentence or adetention order and the requested person did not appear in person at the trial resulting in the decision, unless the arrest warrant states that the person, in accordance with further procedural requirements defined in the domestic law of the issuing State:

(i) in due time:

(A) either was summoned in person and thereby informed of the scheduled date and place of the trial which resulted in the decision, or by other means actually received official information of the scheduled date and place of that trial in such a manner that it was unequivocally established that the person was aware of the date and place of the scheduled trial ;

and

(B) was informed that a decision may be handed down if that person did not appear for the trial;

or

(ii) being aware of the date and place of the scheduled trial, had given a mandate to a lawyer, who was either appointed by the person concerned or by the State, to defend him or her at the trial, and was indeed defended by that lawyer at the trial;

or

(iii) after being served with the decision and being expressly informed about the right to a retrial or appeal in which the person has the right to participate and which allows the merits of the case, including fresh evidence, to be re-examined, and which may lead to the original decision being reversed:

(A) expressly stated that the person did not contest the decision;

or

(B) did not request a retrial or appeal within the applicable time frame;

or

(iv) was not personally served with the decision but:

(A) will be personally served with it without delay after the surrender and will be expressly informed of the right to a retrial or appeal in which the person has the right to participate and which allows the merits of the case, including fresh evidence, to be re-examined, and which may lead to the original decision being reversed;

and

(B) will be informed of the time frame within which the person has to request such a retrial or appeal, as mentioned in the relevant arrest warrant.

2. Where the arrest warrant is issued for the purpose of executing a custodial sentence or detention order under the conditions in point (i) (iv) of paragraph 1 and the person concerned has not previously received any official information about the existence of the criminal proceedings against him or her, that person may, when being informed about the content of the arrest warrant, request to receive a copy of the judgment before being surrendered. Immediately after having been informed about the request, the issuing authority shall provide the copy of the judgment via the executing authority to the person concerned. The request of the person concerned shall neither delay the surrender procedure nor delay the decision to execute the arrest warrant. The provision of the judgment

to the person concerned shall be for information purposes only; it shall not be regarded as a formal service of the judgment nor actuate any time limits applicable for requesting a retrial or appeal.

3. Where a person is surrendered under the conditions in point (i) (iv) of paragraph 1 and that person has requested a retrial or appeal, until those proceedings are finalised the detention of that person awaiting such retrial or appeal shall be reviewed in accordance with the domestic law of the issuing State, either on a regular basis or upon request of the person concerned. Such a review shall in particular include the possibility of suspension or interruption of the detention. The retrial or appeal shall begin within due time after the surrender.

ARTICLE 602

Political offence exception

1. The execution of an arrest warrant may not be refused on the grounds that the offence may be regarded by the executing State as a political offence, as an offence connected with a political offence or as an offence inspired by political motives.

2. However, the United Kingdom and the Union, acting on behalf of any of its Member States, may each notify the Specialised Committee on Law Enforcement and Judicial Cooperation that paragraph 1 will be applied only in relation to:

(a) the offences referred to in Articles 1 and 2 of the European Convention on the Suppression of Terrorism;

(b) offences of conspiracy or association to commit one or more of the offences referred to in Articles 1 and 2 of the European Convention on the Suppression of Terrorism, if those offences of conspiracy or association correspond to the description of behaviour referred to in Article 599(3) of this Agreement; and

(c) terrorism as defined in Annex 45 to this Agreement.

3. Where an arrest warrant has been issued by a State having made a notification as referred to in paragraph 2 or by a State on behalf of which such a notification has been made, the State executing the arrest warrant may apply reciprocity.

ARTICLE 603

Nationality exception

1. The execution of an arrest warrant may not be refused on the grounds that the requested person is a national of the executing State.

2. The United Kingdom, and the Union, acting on behalf of any of its Member States, may each notify the Specialised Committee on Law Enforcement and Judicial Cooperation that that State's own nationals will not be surrendered or that the surrender of their own nationals will be authorised only under certain specified conditions. The notification shall be based on reasons related to the fundamental principles or practice of the domestic legal order of the United Kingdom or the State on behalf of which a notification was made. In such a case, the Union, on behalf of any of its Member States or the United Kingdom, as the case may be, may notify the Specialised Committee on Law Enforcement and Judicial Cooperation within a reasonable time after the receipt of the other Party's notification that the executing judicial authorities of the Member State or the United Kingdom, as the case may be, may refuse to surrender its nationals to that State or that surrender shall be authorised only under certain specified conditions.

3. In circumstances where a State has refused to execute an arrest warrant on the basis that, in the case of the United Kingdom, it has made a notification or, in the case of a Member State, the Union has made a notification on its behalf, as referred to in paragraph 2, that State shall consider instituting proceedings against its own national which are commensurate with the subject matter of the arrest warrant, having taken into account the views of the issuing State. In circumstances where a judicial authority decides not to institute such proceedings, the victim of the offence on which the arrest warrant is based shall be able to receive

information on the decision in accordance with the applicable domestic law.

4. Where a State's competent authorities institute proceedings against its own national in accordance with paragraph 3, that State shall ensure that its competent authorities are able to take appropriate measures to assist the victims and witnesses in circumstances where they are residents of another State, particularly with regard to the way in which the proceedings are conducted.

ARTICLE 604

Guarantees to be given by the issuing State in particular cases

The execution of the arrest warrant by the executing judicial authority may be subject to the following guarantees:

(a) if the offence on which the arrest warrant is based is punishable by a custodial life sentence or a lifetime detention order in the issuing State, the executing State may make the execution of the arrest warrant subject to the condition that the issuing State gives a guarantee deemed sufficient by the executing State that the issuing State will review the penalty or measure imposed, on request or at the latest after 20 years, or will encourage the application of measures of clemency for which the person is entitled to apply under the law or practice of the issuing State, aiming at the non-execution of such penalty or measure;

(b) if a person who is the subject of an arrest warrant for the purposes of prosecution is a national or resident of the executing State, the surrender of that person may be subject to the condition that the person, after being heard, is returned to the executing State in order to serve there the custodial sentence or detention order passed against him or her in the issuing State; if the consent of the requested person to the transfer of the sentence or detention order to the executing State is required, the guarantee that the person be returned to the executing State to serve the person's sentence is subject to the condition that the requested person, after being heard, consents to be returned to the executing State;

(c) if there are substantial grounds for believing that there is a real risk to the protection of the fundamental rights of the requested person, the executing judicial authority may require, as appropriate, additional guarantees as to the treatment of the requested person after the person's surrender before it decides whether to execute the arrest warrant.

ARTICLE 605

Recourse to the central authority

1. The United Kingdom and the Union, acting on behalf of any of its Member States, may each notify the Specialised Committee on Law Enforcement and Judicial Cooperation of, in the case of the United Kingdom, its central authority and, in the case of the Union, the central authority for each State, having designated such an authority, or, if the legal system of the relevant State so provides, of more than one central authority to assist the competent judicial authorities.

2. When notifying the Specialised Committee on Law Enforcement and Judicial Cooperation under paragraph 1, the United Kingdom and the Union, acting on behalf of any of its Member States, may each indicate that, as a result of the organisation of the internal judicial system of the relevant States, the central authority or central authorities are responsible for the administrative transmission and receipt of arrest warrants as well as for all other official correspondence relating to the administrative transmission and receipt of arrest warrants. Such indication shall be binding upon all the authorities of the issuing State.

ARTICLE 606

Content and form of the arrest warrant

1. The arrest warrant shall contain the following information set out in accordance with the form contained in Annex 43:

(a) the identity and nationality of the requested person;

(b) the name, address, telephone and fax numbers and e-mail address of the issuing judicial authority;

(c) evidence of an enforceable judgment, an arrest warrant or any other enforceable judicial decision having the same effect that fall within the scope of Article 599;

(d) the nature and legal classification of the offence, particularly in respect of Article 599;

(e) a description of the circumstances in which the offence was committed, including the time, place and degree of participation in the offence by the requested person;

(f) the penalty imposed, if there is a final judgment, or the prescribed scale of penalties for the offence under the law of the issuing State; and

(g) if possible, other consequences of the offence.

2. The arrest warrant shall be translated into the official language or one of the official languages of the executing State. The United Kingdom and the Union, acting on behalf of any of its Member States, may each notify the Specialised Committee on Law Enforcement and Judicial Cooperation that a translation in one or more other official languages of a State will be accepted.

ARTICLE 607

Transmission of an arrest warrant

If the location of the requested person is known, the issuing judicial authority may transmit the arrest warrant directly to the executing judicial authority.

ARTICLE 608

Detailed procedures for transmitting an arrest warrant

1. If the issuing judicial authority does not know which authority is the competent executing judicial authority, it shall make the requisite enquiries, in order to obtain that information from the executing State.

2. The issuing judicial authority may request the International Criminal Police Organisation ("Interpol") to transmit an arrest warrant.

3. The issuing judicial authority may transmit the arrest warrant by any secure means capable of producing written records under conditions allowing the executing State to establish the authenticity of the arrest warrant.

4. All difficulties concerning the transmission or the authenticity of any document needed for the execution of the arrest warrant shall be dealt with by direct contacts between the judicial authorities involved, or, where appropriate, with the involvement of the central authorities of the States.

5. If the authority which receives an arrest warrant is not competent to act upon it, it shall automatically forward the arrest warrant to the competent authority in its State and shall inform the issuing judicial authority accordingly.

ARTICLE 609

Rights of a requested person

1. If a requested person is arrested for the purpose of the execution of an arrest warrant, the executing judicial authority, in accordance with its domestic law, shall inform that person of the arrest warrant and of its contents, and also of the possibility of consenting to surrender to the issuing State.

2. A requested person who is arrested for the purpose of the execution of an arrest warrant and who does not speak or understand the language of the arrest warrant proceedings shall have the right to be assisted by an interpreter and to be provided with a written translation in the native language of the requested person or in any other language which that person speaks or understands, in accordance with the domestic law of the executing State.

3. A requested person shall have the right to be assisted by a lawyer in accordance with the domestic law of the executing State upon arrest.

4. The requested person shall be informed of the person's right to appoint a lawyer in the issuing State for the purpose of assisting the lawyer in the executing State in the arrest warrant proceedings. This paragraph is without prejudice to the time limits set out in Article 621.

5. A requested person who is arrested shall have the right to have the consular authorities of that person's State of nationality, or if that person is stateless, the consular authorities of the State where that person usually resides, informed of the arrest without undue delay and to communicate with those authorities, if that person so wishes.

ARTICLE 610

Keeping the person in detention

When a person is arrested on the basis of an arrest warrant, the executing judicial authority shall take a decision on whether the requested person should remain in detention, in accordance with the law of the executing State. The person may be released provisionally at any time in accordance with the domestic law of the executing State, provided that the competent authority of that State takes all the measures it deems necessary to prevent the person from absconding.

ARTICLE 611

Consent to surrender

1. If the arrested person indicates that he or she consents to surrender, that consent and, if appropriate, the express renunciation of entitlement to the speciality rule referred to in Article 625(2) must be given before the executing judicial authority, in accordance with the domestic law of the executing State.

2. Each State shall adopt the measures necessary to ensure that the consent and, where appropriate, the renunciation referred to in paragraph 1 are established in such a way as to show that the person concerned has expressed them voluntarily and in full awareness of the consequences. To that end, the requested person shall have the right to a lawyer.

3. The consent and, where appropriate, the renunciation referred to in paragraph 1 shall be formally recorded in accordance with the procedure laid down by the domestic law of the executing State.

4. In principle, consent may not be revoked. Each State may provide that the consent and, if appropriate, the renunciation referred to in paragraph 1 of this Article may be revoked in accordance with the rules applicable under its domestic law. In such a case, the period between the date of the consent and that of its revocation shall not be taken into consideration in establishing the time limits laid down in Article 621. The United

Kingdom and the Union, acting on behalf of any of its Member States, may each notify the Specialised Committee on Law Enforcement and Judicial Cooperation that it wishes to have recourse to this possibility, specifying the procedures whereby revocation of the consent is possible and any amendments to those procedures.

ARTICLE 612

Hearing of the requested person

Where the arrested person does not consent to surrender as referred to in Article 611, that person shall be entitled to be heard by the executing judicial authority, in accordance with the law of the executing State.

ARTICLE 613

Surrender decision

1. The executing judicial authority shall decide whether the person is to be surrendered within the time limits and in accordance with the conditions defined in this Title, in particular the principle of proportionality as set out in Article 597.

2. If the executing judicial authority finds the information communicated by the issuing State to be insufficient to allow it to decide on surrender, it shall request that the necessary supplementary information, in particular with respect to Article 597, Articles 600 to 602, Article 604 and Article 606, be furnished as a matter of urgency and may fix a time limit for the receipt thereof, taking into account the need to observe the time limits provided for in Article 615.

3. The issuing judicial authority may forward any additional useful information to the executing judicial authority at any time.

ARTICLE 614

Decision in the event of multiple requests

1. If two or more States have issued a European arrest warrant or an arrest warrant for the same person, the decision as to which of those arrest warrants is to be executed shall be taken by the executing judicial authority, with due consideration of all the circumstances, especially the relative seriousness of the offences and place of the offences, the respective dates of the arrest warrants or European arrest warrants and whether they have been issued for the purposes of prosecution or for the execution of a custodial sentence or detention order, and of legal obligations of Member States deriving from Union law regarding, in particular, the principles of freedom of movement and non-discrimination on grounds of nationality.

2. The executing judicial authority of a Member State may seek the advice of Eurojust when making the choice referred to in paragraph 1.

3. In the event of a conflict between an arrest warrant and a request for extradition presented by a third country, the decision as to whether the arrest warrant or the extradition request takes precedence shall be taken by the competent authority of the executing State with due consideration of all the circumstances, in particular those referred to in paragraph 1 and those mentioned in the applicable convention.

4. This Article is without prejudice to the States' obligations under the Statute of the International Criminal Court.

ARTICLE 615

Time limits and procedures for the decision to execute the arrest warrant

1. An arrest warrant shall be dealt with and executed as a matter of urgency.

2. In cases where the requested person consents to surrender, the final decision on the execution of the arrest warrant shall be taken within ten days after the consent was given.

3. In other cases, the final decision on the execution of the arrest warrant shall be taken within 60 days after the arrest of the requested person.

4. Where in specific cases the arrest warrant cannot be executed within the time limits laid down in paragraph 2 or 3, the executing judicial authority shall immediately inform the issuing judicial authority of that fact, giving the reasons for the delay. In such cases, the time limits may be extended by a further 30 days.

5. As long as the executing judicial authority has not taken a final decision on the arrest warrant, it shall ensure that the material conditions necessary for the effective surrender of the person remain fulfilled.

6. Reasons must be given for any refusal to execute an arrest warrant.

ARTICLE 616

Situation pending the decision

1. Where the arrest warrant has been issued for the purpose of conducting a criminal prosecution, the executing judicial authority shall either:

(a) agree that the requested person should be heard according to Article

617; or

(b) agree to the temporary transfer of the requested person.

2. The conditions and the duration of the temporary transfer shall be determined by mutual agreement between the issuing and executing judicial authorities.

3. In the case of temporary transfer, the person must be able to return to the executing State to attend hearings which concern that person as part of the surrender procedure.

ARTICLE 617

Hearing the person pending the decision

1. The requested person shall be heard by a judicial authority. To that end, the requested person shall be assisted by a lawyer designated in accordance with the law of the issuing State.

2. The requested person shall be heard in accordance with the law of the executing State and with the conditions determined by mutual agreement between the issuing and executing judicial authorities.

3. The competent executing judicial authority may assign another judicial authority of its State to take part in the hearing of the requested person in order to ensure the proper application of this Article.

ARTICLE 618

Privileges and immunities

1. Where the requested person enjoys a privilege or immunity regarding jurisdiction or execution in the executing State, the time limits referred to in Article 615 only start running when, or if, the executing judicial authority is informed of the fact that the privilege or immunity has been waived.

2. The executing State shall ensure that the material conditions necessary for effective surrender are fulfilled when the person no longer enjoys such privilege or immunity.

3. Where power to waive the privilege or immunity lies with an authority of the executing State, the executing judicial authority shall request that

authority to exercise that power without delay. Where power to waive the privilege or immunity lies with an authority of another State, third country or international organisation, the issuing judicial authority shall request that authority to exercise that power.

ARTICLE 619

Competing international obligations

1. This Agreement does not prejudice the obligations of the executing State where the requested person has been extradited to that State from a third country and where that person is protected by provisions of the arrangement under which that person was extradited concerning the speciality rule. The executing State shall take all necessary measures for requesting without delay the consent of the third country from which the requested person was extradited so that the requested person can be surrendered to the State which issued the arrest warrant. The time limits referred to in Article 615 do not start running until the day on which the speciality rule ceases to apply.

2. Pending the decision of the third country from which the requested person was extradited, the executing State shall ensure that the material conditions necessary for effective surrender remain fulfilled.

ARTICLE 620

Notification of the decision

The executing judicial authority shall notify the issuing judicial authority immediately of the decision on the action to be taken on the arrest warrant.

ARTICLE 621

Time limits for surrender of the person

1. The requested person shall be surrendered as soon as possible on a date agreed between the authorities concerned.

2. The requested person shall be surrendered no later than ten days after the final decision on the execution of the arrest warrant.

3. If the surrender of the requested person within the time limit in paragraph 2 is prevented by circumstances beyond the control of any of the States, the executing and issuing judicial authorities shall immediately contact each other and agree on a new surrender date. In that event, the surrender shall take place within ten days of the new date thus agreed.

4. The surrender may exceptionally be temporarily postponed for serious humanitarian reasons, for example if there are substantial grounds for believing that the surrender would manifestly endanger the requested person's life or health. The execution of the arrest warrant shall take place as soon as those grounds have ceased to exist. The executing judicial authority shall immediately inform the issuing judicial authority and agree on a new surrender date. In that event, the surrender shall take place within ten days of the new date agreed.

5. Upon the expiry of the time limits referred to in paragraphs 2 to 4, if the requested person is still being held in custody, that person shall be released. The executing and issuing judicial authorities shall contact each other as soon as it appears that a person is to be released under this paragraph and agree the arrangements for the surrender of that person.

ARTICLE 622

Postponed or conditional surrender

1. After deciding to execute the arrest warrant, the executing judicial authority may postpone the surrender of the requested person so that the

requested person may be prosecuted in the executing State or, if the requested person has already been sentenced, so that the requested person may serve, a sentence passed for an act other than that referred to in the arrest warrant in the territory of the executing State.

2. Instead of postponing the surrender, the executing judicial authority may temporarily surrender the requested person to the issuing State under conditions to be determined by mutual agreement between the executing and the issuing judicial authorities. The agreement shall be made in writing and the conditions shall be binding on all the authorities in the issuing State.

ARTICLE 623

Transit

1. Each State shall permit the transit through its territory of a requested person who is being surrendered provided that it has been given information on:

(a) the identity and nationality of the person subject to the arrest warrant;

(b) the existence of an arrest warrant;

(c) the nature and legal classification of the offence; and

(d) the description of the circumstances of the offence, including the date and place.

2. The State, on behalf of which a notification has been made in accordance with Article 603(2) to the effect that its own nationals will not be surrendered or that surrender will be authorised only under certain specified conditions, may, refuse the transit of its own nationals through its territory under the same terms or submit it to the same conditions.

3. The States shall designate an authority responsible for receiving transit requests and the necessary documents, as well as any other official correspondence relating to transit requests.

4. The transit request and the information referred to in paragraph 1 may be addressed to the authority designated pursuant to paragraph 3 by any means capable of producing a written record. The State of transit shall notify its decision by the same procedure.

5. This Article does not apply in the case of transport by air without a scheduled stopover. However, if an unscheduled landing occurs, the issuing State shall provide the authority designated pursuant to paragraph 3 with the information referred to in paragraph 1.

6. Where a transit concerns a person who is to be extradited from a third country to a State, this Article applies *mutatis mutandis*. In particular, references to an "arrest warrant" shall be treated as references to an "extradition request".

ARTICLE 624

Deduction of the period of detention served in the executing State

1. The issuing State shall deduct all periods of detention arising from the execution of an arrest warrant from the total period of detention to be served in the issuing State as a result of a custodial sentence or detention order being passed.

2. All information concerning the duration of the detention of the requested person on the basis of the arrest warrant shall be transmitted by the executing judicial authority or the central authority designated under Article 605 to the issuing judicial authority at the time of the surrender.

ARTICLE 625

Possible prosecution for other offences

1. The United Kingdom and the Union, acting on behalf of any of its Member States, may each notify the Specialised Committee on Law Enforcement and Judicial Cooperation that, in relations with other States to which the same notification applies, consent is presumed to have been given for the prosecution, sentencing or detention of a person with a view to the carrying out of a custodial sentence or detention order for an offence committed prior to the person's surrender, other than that for which that person was surrendered, unless in a particular case the executing judicial authority states otherwise in its decision on surrender.

2. Except in the cases referred to in paragraphs 1 and 3, a person surrendered may not be prosecuted, sentenced or otherwise deprived of liberty for an offence committed prior to that person's surrender other than that for which the person was surrendered.

3. Paragraph 2 of this Article does not apply in the following cases:

(a) the person, having had an opportunity to leave the territory of the State to which that person has been surrendered, has not done so within 45 days of that person's final discharge or has returned to that territory after leaving it;

(b) the offence is not punishable by a custodial sentence or detention order;

(c) the criminal proceedings do not give rise to the application of a measure restricting personal liberty;

(d) the person could be liable to a penalty or a measure not involving the deprivation of liberty, in particular a financial penalty or a measure in lieu of a financial penalty, even if the penalty or measure may give rise to a restriction of the person's personal liberty;

(e) the person consented to be surrendered, where appropriate at the same time as the person renounced the speciality rule, in accordance with Article 611;

(f) the person, after the person's surrender, has expressly renounced entitlement to the speciality rule with regard to specific offences preceding the person's surrender; renunciation must be given before the competent judicial authority of the issuing State and be recorded in accordance with that State's domestic law; the renunciation must be drawn up in such a way as to make clear that the person concerned has given it voluntarily and in full awareness of the consequences; to that end, the person shall have the right to a lawyer; and

(g) the executing judicial authority which surrendered the person gives its consent in accordance with paragraph 4 of this Article.

4. A request for consent shall be submitted to the executing judicial authority, accompanied by the information referred to in Article 606(1) and a translation as referred to in Article 606(2). Consent shall be given where the offence for which it is requested is itself subject to surrender in accordance with the provisions of this Title. Consent shall be refused on the grounds referred to in Article 600 and otherwise may be refused only on the grounds referred to in Article 601, or Article 602(2) and Article 603(2). The decision shall be taken no later than 30 days after receipt of the request. For the situations laid down in Article 604 the issuing State must give the guarantees provided for therein.

ARTICLE 626

Surrender or subsequent extradition

1. The United Kingdom and the Union, acting on behalf of any of its Member States, may each notify the Specialised Committee on Law Enforcement and Judicial Cooperation that, in relations with other States to which the same notification applies, the consent for the surrender of a person to a State other than the executing State pursuant to an arrest warrant or European arrest warrant issued for an offence committed prior

to that person's surrender is presumed to have been given, unless in a particular case the executing judicial authority states otherwise in its decision on surrender.

2. In any case, a person who has been surrendered to the issuing State pursuant to an arrest warrant or European arrest warrant may be surrendered to a State other than the executing State pursuant to an arrest warrant or European arrest warrant issued for any offence committed prior to the person's surrender without the consent of the executing State in the following cases:

(a) the requested person, having had an opportunity to leave the territory of the State to which that person has been surrendered, has not done so within 45 days of that person's final discharge, or has returned to that territory after leaving it;

(b) the requested person consents to be surrendered to a State other than the executing State pursuant to an arrest warrant or European arrest warrant; consent must be given before the competent judicial authorities of the issuing State and be recorded in accordance with that State's domestic law; it must be drawn up in such a way as to make clear that the person concerned has given it voluntarily and in full awareness of the consequences; to that end, the requested person shall have the right to a lawyer; and

(c) the requested person is not subject to the speciality rule, in accordance with point (a), (e), (f) or (g) of Article 625(3).

3. The executing judicial authority shall consent to the surrender to another State in accordance with the following rules:

(a) the request for consent shall be submitted in accordance with Article 607, accompanied by the information set out in Article 606(1) and a translation as referred to in Article 606(2);

(b) consent shall be given where the offence for which it is requested is itself subject to surrender in accordance with the provisions of this Agreement;

(c) the decision shall be taken no later than 30 days after receipt of the request; and

(d) consent shall be refused on the grounds referred to in Article 600 and otherwise may be refused only on the grounds referred to in Article 601, Article 602(2) and Article 603(2).

4. For the situations referred to in Article 604, the issuing State shall give the guarantees provided for therein.

5. Notwithstanding paragraph 1, a person who has been surrendered pursuant to an arrest warrant shall not be extradited to a third country without the consent of the competent authority of the State which surrendered the person. Such consent shall be given in accordance with the Conventions by which that State is bound, as well as with its domestic law.

ARTICLE 627

Handing over of property

1. At the request of the issuing judicial authority or on its own initiative, the executing judicial authority shall, in accordance with its domestic law, seize and hand over property which:

(a) may be required as evidence; or

(b) has been acquired by the requested person as a result of the offence.

2. The property referred to in paragraph 1 shall be handed over even if the arrest warrant cannot be carried out owing to the death or escape of the requested person.

3. If the property referred to in paragraph 1 is liable to seizure or confiscation in the territory of the executing State, that State may, if the property is needed in connection with pending criminal proceedings, temporarily retain it or hand it over to the issuing State on condition that it is returned.

4. Any rights which the executing State or third parties may have acquired in the property referred to in paragraph 1 shall be preserved. Where such rights exist, the issuing State shall return the property without charge to the executing State as soon as the criminal proceedings have been terminated.

ARTICLE 628

Expenses

1. Expenses incurred in the territory of the executing State for the execution of an arrest warrant shall be borne by that State.

2. All other expenses shall be borne by the issuing State.

ARTICLE 629

Relation to other legal instruments

1. Without prejudice to their application in relations between States and third countries, this Title, from the date of entry into force of this Agreement, replaces the corresponding provisions of the following conventions applicable in the field of extradition in relations between the United Kingdom, on the one side, and Member States, on the other side:

(a) the European Convention on Extradition, done at Paris on 13 December 1957, and its additional protocols; and

(b) the European Convention on the Suppression of Terrorism, as far as extradition is concerned.

2. Where the Conventions referred to in paragraph 1 apply to the territories of States or to territories for whose external relations a State is responsible to which this Title does not apply, those Conventions continue to govern the relations existing between those territories and the other States.

ARTICLE 630

Review of notifications

When carrying out the joint review of this Title as referred to in Article

691(1), the Parties shall consider the need to maintain the notifications made under Article 599(4), Article 602(2) and Article 603(2). If the notifications referred to in Article 603(2) are not renewed, they shall expire five years after the date of entry into force of this Agreement. Notifications as referred to in Article 603(2) may only be renewed or newly made during the three months prior to the fifth anniversary of the entry into force of this Agreement and, subsequently, every five years thereafter, provided that the conditions set out in Article 603(2) are met at that time.

ARTICLE 631

Ongoing arrest warrants in case of disapplication

Notwithstanding Article 526, Article 692 and Article 693, the provisions of this Title apply in respect of arrest warrants where the requested person was arrested before the disapplication of this Title for the purposes of the execution of an arrest warrant, irrespective of the decision of the executing judicial authority as to whether the requested person is to remain in detention or be provisionally released.

ARTICLE 632

Application to existing European arrest warrants

This Title shall apply in respect of European arrest warrants issued in accordance with Council Framework Decision 2002/584/JHA[490] by a State before the end of the transition period where the requested person has not been arrested for the purpose of its execution before the end of the transition period.

TITLE VIII

MUTUAL ASSISTANCE

ARTICLE 633

Objective

1. The objective of this Title is to supplement the provisions, and facilitate the application between Member States, on the one side, and the United Kingdom, on the other side, of:

(a) the European Convention on Mutual Assistance in Criminal Matters, done at Strasbourg on 20 April 1959 (the "European Mutual Assistance Convention");

490 Council Framework Decision 2002/584/JHA of 13 June 2002 on the European arrest warrant and the surrender procedures between Member States (OJ EU L 190, 18.7.2002, p. 1).

INDEX

MORE BOOKS BY LAW BRIEF PUBLISHING

'The Electronic Communications Code: A Practical Guide – Second Edition' by Kerry Bretherton KC, James Castle, Mark Loveday
'A Practical Guide to the Independent School Standards – September 2023 Edition' by Sarah McKimm
'A Practical Guide to Estate Administration and Crypto Assets' by Richard Marshall
'A Practical Guide to Parental Alienation in Private and Public Law Children Cases' by Sam King QC & Frankie Shama
'Contested Heritage – Removing Art from Land and Historic Buildings' by Richard Harwood QC, Catherine Dobson, David Sawtell
'The Limits of Separate Legal Personality: When Those Running a Company Can Be Held Personally Liable for Losses Caused to Third Parties Outside of the Company' by Dr Mike Wilkinson
'A Practical Guide to Transgender Law' by Robin Moira White & Nicola Newbegin
'A Practical Guide to 'Stranded Spouses' in Family Law' by Mani Singh Basi
'A Practical Guide to Residential Freehold Conveyancing' by Lorraine Richardson
'A Practical Guide to Pensions on Divorce for Lawyers' by Bryan Scant
'A Practical Guide to Challenging Sham Marriage Allegations in Immigration Law' by Priya Solanki
'A Practical Guide to Digital Communications Evidence in Criminal Law' by Sam Willis
'A Practical Guide to Legal Rights in Scotland' by Sarah-Jane Macdonald
'A Practical Guide to New Build Conveyancing' by Paul Sams & Rebecca East
'A Practical Guide to Inherited Wealth on Divorce' by Hayley Trim
'A Practical Guide to Practice Direction 12J and Domestic Abuse in Private Law Children Proceedings' by Rebecca Cross & Malvika Jaganmohan
'A Practical Guide to Confiscation and Restraint' by Narita Bahra QC, John Carl Townsend, David Winch
'A Practical Guide to the Law of Forests in Scotland' by Philip Buchan
'A Practical Guide to Health and Medical Cases in Immigration Law' by Rebecca Chapman & Miranda Butler
'A Practical Guide to Bad Character Evidence for Criminal Practitioners by Aparna Rao
'A Practical Guide to Hoarding and Mental Health for Housing Lawyers' by Rachel Coyle
'Stephens on Contractual Indemnities' by Richard Stephens

'A Practical Guide to the EU Succession Regulation' by Richard Frimston
'A Practical Guide to Solicitor and Client Costs – Second Edition' by Robin Dunne
'Constructive Dismissal – Practice Pointers and Principles' by Benjimin Burgher
'A Practical Guide to Religion and Belief Discrimination Claims in the Workplace' by Kashif Ali
'A Practical Guide to the Law of Medical Treatment Decisions' by Ben Troke
'Fundamental Dishonesty and QOCS in Personal Injury Proceedings: Law and Practice' by Jake Rowley
'A Practical Guide to the Law in Relation to School Exclusions' by Charlotte Hadfield & Alice de Coverley
'A Practical Guide to Divorce for the Silver Separators' by Karin Walker
'The Right to be Forgotten – The Law and Practical Issues' by Melissa Stock
'A Practical Guide to Planning Law and Rights of Way in National Parks, the Broads and AONBs' by James Maurici QC, James Neill et al
'A Practical Guide to Election Law' by Tom Tabori
'A Practical Guide to the Law in Relation to Surrogacy' by Andrew Powell
'A Practical Guide to Claims Arising from Fatal Accidents – Second Edition' by James Patience
'A Practical Guide to Asbestos Claims' by Jonathan Owen & Gareth McAloon
'A Practical Guide to Stamp Duty Land Tax in England and Northern Ireland' by Suzanne O'Hara
'A Practical Guide to the Law of Farming Partnerships' by Philip Whitcomb
'A Practical Guide to the Law of Unlawful Eviction and Harassment – Second Edition' by Stephanie Lovegrove
'A Practical Guide to Costs in Personal Injury Claims – Second Edition' by Matthew Hoe
'A Practical Guide to the General Data Protection Regulation (GDPR) – Second Edition' by Keith Markham
'A Practical Guide to Working with Litigants in Person and McKenzie Friends in Family Cases' by Stuart Barlow
'Protecting Unregistered Brands: A Practical Guide to the Law of Passing Off' by Lorna Brazell
'A Practical Guide to Secondary Liability and Joint Enterprise Post-Jogee' by Joanne Cecil & James Mehigan
'A Practical Guide to the Pre-Action RTA Claims Protocol for Personal Injury Lawyers' by Antonia Ford

'A Practical Guide to Neighbour Disputes and the Law' by Alexander Walsh
'A Practical Guide to Coercive Control for Legal Practitioners and Victims' by Rachel Horman
'A Practical Guide to the Law of Driverless Cars – Second Edition'
by Alex Glassbrook, Emma Northey & Scarlett Milligan
'A Practical Guide to TOLATA Claims' by Greg Williams
'A Practical Guide to Elderly Law – Second Edition' by Justin Patten
'A Practical Guide to Responding to Housing Disrepair and Unfitness Claims' by Iain Wightwick
'A Practical Guide to the Law of Bullying and Harassment in the Workplace' by Philip Hyland
'How to Be a Freelance Solicitor: A Practical Guide to the SRA-Regulated Freelance Solicitor Model' by Paul Bennett
'A Practical Guide to Prison Injury Claims' by Malcolm Johnson
'A Practical Guide to Advising Clients at the Police Station' by Colin Stephen McKeown-Beaumont
'A Practical Guide to Antisocial Behaviour Injunctions – Second Edition' by Iain Wightwick
'Practical Mediation: A Guide for Mediators, Advocates, Advisers, Lawyers, and Students in Civil, Commercial, Business, Property, Workplace, and Employment Cases' by Jonathan Dingle with John Sephton
'The Mini-Pupillage Workbook' by David Boyle
'A Practical Guide to Crofting Law' by Brian Inkster
'A Practical Guide to the Law of Domain Names and Cybersquatting' by Andrew Clemson
'A Practical Guide to the Law of Gender Pay Gap Reporting' by Harini Iyengar
'NHS Whistleblowing and the Law' by Joseph England
'Employment Law and the Gig Economy' by Nigel Mackay & Annie Powell
'A Practical Guide to Noise Induced Hearing Loss (NIHL) Claims' by Andrew Mckie, Ian Skeate, Gareth McAloon
'An Introduction to Beauty Negligence Claims – A Practical Guide for the Personal Injury Practitioner' by Greg Almond
'Intercompany Agreements for Transfer Pricing Compliance' by Paul Sutton
'Zen and the Art of Mediation' by Martin Plowman
'A Practical Guide to Adoption for Family Lawyers' by Graham Pegg
'A Practical Guide to Industrial Disease Claims' by Andrew Mckie & Ian Skeate

‘A Practical Guide to Conducting a Sheriff Court Proof’ by Andrew Stevenson
‘A Practical Guide to Vicarious Liability’ by Mariel Irvine
‘A Practical Guide to Applications for Landlord’s Consent and Variation of Leases’ by Mark Shelton
‘A Practical Guide to Relief from Sanctions Post-Mitchell and Denton’ by Peter Causton
‘A Practical Guide to Equity Release for Advisors’ by Paul Sams
‘A Practical Guide to Financial Services Claims’ by Chris Hegarty
‘A Practical Guide to Financial Ombudsman Service Claims’ by Adam Temple & Robert Scrivenor
‘A Practical Guide to Running Housing Disrepair and Cavity Wall Claims – Second Edition’ by Andrew Mckie & Ian Skeate
‘A Practical Guide to Holiday Sickness Claims – Second Edition’ by Andrew Mckie & Ian Skeate
‘Arguments and Tactics for Personal Injury and Clinical Negligence Claims’ by Dorian Williams
‘A Practical Guide to Drone Law’ by Rufus Ballaster, Andrew Firman, Eleanor Clot
‘On Experts: CPR35 for Lawyers and Experts’ by David Boyle
‘An Introduction to Personal Injury Law’ by David Boyle

These books and more are available to order online direct from the publisher at www.lawbriefpublishing.com, where you can also read free sample chapters. For any queries, call us on 0844 587 2383 or email us at mail@lawbriefpublishing.com.

Our books are all generally in stock at www.amazon.co.uk with free next day delivery for Prime members, and at good legal bookshops such as Wildy & Sons.

We are regularly launching new books in our series of practical day-to-day practitioners' guides. Visit our website and join our free newsletter to be kept informed and to receive special offers, free chapters, etc.

You can also follow us on Twitter at www.twitter.com/lawbriefpub.

www.ingramcontent.com/pod-product-compliance
Lightning Source LLC
LaVergne TN
LVHW052243200926
848481LV00002B/250

Daniel Sternberg is a District Judge (Magistrates' Courts) based at Westminster Magistrates' Court hearing first instance extradition, crime, terrorism and POCA matters. He also sits as a Deputy Upper Tribunal Judge in the Immigration and Asylum Chamber.

Nick Dobbs is an experienced trial advocate and extradition practitioner, representing requested persons in proceedings before the Westminster Magistrates' Court and the High Court. He has handled a wide range of grounds for refusal to surrender, successfully defending clients facing extradition requests from various countries in Europe. His practice includes advising HM Treasury on investigations into breaches of financial sanctions, as well as assisting clients involved in inquests and public inquiries.

Kathryn Howarth has developed her expertise in extradition over the last decade and has been instructed in numerous leading cases. She is recognised in Chambers & Partners as a "quiet superstar" of the extradition bar and in the Legal 500 as combining "intellectual strength with an imperturbable, yet reassuring, court manner". She also has expertise in international criminal law and is the author of "A Practical Guide to International Crimes in Proceedings before the Courts of England and Wales". Kathryn sits as a Deputy Judge in the Upper Tribunal (Immigration and Asylum Chamber).

Anisa Kassamali practices in public and private law. She has particular expertise in public law (including unlawful detention, human rights, immigration and asylum, and national security matters), group litigation with international elements, business and human rights, and extradition.

Nancy Kelehar has a broad practice across both private and public law, with particular emphasis on extradition, personal injury, and inquests and inquiries. She represents requested persons and requesting states in extradition proceedings before Westminster Magistrates' Court and the High Court. Nancy has recently been seconded to the CPS Extradition Unit as a Senior Crown Prosecutor, regularly advising and acting on behalf of various judicial authorities.

Émilie Pottle is an extradition, public and international law specialist. She is recommended in the directories across multiple practice areas and has appeared before the Supreme Court, Court of Appeal and Divisional Court. She represents UK and foreign government departments, individuals and NGOs. She is ranked in the Chambers and Partners Guide to the Bar 2020, with sources stating that she is *"a smart and able up-and-coming barrister who is frequently instructed in cases concerning European Arrest Warrants"*. She also has expertise in cases concerning international criminal law.

Benjamin Seifert practises in extradition and public law. He appears at Westminster Magistrates' Court, the High Court and in the Supreme Court in extradition cases representing both requesting states and requested persons. His practice also includes inquests, inquiries and immigration law. Chambers and Partners 2021 describes him as *"an excellent advocate who is always thoroughly prepared"* and *"He goes the extra mile and argues his points very well"*.

Saoirse Townshend has a dynamic court and advisory practice specialising in extradition and public law. Saoirse is instructed alone and is led in complex and novel points of law before the Supreme Court and the Divisional Court. She represents requested persons and requesting states in extradition proceedings; as well as interested parties in inquests concerning deaths in custody, and is instructed on prison law matters. She is currently instructed as first junior counsel to the Brook House Inquiry.